Words in the Wilderness

SUNY series,

INTERRUPTIONS: Border Testimony(ies) and Critical Discourse/s

Henry A. Giroux, editor

Words in the Wilderness

Critical Literacy in the Borderlands

Stephen Gilbert Brown

Foreword by Gary A. Olson

STATE UNIVERSITY OF NEW YORK PRESS

Chapter 6, "De-Composing the Canon: Alter/Native Narratives from the Borderlands," was originally printed in *College Literature,* Volume/Issue 25.2, Spring 1998, (pp. 30–44). Reprinted by permission of *College Literature.*

Production by Ruth Fisher
Marketing by Dana E. Yanulavich

Published by
State University of New York Press, Albany

For information, address State University of New York Press, State University Plaza, Albany, NY 12246

Library of Congress Cataloging-in-Publication Data

Brown, Stephen Gilbert, 1949–
    Words in the wilderness : critical literacy in the borderlands / Stephen Gilbert Brown ; foreword by Gary A. Olson.
        p.   cm. — (SUNY series, interruptions — border testimony(ies) and critical discourse/s)
    Includes bibliographical references and index.
    ISBN 0-7914-4405-8 (alk. paper). — ISBN 0-7914-4406-6 (pbk. : alk. paper)
    1. Athabascan Indians—Education—Alaska.   2. Brown, Stephen Gilbert, 1949– —.—3. Critical pedagogy.   4. Literacy.
    5. Teachers—Alaska—Biography.   I. Title.   II. Series.
    E99.A86B76   2000
    371.829'972—dc21   99-38732
                                                                          CIP

10 9 8 7 6 5 4 3 2 1

This work is dedicated to the Native Peoples of Alaska,
to B.N.W. and to my father, Harry Brown,
to my colleagues in Rhetoric and Composition
at the University of South Florida,
to Professor Gary A. Olson,
and in loving memory of
Regina Joan Brown

◆ Contents ◆

❖ Foreword ❖

Critical Literacy for a New Generation

Not since *Pedagogy of the Oppressed* have I read a work so passionate in its concern for the dispossessed, so eminently practical in its attempt to theorize and implement a liberatory pedagogy, so inspiring yet disturbing to read. *Words in the Wilderness* is a masterpiece of scholarship on critical literacy.

Part autobiography, part case study, part ethnography, and part sophisticated theoretical examination, this book is an ingenious mosaic of theory and practice. In a moving narrative that at times borders on the literary, Steve Brown transports us into the breathtaking landscape of Alaska and the stark, gritty realities of an Athabascan Indian reservation, where we see first hand the debilitating effects of racism and cultural imperialism, the crushing weight of a white educational system on the backs of a despairing populace, and one teacher's journey of self-understanding—from complicitous colonizer to unself-reflexive missionary to champion of resistance pedagogy.

Brown quickly learns that the educational system he represents works overtime to reproduce power hierarchies that perpetuate the marginalization of borderland students and that erase their indigenous culture; he therefore struggles to devise a pedagogy that disrupts the workings of this Ideological State Apparatus, a pedagogy that values agency over acculturation, that encourages

ix

borderland students to become active makers of their own knowledge rather than passive imbibers of the colonizer's knowledge. Along the way, Brown must first learn an important lesson—one we should all heed: simply teaching consciousness raising in the classroom is insufficient because such a process reinscribes the relations of domination, albeit in a kinder gentler way; subverting pedagogies of assimilation and domination must begin with "educating the educator," with raising the consciousness *of the critical educator*. Only then can the educational process be truly liberatory.

In effect, Brown attempts to reverse the misappropriation of Freirean pedagogy: the tendency to reduce Freire's teachings to a mere academic exercise, to incorporate it into our pedagogy but not into our politics. He reminds us all too graphically that teaching for critical literacy is deadly serious business, that our actions as teachers have serious consequences in the material, intellectual, and spiritual lives of our students. This is why he hopes that his book will not simply be read but will be "acted upon."

Brown hopes that *Words in the Wilderness* will serve not as an imaginative tour into the exotic landscape of Alaska—though it certainly is that, too—but as a "blueprint for redesigning pedagogy in the borderlands." It would be wrong to assume, however, that *Words in the Wilderness* applies only to education remote from our own daily realities. Brown's narrative is a parable for all education in all places; it has implications for every teacher struggling to promote critical literacy.

At dawn on May 2, 1997, Paulo Freire passed away. Part of his legacy is that he made us all sensitive to the transformative potential of critical education. Steve Brown represents the next generation of Freireans—a generation of teacher/scholars who will take up the struggles of critical literacy in a postmodern world. *Words in the Wilderness* signals the beginning of that struggle.

Gary A. Olson
University of South Florida

❖ Acknowledgments ❖

In writing this work I have benefited from the guidance of several colleagues whose contributions I wish to acknowledge. First, I would like to express my gratitude to Victor Villanueva, Tom Fox and Irene Ward for providing careful readings, thought-provoking questions, and useful suggestions for revising key portions of this work. I also owe a debt of gratitude to Professors Debra Jacobs, Tom Ross, Sara Deats, and Ab Zilstra at the University of South Florida for their helpful support and suggestions. I would similarly like to thank editors Sid Dobrin (*Journal of Advanced Composition*), Henry Giroux (*Review of Education*), and Kostas Myrsiades (*College Literature*) for providing useful comments and/or permission to reprint materials. Although not cited in the text, there are a number of compositionists, literacy scholars, and postcolonial theorists whose influence on my own writing I would like to acknowledge: David Bartholomae, Patricia Bizzell, William Dowling, Franz Fanon, Shirley Bryce Heath, Linda Hutcheon, C. H. Knoblauch, Andrea Lunsford, John Trimbur, and Robert Young (see References for full citation of these sources). I would like to especially thank Gabriel Horn, in whom the spirit still lives, radically rejuvenated. Finally, I owe a special thanks to Priscilla Ross, Editor in Chief at SUNY Press, for her patience, encouragement, and suggestions over the last two years; to Dr. David Marcus and to Bobbi for being there through the thick and thin of it; and to my Dad for stressing the value of a college education, and for the commitment that made it a reality.

Introduction
Of Words in the Wilderness

> But the institution of the Word in the wilds is also an *Enstellung*,
> a process of displacement, distortion, dislocation, repetition—the
> dazzling light of literature sheds only darkness.
> —Homi Bhabha, "Signs" 31

There are a number of qualifications I want to set forth from the outset concerning this work. First, I would like to say a word about its interpretive framework: this project was never intended to be purely an ethnographic inquiry, nor a case study, nor an autobiographical/cultural memoir, though it contains elements of each of these modes of discourse. Those readers looking for a "study" that privileges "scientific" modes of research in which "hypotheses" are proffered, "data" scientifically and systematically collected and collated in tandem with "control" groups in support of "conclusions" which are drawn based on this "evidence" will be disappointed. What I am attempting to do in this work is to theorize pedagogy in a very real-world situation: an Athabascan Indian reservation in Alaska. Specifically, I use postcolonial discourse as an analytical tool to assess current scholarship in the field of Rhetoric and Composition, and in particular to enrich and revise traditional basic writing pedagogy in order to wed it to radical composition theory, to configure a more emancipatory borderland pedagogy. Thus, one of the aims of this work is to narrow the disjunction between radical composition theory and practice by concretizing theory in this localized, politicized, and colonized pedagogical terrain. The work is thus as hybridized as the bicultural milieu that comprises the setting of it: a compendium of autobiography, Native American resistance struggle, postcolonial discourse, radical composition theory, case study, and ethnography. An additional aim of this project is to broaden the conversation in composition studies by bringing it into dialogic contact with the conversations in these other disciplines.

In the search for the "pedagogical arts of this contact zone," I therefore critique several pedagogies, including my own: traditional cognitivist pedagogy, basic writing practice, "contact zone" pedagogy, conflict-oriented pedagogy, and Foxfire pedagogy. My aim throughout is to illustrate the possibilities for a pedagogy in the bicultural borderlands that more truly serves the interests and needs of the marginalized, borderland learner: a pedagogy whose goal is not acculturation, but agency; that is not predicated on the transmission of knowledge, but on the transference of authority; that does not foreground assimilation into the dominant culture, but spiritual redemption through reconnection to an indigenous subculture. Among other things, this narrative is an investigation of the manner in which race and ethnicity, deracination and acculturation affect the acquisition of literacy. It is as well an interrogation of the traditional uses to which literacy in the borderlands has been put, an interrogation of a colonizing strategy that uses literacy as a vehicle of cultural imperialism.

Representing the Other:
The Margins of Signification in the Moose Culture

> And wherein lies\ the offense
> that men should thus attain to know?
> What can your knowledge hurt him?
> —Paradise Lost IX, 725–27.

Some readers may question my right as a white male to "name" or otherwise "represent" the Other, arguing that such representation reinscribes colonizing gestures of domination insofar as the native's voice is subsumed in my own. If, as Homi Bhabha asserts, the subaltern can speak, what is less certain is that the subaltern can be spoken about. This assertion, however, is based on the questionable assumption that the Native American can ever be absolutely contained in language, words, or signification. In Chapter Two, I describe various subject positions assumed by the Athabascan students relative to the dominant culture and to the Athabascan subculture in an effort to convey to the reader a sense of the group dynamics within this borderland classroom. Some will argue that this attempt to categorize the Other is dehumanizing insofar as it reduces the Other to a series of exotic types and inasmuch as it reinscribes colonizing gestures of possession. I would argue that on the contrary it humanizes the Other by individualizing him or her, by subverting the myth that all Others are the same, by enunciating a multiplicity of hybrid identities, each enacting its own resistance across the bicultural terrain. It foregrounds a view of Otherness that is multiple, fragmented, elusive and therefore not easily contained in centralizing, unitary systems of signification that would construct all others as The Other in order to colonize, marginalize, or demonize them. Whereas the signifying practices of the colonizer privilege the Sameness of Otherness, my observations of the group dynamics within this borderland classroom reinscribe Bhabha's observations on "native difference." As Benita Parry writes,

> By showing the wide range of stereotypes and the shifting subject positions assigned to the colonized . . . [Bhabha] sets out to liberate the colonial from its debased inscription as Europe's monolithic and shackled Other, and into an autonomous native "difference." (40)

The fact that such representations are mediated by language problematizes the assumption that they "contain" anything at all. Words, signs, are not presences but absences. They are defined not by what they possess, but only by their differences from other signs. The real Other floats freely outside our signifying schemes, outside Theory, beyond Knowledge—a trickster coyote that leaves

nothing more than its tracks, who can be named but never captured by naming. If we would look for the Native American Other,
we should seek for him or her not in the words we use to name
Otherness, but in the spaces between our words, in the "white hush
between two lines" (Walcott 428), in the white margins that "surround" our text—the text in which we imagine the Other to be held
captive. If we "own" the text, the Other possesses the context—the
margins, the borders, the spaces where alas our words can never
go. In the last analysis, the Other exists beyond the predatory and
possessive reach of The Word, which is forever imprisoned upon
the page in the chains of its own signification.

A view of Otherness that foregrounds a multiplicity of hybrid
identities humanizes the Native American Other inasmuch as it
signifies a radical red subjectivity that is not fixed but fragmented,
not unitary but multiple, not easily possessed by signs but slippery
in the grasp of signification. This subjectivity is designed to escape
containment by homogenizing signifying systems that would reduce all others to The Other, the better to consume and subsume
them in an alien culture where they are relegated to the margins.
Instead, Native American subjectivity wraps itself in a mystifying,
shifting identity that resists conscription by virtue of a complexity
and multiplicity. The Native American Other can never be seen in
its entirety, only glimpsed in its partiality—Mt. Denali shrouded in
its summit cloudbank, the shifting currents and colors of the aurora
borealis, or the sinuous track of a coyote that navigates and nego-
tiates the borders between two worlds, tripping the signifying traps
laid for it, adapted to either realm, floating freely between them,
elusive, enigmatic, enduring.

These subject positions are not closed categories that capture
the Native American Other, but shifting and strategic sites that
confound containment insofar as they foreground difference, not
only between native and white, but between native and native. To
reiterate, knowledge-making and morality in this arena are not
incompatible, as long as the quest for knowledge is not reduced to
an end in itself, but yoked to a nobler purpose: the counterhegemonic
resistance of the Native American. This is the only justification for
the acquisition of knowledge about the native and for the acquisition of literacy by the native. A pedagogy that reduces the native
to an object of academic inquiry and nothing more is as immoral as

one that yokes the acquisition of literacy to cultural genocide. Instead of a pedagogy that reduces the Other to a passive learner of the colonizer's knowledge, pedagogy must permit the Athabascans to become active makers of their own knowledge; to say their own Word instead of mimicking the word of their colonizers; to use language not as a tool of mimicry, but as an instrument of self-creation, so that language on the tongue of the indigene arises not as "an echo from without, but a resonance from within" (Proust 64). Such a pedagogy would reinscribe the emergence motifs of Native American mythology inasmuch as it would foreground the emergence of a new, radical red subjectivity, one that reverses the direction of acculturation by privileging reconnection to an ancestral topos and subculture, and one that transforms marginality from a fixed location of oppression to a shifting landscape of liberatory resistance.

I would therefore assert that the Native American Other always and forever exists beyond the scope of signification, theory, and representation. Ontology can no more complete the "surround" of the Native American than it can capture the winds that howl across the open prairie. Thus, even if I desired to capture the Native American in words, I could not do so. Because of the inevitable disjunction between signifier and signified, all I can ever hope to do is project onto the Other a series of signs that no more "contain" the Other than the tracks in the snow contain the Trickster Coyote of Native American myth. In the end, our gaze into the depths of Otherness is obscured by the image of our own reflection projected onto the surface of Otherness. What our vision of the Other gives back to us is an image of ourselves. We are blind to all that lies beneath the surface of Otherness by our own quivering word reflections that we project onto it. I have no pretensions that this work is anything more, nor less, than a trace of my own reflections. The Native American Other is eternally "absent" from any work authored by a nonnative.

Some elusive, enigmatic, freedom-craving aspect of the Other resists containment within a well-woven web of words—a single red thread that disrupts the pattern of a Navajo blanket that transgresses the borders that would enclose it, regaining the margins that lie just beyond the domain of signification that indeed encompass the pages that would encompass him or her, framing the "talking leaves" of the colonizer in a vast web of unsignified silence, a fitting trope indeed for the direction and destiny of Native American resistance struggle.

Why Is the Teacher Here?

If borderland students have already had their consciousness raised outside the classroom, what need have they for a radical practitioner whose pedagogy foregrounds consciousness-raising? The question is a significant one insofar as it interrogates the need for radical pedagogy in such a borderland terrain. First, the privileging of consciousness-raising within the classroom is critical if for no other reason than for raising the consciousness of the borderland teacher, as a precondition for subverting pedagogies of assimilation and domination. The borderland classroom occupies a strategic site in the terrain of cultural imperialism insofar as it reinscribes relations of domination. Any attempt to reconfigure these relations must begin with the education of the educator.

Second, while many native students may have had their consciousness raised outside the classroom, few have been accorded the opportunity to exercise that consciousness within the classroom. Could not such a repositioned pedagogy be expected to reduce some of the debilitating effects of alienation by narrowing the gap between literacy and lived reality? Further, exposing students, native and white, to a heterglossia of discourses, as opposed to a single, teacherly discourse, not only raises consciousness, but helps reinforce their own identity, as students position and reposition themselves relative to these discourses. But how are such students to gain a sense of self if they are never given the opportunity to say their own words, to hear others speak, to apprehend the rich possibilities of subaltern signification and subjectivity, to discover the complex continuum of hybrid identities, to position and reposition themselves relative to the dominant culture and indigenous subculture according to their changing consciousness?

What demands that such consciousness-raising be undertaken in the classroom is the very fact that many students have already had their consciousness raised outside it, have already been politicized by the experiences of discrimination, marginalization, and colonization. The work of having to "raise" their consciousness has already been done by reality. It only remains for the borderland practitioner to catch a little of this insurrectional lighting in a pedagogical bottle, as it were, and free it within the classroom. If practitioners are really intent on bringing "light" into the native's "darkness," let them begin by bringing a little light into the darkness of the colonized classroom, a flame as real as it is red, which can not only help the native endure the long night of colonization, but guide his or her footsteps toward a new, decolonized dawn.

If these marginalized students have already been politicized, why shouldn't the classroom become as equally politicized? Why shouldn't the classroom become as politicized as the terrain around it? The borderland practitioner would be remiss to ignore this wealth of "raw material," this critical consciousness that is already there, waiting to be tapped, just beneath the surface of Velma's introspective silence and Mark's sly civility, of Will's mimicry, David's narcissistic alienation, and Erin's confrontational hostility, of all these resistances: a reservoir of pedagogical possibilities as rich as the vast deposits of coal, oil, and other fossil fuels discovered on Athabascan lands—fuels which have been produced by the oppressive and compacting weight of the native earth over eons. This consciousness is occasionally exposed when it is rubbed raw by the erosive forces of deracination and acculturation, like so many chips of coal exposed along the seashore by the relentless reflux of the bore tides. And like these coal chips, this consciousness has value insofar as it may kindle fires of a different variety, fires that may repel the native darkness, warming the Athabascan with the decolonizing heat released by this consciousness once it has been tapped and transformed into energy. The pedagogical mining of this rich ore of critical consciousness is potentially more valuable to the Athabascan's future than all the mineral deposits on reservation lands yet to be sold to transnational corporations.

And this is why the teacher is here.

The Category of "The Native"

I would also like to offer some comments regarding the category of the "native." Throughout this narrative I privilege the use of this term as opposed to the Other to "represent" the Native American for the simple reason it appears in the name, "Native American."

I also deploy the sign "indigene" as opposed to "subaltern" because it is not encumbered with as much stereotypic baggage as the latter term. This is not to suggest, however, that the sign "native" is an uncontested one. For some the sign of the "native" is a negative signifier, connoting primitivism, heathenism, and savagery. For others it resonates with more positive connotations, signifying the "local," the "natural" or the "indigenous," exhaling something of the spirit of the place. Thus, the category of "native" was not uncontested among Athabascans. For some students (Mark) and some elders (Max) it became the object of a nostalgic gaze, signifying a pre-contact, Edenic moment, an originary paradise lost awaiting reoccupation. For other students, like David, the category of the "native" was something to be buried, abandoned, denied, renounced. "Native" signified a shackle they were anxious to free themselves of and distance themselves from. For others, such as Erin, it kindled ambivalent feelings of pride and disgust—pride in those aspects of the "native" that connoted difference, disgust with those elements of the "native" that were complicit in the enterprise of colonization, which facilitated the near-genocide of their own culture. It was, in the last analysis, a category that signified many things to many people, Athabascan as well as white, whose meaning was not fixed but contested across a range of signification. If my use of the category was stable, the category itself was destabilized by the various uses to which it was put by others. For some it was a sign of orthodox identity, for others a talisman of resistance, for others still a sign of oppression. It was, in the final analysis, a signifier that floated freely throughout the bicultural borderlands and assumed many shapes, like the shifting auroras that flowed over the rooftops of the Athabascan homes on clear wintry nights: to some the reincarnated spirits of the dead, or "spirit lights"; to others, nothing more than celestial dust illumined by starlight, a purely scientific phenomenon. However, this multiplicity of meanings renders the aurora, and the category of the "native" itself, apt tropes for the enigmatic identity of the Athabascan.

Hybridity versus Biculturalism

As these signifiers recur throughout this narrative, I feel it is necessary to comment on their distinctive connotations, for they are not deployed interchangeably. If biculturalism connotes the fragmentation of the colonial moment, then, conversely, hybridity signifies the fusion of the postcolonial moment. If biculturalism connotes a disabling alienation, then hybridity suggests an enabling agency, and if biculturalism connotes the absence of the Other who is in-between, then hybridity implies the presence of the Other who moves beyond colonization into the utopian possibilities of the postcolonial moment. If biculturalism connotes stagnation, then hybridity connotes a fresh movement toward a becoming self-consciousness, the emergence of a radical red subjectivity spawned in anticolonizing resistance. If biculturalism is the December ice that freezes the current between its two banks, then hybridity is the eruptive force of that self-same current breaking free of its April shackles, once more touching the shores of the two banks it flows between and beyond, resuming in the postcolonial moment the ancient journey interrupted in the long silent stasis of its colonizing capture. If biculturalism connotes disintegration into passive nonbeing, then hybridity signifies the reintegration of an active becoming. If biculturalism connotes the metonymic dismemberment of a colonial epoch, then hybridity signifies the metaphoric "rememberment" of the postcolonial and the precolonial moments, a bridge of identity raised across the abyss of absence; a red, wind-hewn rock arching through the air of the American southwest.

The Colonizer-Colonized Binary

I also want to say a word or two about the binary opposition of colonizer-colonized. Some readers may feel that my treatment of this opposition is reductive insofar as it effaces the dynamics of that relationship. However, one of the most intriguing aspects of this relationship is what Sara Suleri terms "the peculiar intimacy" of it (756). Where relevant, I have attempted to elaborate the aspects of the colonizer-colonized relationship that reflect cross-contamination: the indiginization of the colonizer, for example, who attempts to "go native," is given as much play as the colonization of the indigene through mimicry and assimilation. Similarly, I discuss this peculiar intimacy within the context of "resistance literature," noting how the tropes of resistance literature are "contaminated" by their contact with the tropes of the realist novel: magic realism, irony, parody, satire, allegory can only exist in opposition to the realist novels they subvert. The view I attempt to project of the colonizer-colonized relationship is one that reflects its ambiguities, ambivalences, complexities, contaminations, and peculiar intimacies.

A Warning to Freireans

Finally, I want to say a word about the pitfalls of applying Freirean praxis to other pedagogical settings, of misappropriating Freire for the borderland classroom. The greatest of these dangers, in my view, is the tendency to reduce Freirean praxis to an academic exercise, to incorporate it into our pedagogy, but not into our politics; to practice it in the classroom, but not in the community whose oppressive conditions are ultimately the logical destination of such praxis. The greatest risk, in other words, consists in forgetting the second half of the Freirean pedagogical equation: How can this pedagogy serve as a springboard for meaningful action in the local community?

A second danger is posed by the practitioner's tendency to relax his or her vigilance for practices that reinscribe colonizing gestures of domination while purporting to subvert or resist them. Here I am thinking of the teacher's almost ingrained tendency to lead, to speak, to know, to wield authority, which inevitably reproduces the hierarchical dynamic of the colonizer-colonized relation insofar as the student's voice is subsumed in that of the teacher who retains the status of knowing subject while students are yet relegated to the status of passive objects, comprising no more than a backdrop for the practitioner's pedagogical "conversion."

Therefore, it is my fondest wish that this book will not only be read, but acted upon; that it will serve not only as a book, but as a weapon—a linguistic rock to be hurled into the face of colonizing practices of education; that it will serve not only as a package in which knowledge is contained, but as a blueprint for redesigning pedagogy in the borderlands as a precondition for altering the landscape of borderland residency; that it will serve not only as a personal memoir but as a pedagogical manifesto that humanizes the use of words in the wilderness.

1

How I Came to Be
a Bush Teacher

O might I here\ In solitude live savage,
in some glade\ Obscured
— Paradise Lost IX, 1084–86

My career as an Alaskan bush teacher really began in San Francisco, California: at San Francisco State University to be precise. Five months before I signed my first teaching contract, seven months before I assumed the podium at the front of my first class, and four thousand miles of highway to the south of the Athabascan village of Nyotek where I first came to ply my craft, I found myself sitting in a classroom on the campus of San Francisco State University with two dozen other unemployed teachers. We had come to hear the presentation of two recruiters from the Alaska Teachers' Placement office of the University of Alaska–Fairbanks.

Every spring I'd watched the migratory birds winging northward over the rooftops of Encino, envious that they were bound for a place I could only envision. Now it was time to see for myself, to go where the mallards, coots, and Canadian geese had long since been going. I gazed on their winging wedges, dark and cacophonous, with envy, knowing they would be visiting a land I felt compelled to see for myself and had visited in my dreams quite often. Their long, honking throats seemed to proclaim their joy at being Alaska-bound. Every ring-necked note seemed to resound with its pristine reaches, with its glacier-mirroring fjords and columbine-colored tundra. A similar impulse to take flight was animating an unnameable quarter of my own soul.

That is how I came to be one of the twenty-odd aspiring bush teachers sitting in Room 111 of the Education Department at San Francisco State that Saturday morning in February.

An Unconventional Recruiter

The course of my life was changed by what I heard in that room on that day. Bob Egan was a slender, six-foot, slightly rumpled figure, whose thick reading glasses surmounted a friendly smile. He had an engaging air of informality about him that I immediately liked, as if the expansive, unfettered spirit of the great land itself still clung to him. The unbuttoned collar, the rolled up sleeves, the natural smile hinted of the unfettered spaces of the tundra. He exuded that free and easy confidence, that aura of shaggy informality that identifies the Alaskan wherever he or she goes. He also cut straight to the chase.

"Hi. I'm Bob Egan, the Director of the Teacher Placement Program for the University of Alaska–Fairbanks. The good news for you is that we have a chronic shortage of teachers in Alaska. But before I expand on the upside of the job market there, let me say a few things. If I can burst a few bubbles, I'll be doing you a great service. Not everyone should go to Alaska. It's not anything like teaching in Long Beach, zooming to and from work on freeways. I mention Long Beach 'cuz that's my hometown. I went from there straight to Nome, Alaska, where I taught for a year. I immediately fell in love with the whole state, especially the salaries for teachers. Now, I know you've all heard about the high salaries, and that may be the reason you're interested in going, which is fine. There's nothing wrong in that. But there's more to consider than just the high salaries. If you teach in the Pribiloffs, you will be lucky if you get your mail once a month! In Barrow, it's dark right now at 1:00 p.m. In fact, it's dark all day long! On the North Slope, living conditions range from urban Barrow to remote Eskimo villages. The environment may be significantly different from what you've grown accustomed to. You have to ask yourself, am I really willing to live in a remote Indian village? Are you mechanically inclined, able to do your own plumbing repairs, engine repairs, carpentry repairs? Handy with first aid? Willing to house visitors overnight, such as the Superintendent of Schools? Can you live with a rationed water supply? Are you content with facilities other than a flush toilet? Can you adjust to no television? Willing to live in an area where no medical attention may be available? Willing to live with only periodic communication with the outside world?"

He paused to take a sip of water.

"These are questions you need to think about. I've seen a lot of teachers bite the dust. And it's not a pretty sight. They arrive with high hopes and false notions and when the reality sinks in, they cave in. Quit their jobs in midyear and catch the first flight out of the bush. That's my worst nightmare too. 'Cuz I'm the one who has to deal with the fallout, who has to find their replacements. Do you know how hard it is to find a teacher willing to go into the Alaskan bush in the middle of February? So, I try to avoid that situation at all costs, which is why we're having this talk now, why I start out this way. The last two Californians I hired lasted exactly one week. Barely long enough to get unpacked."

He surveyed our faces, assessing the impact of his words.

"Let me give you a little background on the State. It's really five distinct states. The Southeast is a prettier version of Oregon. Rain forests. Tlinget Indian predominantly. Small fishing communities. Most likely you'd be the only white person in the village. Except for the other teachers of course. Compared to the rest of the state, the climate is easy. Piece of cake. So, these positions are very popular. There's little turnover, so they're hard to come by. To secure one, you need a strong teaching specialty. Better to set your sights on one of the less appealing regions. The second most popular region is the South Central, the Kenai Peninsula."

I suddenly recalled that I had mailed an application to this district, though at the time I had no idea where it was located. It

was merely an address on a bulletin board at the University placement office.

"Mountains. Which means snow. Winters not too severe though.
That's 'cuz it's on the ocean. Northern Pacific. Not the Bering Sea.
Big difference. It's a bit like Montana. If you land a position here,
Anchorage will be within easy access by plane or even car in some
cases. Anchorage has all the diversions of any metropolis anywhere.
And after a stint in the Alaskan bush, you come to appreciate such
amenities and diversions. It's also a supply depot for the bush.
Most districts pay their teachers a stipend to fly to Anchorage
several times a year. 'Mental health money,' we call it. 'Cabin fever
funds,' I've also heard it called. The mind that came up with that
idea was truly enlightened. Makes my job a lot easier."

This was sounding a little better. My spirits began to rise just a
little from the abyss into which his first words had plunged them.

"Anyway, the Kenai Peninsula is truly one of the wonders of the
state. A favorite recreation area in summer. And a very popular
place to teach. So I wouldn't set your sights on there either. They
rarely have to recruit through our office to fill whatever openings
they might have. Same with the Anchorage School District. They
don't recruit; teachers come to them. Most of them have a Master's
and five years experience."

Where had I heard this before?

"You can forget about landing a position there as well. Especially
if your field is Language Arts or Social Studies. They already have
a backlog of those waiting to get in. The Matanuska Valley School
District is the same. One of the most beautiful areas of the state.
Just north of Anchorage. Rich, fertile soil. Ringed by mountains. A
little Tibet on the roof of the North American continent. Quite
lovely."

He stopped, tilting his head down to peer over the rim of his
glasses.

"Kodiak Island School District is another with little turnover.
It's a hub of commercial fishing. With a sprinkling of rural villages.
Athabascan Indian mostly. They will not hire couples. It's a strong,
innovative, heads-up district. Good superintendent. Old friend of
mine. Well, that's it for the popular spots. So I would forget about
a position in any of these places. If you're coming to Alaska to live
in one of them, I suggest you reconsider."

A sip of water. Another assessing glance over the rim of his glasses.

"That leaves the "undesirables," as I call them. First, there's the Aleutians. They don't celebrate Christmas, so you don't get out for Christmas. Once you're there, you're there. Also a good superintendent. In the Pribiloffs there is a lot of turnover every other year. It's like a lot of boroughs. Good openings this coming season. Dillingham in the Bristol Bay School District is a nice fishing village. Grim winters though. The Lake and Peninsula District is inland. Remote. Athabascan mostly. Bethel and Nome, I think, are the most rewarding. Eskimo. Maybe that's why. They're so different from the Athabascans. Less shy. More gregarious. Friendlier toward nonnatives. Despite that, there's also a high teacher turnover. Severe winters. Low tundra. Not scenic. Lots of poverty, alcoholism, racial tension. Plenty of time to do a lot of soul searching, and not much else. There's a very high probability of finding a job on the West Coast. Places like Nome, the Bering Straits don't get your low temps like the interior. The North Slope district is a very rich school district. Highest salaries in the state. But it's also the most isolated and has the harshest winters. The complete lack of daylight can be emotionally difficult. The Fairbanks School District is mostly Athabascan Indian. It's a more cross-cultural experience. Students speak pidgin English."

My students in Hawaii had spoken pidgin, and the cross-cultural nature of that experience lessened my fears of this one to a degree.

"If you're still interested in coming north, what you need to do is to write and register with Juneau. It'll cost $30 and take anywhere from 30 to 60 days to get the form for an Alaska Teaching Certificate. They have a reciprocal agreement with Hawaii, Oregon, and California. So if you already hold a certificate from those states, all you have to do is pay the thirty dollars and send in the form. Now the good part: salaries! Salaries are the highest in Barrow and Nome at 40K and rising at the rate of 2K per year. The Southeast pays 35 to 40K. They're also rising at 2K per. In fact, statewide you can expect salaries to go up about 2K per year as part of what's called your "step increase." For every year of experience and for every graduate degree earned you receive a step increase. Doesn't even have to be negotiated. Or more precisely, it's already been negotiated. You'll find that the State of Alaska has the best teaching

contract of any state in the union, including a twenty-year retirement plan that allows you to retire at fifty percent of your salary.
Most teachers are still in their forties and fifties when they retire.
But, I'll say it again: if money is your number one priority, don't
come to Alaska 'cuz you're gonna get very bitchy. None of us are
starving to death. I left Southern California 'cuz I couldn't cope
with the lifestyle any longer. Maybe some of you feel the same way.
Something has been lost in the rush toward progress if you ask me.
Twenty, thirty years ago, it was different. You could still see the
San Gabriel Mountains. But what good are mountains if you can't
see them for the smog? Might as well not even be there. In Alaska
I built my own home. I don't have to put up with any traffic. There
isn't a parking meter in the entire state. And I live on five acres of
land that I got for free through the homestead lottery."

He paused for another sip of water.

"Let's talk accommodations. Housing is no guarantee. But many
districts will provide it. Those that don't will give teachers a housing stipend as well as a travel stipend. So that the money you
make is yours. No overhead. Not even rent. We do this to heighten
the appeal of the experience. All we're looking for from you is two
years. That's the length of the contract. If you play your cards
right, you can come out of that two years with a nest egg amount-
ing to one year's salary. I've seen it done many times. In some
districts you'll have a modern house to live in with central heating
and running water. In others, a one-room cabin with no running
water, a wood-burning stove, and a "honey-bucket" instead of an
outhouse. It just depends where you wind up. But even if you have
running water, you can count on the pipes freezing once or twice
during the winter, on having to squirm under the house with an
acetylene torch to unfreeze them."

"Now, for those of you who are still interested, we conduct a job
fair on the Fairbanks campus the first week in June. Principals
from all over the bush come to the campus to conduct interviews
and do their hiring. It's not unusual for one of our candidates to
have eight or nine interviews in a week, to have several offers to
choose from. As I say, there's more openings than candidates. Many
of our recruits pitch their tents in the woods adjacent to campus to
cut down on expenses. They shower in the locker rooms, eat in the
cafeteria, sleep in their tents. Weather's usually nice that time of

year. Eighty degrees. Clear skies. Little rainfall. Kinda like Arizona with pine trees! As an added attraction, the Second Annual Midnight Sun Writer's Conference will be going on at the same time. It was a big success last year. Some well-known names will be attending this year: William Stafford, Geary Hobson, John Haines, Jack Cady, just to name a few. Last year we placed all but four of our one hundred candidates who came up from the Lower Forty-eight, and four hundred out of a thousand applicants we had overall. Those are pretty good odds. So, if you do come, I can practically guarantee you a job."

The scales were already tipping in favor of making the trip when he mentioned the Midnight Sun Writer's Conference.

"The greatest placement occurs in June, July, and August. Best jobs will go in early June. So that's the ideal time to be there. A second wave gets hired in July. And then there's always a flurry of last-minute hirings in August for those who changed their minds and for positions that get funded at the last minute. So, your chances of getting hired improve dramatically if you can extend your stay for a month or so, to include that second hiring flurry. We feature a very personalized, individualized, and unconventional placement service. All it costs you is $20 for the registration fee, and whatever it costs to have your placement file sent from the university where you did your teacher training. If you want to stay on campus in the dorm, you must make prior arrangements. Don't show up expecting to find dorm space 'cuz it goes quickly. But as I said, some of our jobseekers just pitch a tent in the forest for free. The local authorities might not like it, but the local mosquitoes sure do."

Of the two options he mentioned regarding accommodations, I found the second more appealing, as it better suited my shoestring budget. If I made the long journey north, it would be with a minimum of cash.

"What we need from you is your placement file, twenty bucks, a recent photograph, and a coherent letter of application. You'd be amazed at how many illiterate letters we get from teachers. In the letter, say some things about yourself we won't find in the placement file. Address it to me. My address is on the board. And leave out the outdoorsy stuff. We get a lot of that. Another thing to keep in mind: rural Alaska is extremely religious. What we really need this year are reading specialists and curriculum coordinators. The teacher surplus is over, folks. I hear there's sixty positions in Montana they can't fill. Well, good luck and hope to see ya in Alaska."

I joined the crowd of people around Bob Egan's podium and when my turn to speak came, said I'd like to come north. My mind had been made up. He shook my hand and our eyes met in a brotherly embrace, as if we now shared something in common. "Problem is, I'll be making the trip on a shoestring." How frayed a shoestring I didn't know at that time.

"If you can make it up there, I'll guarantee you a job!"

Those were the only words I needed to hear. Now that I had a familiar face waiting for me at the other end of the long Northern road, and a strong assurance that a well-paying job in my chosen field would be waiting for me there, I vowed to surmount any obstacle that might get in my way.

Once more I felt I had a direction in life. The disquieting sensation of just drifting along vanished. I set my course for due north and embarked with the energy and excitement of a migratory bird on its fledgling flight into the arctic. I was about to enter my own Big Scrub country, even as my imagination once upon a time had followed Jody and Flag into the Florida backwoods. With this vital difference: that big scrub was figurative and this one was all too real. But somehow, Marjorie Kinnan Rawlings' *The Yearling* prepared the way for this leap from the imaginary into the literal, from the page into the unfettered interior of the Far North. If in *The Yearling* I had made an inward journey into an outdoor realm, now I was making a journey outward into the interior of Alaska.

The Great North Road

On a morning in the middle of May, I boarded a train in Oakland for the first thousand-mile leg of my journey. I had two hundred dollars in my pocket and everything I thought I would need for the trek stuffed into my blue ski-touring pack—a veteran piece of equipage that had accompanied me through the Sierras, the Tetons, the Rockies, and the Na Pali coast of Kauai. My most prized possessions, however, were the last words Bob Egan had spoken to me: "You make it to Fairbanks and I'll guarantee you a job!" I held onto this promise as if clutching a ticket to an exotic destination, reciting it in moments of fear, skepticism, and restlessness.

I spent many hours in the dome car, admiring the familiar scenery of California, Oregon, and Washington, thinking of other trips I had taken through this part of America. This time, however, I was heading far beyond the northernmost limits of previous treks, which had extended to the Western shore of Vancouver Island. In Seattle, I bought a ticket as a foot passenger and boarded a ferry of the Alaska Maritime System, the Sitka Star, for the trip up the Inside Passage to Haines Junction, the second thousand-mile leg of the journey. I slept in my down bag in the solarium on the upper deck, by night gazing at stars in positions I had never seen, by day gazing at a primeval forest that slipped by our bow for days on end without so much as a sign of civilization.

This I liked.

We were escorted north by a pod of orcas that rode our bow wave—a trick they must have learned from the porpoises. Each four-foot, keel-like dorsal sliced the water like a knife through syrup, their hull-long shapes weaving through the subsurface at surprising speed, criss-crossing our bow in cosign waves under a waveless body of water as serene as the surrounding terrain was rugged. This syrup-sea was a palette for the reflections of unnamed subarctic Alps. The sheer immensity of the land was intimidating, and beyond the scope of words.

Until I traveled into the Far North, I assumed I occupied a significant place in the universe. Alaska put me back in my place. Such a monolithic landscape has a way of cutting the male ego down to size, of taking it down a peg or two. I was immediately humbled by the anonymity of these numberless ranges of mountains. The wilderness seemed to be saying: "Here is your place. Don't forget it. One misstep and you're done." It was a message I never forgot in the Far North. I was painfully conscious of my status as a greenhorn, a Cheeckako, a newcomer to this inhospitable realm. And the horror stories of other travelers who had come north, who had forgotten their place, and who had suffered the unforgiving consequences never left my mind. They were too legion to dismiss. And seeing this giant landscape in person, having it stare me straight in my face, it was easy to understand how one false step, how a false sense of one's own abilities, could lead to disaster.

The Sitka Star was also escorted north by a flock of bald eagles that shadowed our wake scavenging the scraps and the detritus of the ship. Species that were endangered or extinct in the lower forty-eight states, abounded here—from the old growth, primeval forests that marched down to the sea from a precipitous, Norwegianesque coastline to the orcas, eagles, salmon, and bears. The sheltered fjords of the Inside Passage were as pristine as they were serene, as anonymous as they were numerous, shrouded in a sea-clinging mist that added a dreamy texture to the place. All linguistic paradigms for bigness were useless for depicting this landscape. The language had yet to be invented that could achieve its linguistic capture. It resisted any effort to name, much less to tame, it. It had more coastline than the rest of the United States combined, and was one-fifth the size of the forty-eight states combined. Yet, the place-names evoked something of the place itself: Wrangell, Ketchikan, Skagway, Sitka, Juneau, the Red Dog Saloon. Strange-sounding names, fresh, wild, indigenous-sounding—as native to the place as its fjords and orcas, its mists and coastal waterfalls, its microscopic blossoms and native peoples.

It felt thrilling to be following in the footsteps of other writers I admired, of London and Muir, whose works I read as I retraced their routes through this same Northern realm—works I would soon come to use in the borderland classroom. The fact I could be so far from my Yosemite cabin and yet still be reading Muir's descriptions of the land before me made me feel less alone. From his *Travels in Alaska* I read:

> Wrangell was a tranquil place. I never heard a brawl in the streets or a clap of thunder. . . . The cloudless days are calm, pearl gray, and brooding in tone, inclining to rest and peace; the islands seem to drowse and float on the glassy water and in the woods scarcely a leaf stirs. (28)

I came across a sign while wandering the wooden sidewalks of Wrangell that led me to believe that the hospitality of the locals was yet the result of being drunk on nature: "What sunshine is to flowers, smiles are to humanity."

"Perhaps I'll end up teaching in this part of the state."

But something in me balked at the idea, for the weather was too inclement, the skies too overcast, the rains too frequent for my tastes. "Toad-strangling weather," my dad called it. While camped in my tent on Sitka Island, I nearly caught pneumonia—an ill omen for a teaching career in The Panhandle.

At Haines Junction I reluctantly left the Sitka Star. It had been a comforting refuge from the reality of the landscape. Now there was nothing standing between it and me. Now I faced the most uncertain part of this journey, the third thousand-mile leg that would take me overland through one of the most uninhabited places on the planet: The Yukon Territory. My plan had been to hitchhike the rest of the way to Anchorage. But as I dropped my pack by the side of the deserted road leading out of Haines, I seriously questioned the practicality of this plan, and wished I had had the resources to fly from Seattle to Anchorage instead. The traffic was non-existent, the streets deserted. A sense of desolation touched my heart. However, if there is one thing my travels have taught me, it is that the further you get from civilization the friendlier people are.

The first car to come my way was driven by a young woman who stopped to pick me up. She was headed to Dawson, the old gold rush town situated in the heart of the Yukon Territory, three hundred miles into the interior. I was glad to be on the move again. Movement was the one staple my spirits could not do without. As long as I was making progress toward my destination, toward Fairbanks, Bob Egan, and the Teacher Placement Center, I could endure whatever hardships the road might place in my way. Now I understood the compulsion that drives the salmon upstream, and I derived inspiration from their steel-like shafts defeating torrents and falls until they reached the tranquil tributary of their journey's end.

The Haines Highway began in coastal forests, climbed Chilkoot Pass, then descended into purple tundra ringed by mountains unlike any I had ever seen. No alpine meadows here. Just these peaks: naked, windswept, icebound, lunar-looking, monochromatic, iron-hued. It was a glaciated space, traversed by glacial streams and opal lakes. To the north I received my first, heart-jolting sight of the St. Elias Range, with its unbroken chain of eight-thousand-foot summits.

As we left the sea, we also left the rains. This was a welcome change, and one that helped soften the shock of these mountains. There were other changes as well. Whereas I had been surrounded by these lush, heaven-reaching, old-growth forests, now there were no trees whatsoever. The landscape seemed emptier, larger, and

quieter—disquietingly so, in fact. It was as silent as it was limitless, inspiring awareness of my own limitations. In fact, its limitless expanses seemed to mock my own limitations, its infinite
reaches my own finite being. The Sierras seemed like anthills compared to these ranges, seemed unworthy of the name mountain
range. It was difficult to grasp the fact I was now in the same
Yukon Territory I had just been reading about in the pages of Jack
London's *Call of the Wild*.

And so I reached that vital crossroads of Haines Junction and
the Alkan Highway. The very sight of the Alkan lifted my spirits,
knowing I had reached the highway that led to Alaska, to Fairbanks,
and to Bob Egan. I was close enough now to sense the end of the
highway, though it was still 700 miles of wilderness away.

No less evocative of the Yukon than its mountains and place-
names was the humor of its native-wits. In a little roadside café
outside of White Horse, I eavesdropped on the badinage of a group
of older locals. A tourist approached the old sourdough who ran the
café while he was taking a coffee break with this group of old-timers.

"Do you have showers?"

"They're forecast," he replied.

There was a pregnant pause in the conversation of his friends
before all exploded in laughter.

The tourist ignored his answer.

"How much are they?"

$1.50 a drop. It's just a pipe that leaks."

"How much you want for that king crab on the wall?"

"It's not a king crab. That's a Kodiak spider!"

His friends howled their delight. As I soon discovered, having
fun with the tourists was a favorite summer sport in the Yukon,
especially if they were American tourists bound for Alaska. There
was a cutting edge to the old-timer's wit, a note of Canadian pride
in his voice.

"Alright then, you have any stamps?"

"Sure. Here!" he said. He raised a booted foot and stomped it on
the wooden floor.

I thought for sure that this sourdough's backwoods wit would
have pleased Penny in *The Yearling*, for there are few things such
folk enjoy as much as a good laugh at the expense of an outsider,
a city slicker, a Cheechako.

"Very well, then. Can we have some milk."

"I only serve milk to sourdoughs."

"What's that?"

"Well, to be a sourdough you have to do three things: pee in the Yukon, wrestle a bear, and sleep with an Eskimo. 'Course, when you see an Eskimo you might prefer to wrestle with her and sleep with the bear!'"

Another round of laughter, and my first glimpse of the stereotypic attitudes that still prevailed in many parts of the Far North toward the native Other.

In the dirt parking lot outside the café, I saw a bumper sticker on a car with Alaska plates that afforded yet another example of humor in the Far North: "Preserve sport fishing; can Hammond." Jay Hammond was the Governor of Alaska, a big, burly, bearded throwback to the rough and tumble days that preceded statehood. Apparently, not even the highest political figure in the land was immune to the slings and arrows of these native wits.

As I paid my bill, the old sourdough couldn't resist having a little fun with me.

"Watchout for those yahoots, now."

"What are those?"

"Mean you never heard? They're a little smaller than a kiyote. Real wily like. Tug your hair while you're asleep. They have these green eyes that glow in the dark."

"Are you sure they aren't purple?"

He looked up at me as if to say, "Hey, I'm not kidding."

As I sped through the Yukon in the back of a pickup, gazing at the ring of treeless, monochromatic mountains, I felt as if I'd passed a significant watershed on my journey. Gone for good were the low-spirits experienced in The Panhandle, induced by the rains that made the heart as heavy and low and soggy as the overcast skies. I was still on an incredible run of good luck, and prayed it would last a little longer. As my fellow travelers were heading to Anchorage, I was now assured of reaching my destination—a thousand miles through the Yukon and Alaska in two rides and forty-eight hours!

I sat in the bed of the pickup, using the touring pack for a backrest, my feet dangling out the tailgate, my eyes contemplating the extraterrestrial look of the Yukon. We toured on through the Mentasta and Wrangell Ranges. The scenery set me to thinking about teaching in this part of the state, to fantasizing about a log cabin in this wilderness. As we crossed the border into Alaska the land became lusher, the forests returned. It took on the look of an alpine environment again, with jade lakes nestled in timbered, white-capped bowls. We stopped to let the occasional moose or black bear cross the gravel Alkan. Even the moose here were different, were evocative of the Far North, with their shorter, shallower racks, their longer dewlaps, their humped shoulders—changes I noted while watching one nibble red willow buds alongside the highway.

Here was country so beautiful I regretted being in transit through it. I had to resist a mad urge to leap out of the truck and explore it at leisure. Then there appeared a mountain so disproportionate to the ranges we had seen, I could only stare in disbelief. It was an entire range unto itself, a subcontinent of ice dominating the horizon and all other ranges to the south. The clouds that capped other peaks were in turn surmounted by its shoulders. As my gaze lifted above the cloud layer, I gasped in disbelief, for the whiteness I had mistaken for cloud-stuff was in reality a massive shoulder of this mountain still rising through the air! Into a second cloud bank it disappeared, only to reappear above it as well. I was again humbled to be in a place that could spawn such goliaths: whether mountains, bears, or redwoods. A reverent awe, surpassing any I have felt in the world's most famed cathedrals and temples, such as Notre Dame, Il Duomo, Chichen Itza, filled my heart. Finally, there in the sky, seemingly nearer to heaven than Earth, it culminated in a white pyramid worthy of a Pharaoh.

"Is that it way up there too?" someone asked.

Its watershed extended for hundreds of miles in all directions.

"What's it called?"

"According to my map, Mount Sanford."

I laughed. "What a ridiculous name! I wish I knew what the Indians called it. What elevation is it?"

"19,200 feet."

I imagined the Grand Teton, whose roseate face I had seen from my cabin window many mornings, then imagined a mountain 6,000 feet taller!

I awoke from my bed in the back of the pickup to find myself surrounded by skyscrapers.

"Welcome to Anchorage!"

The reflecting glass was tinted pink in the predawn hour. Wrappers were blowing down the deserted street in a chilly wind that made me tighten the collar around my throat and wrap myself more snugly in the folds of my down sleeping bag. We found a café and nursed ourselves awake over sour coffee in styrofoam cups, then resumed the last leg of our trip, taking the highway that led south down the Kenai Peninsula to my friend, Ron's home.

I was eager to reach the end of the road, to resume a more civilized existence. I'd had the same clothes on for three days, hadn't showered, shaved, or brushed my teeth in that same period. I was tired of sleeping on the floor of ferries, in the back of trucks, and on the ground. I was tired of waging war with the mosquitoes, which seemed as loud and large as honeybees. Though it was late May, my breath was still visible on the air. However, tucked inside my down sleeping bag, in my wind pants, down booties, down jacket, and down hood, I was positively crispy. I was also down to my last one hundred dollars and must somehow find a way of replenishing my funds. I would check the docks in Homer, a fishing village at the end of the road where my friend Chuck lived, to see if I could find work in a cannery. It was the peak of herring season, and whenever a ship arrived there was always a hiring frenzy at the canneries.

The destination of my fellow travelers was Homer, mine was Soldotna, where my old high school fishing buddy, Ron had established a practice as a dentist. As luck would have it, Soldotna was also the headquarters of the Kenai Peninsula School District. Despite Bob Egan's assessment that the popular Kenai District offered little hope for inexperienced teachers, I nevertheless resolved to fill out an application since I would be there anyway.

My travel companions dropped me off outside Ron's office in a new, wooden medical center. Ron had found his own paradise: a two-story, four-bedroom home on the Kenai River, his own boat landing, his own eighteen-foot aluminum fishing boat, his walls mounted with trophy-sized king salmon, a sauna in the backyard, two freezers in the garage stuffed with fresh salmon, halibut, and moose meat, a partner who owned a bush plane and who flew him into the best fishing and moose-hunting habitat the state could offer, and a profitable practice. It was a long way from the medical center at the University of California, San Francisco, where he had done his internship and had once worked on my teeth, or the shoals of Cave Rock at Lake Tahoe where we had "limited" on trout one summer after our sophomore year in college. Judging by the smile on Ron's face and the vitality in his voice, the trip had been worth every mile of Alkan Highway he had had to travel.

He told me that he had arranged a "blind date" for me with his girlfriend's friend, and that the four of us would be double-dating that same night. From his house I made an appointment with the personnel director of the Kenai Peninsula School District for the next morning. As luck would have it, my blind date turned out to be the daughter of the Assistant Superintendent of Schools. At the end of our date that night, she invited me into their house. We stayed up talking in her living room until 1:00 a.m., at which point a door opened down the hall, followed by slow footsteps. A moment later Dr. Walls rounded the corner in his bathrobe. We had awakened him from a sound sleep. We shook hands as his daughter performed the introductions, then he retired entreating us to keep our voices down. I took this as my cue to leave and did so, not knowing whether this had been a good or a bad omen. To this day I'm not sure which it was, for everything that followed happened as a consequence of this chance encounter with the Assistant Superintendent of Schools on the eve of my interview with the Kenai Peninsula School District.

Next morning at 9:00 a.m. sharp I entered the district offices, a copy of my resume in hand. Walt recognized me as he emerged from his office, and made a detour to shake my hand. He called one of the secretaries over and introduced me, then told me to see him in his office before I left. The secretary asked if I had any other documents. Suddenly a light went on.

"You should already have them! I applied for a position in this district last year when I was doing my student-teaching in Hawaii."

Her face lit up.

"Wait just a minute," she said, retreating into the records room while I prayed my file hadn't been tossed. She emerged a few minutes later wearing a big smile and bearing my file in her right hand.

"You're in luck! Here it is."

Was I ever. She was as amazed as I was.

"I can't believe it. We received your application from Hawaii last year. And now here you are in person! I am impressed. Just a minute."

She gave me a wink as she said this. And I knew at that point I would be hired. I rolled my eyes heavenward in a silent prayer of thanksgiving for this string of lucky occurrences: Ron's living in the same town as the district office, a blind date who turns out to be the daughter of the Assistant Superintendent of Schools, with whom I just happened to have an appointment the next morning, and now the file! Whoever was pulling the strings up there must have wanted me to work in the Kenai Peninsula School District very badly. But whether he was pulling them for my benefit or for his own diabolical amusement I have not been able to determine to this day.

The secretary disappeared into Dr. Walls' office with my file. I could almost hear her telling him of the extraordinary coincidence. And so as a result of these lucky occurrences I vaulted over all those other aspiring and unemployed teachers who had applied for a position in this popular district. A few minutes later she emerged, and with a knowing smile motioned me into Dr. Walls' office.

His welcome was the big, hearty, informal welcome of the Far North—a verbal bear-hug.

"So, there's the man who had me up all hours of the night with my daughter!"

We talked of his daughter's plans to attend the University of Colorado. I spoke of my travels in that state. And then he got straight to the point.

"Well, I can't promise you anything right now. But we do antici- pate having a few openings in your area. I will take my recommen- dation to the next board meeting. They meet in two weeks. Can you leave me a phone number where you can be reached?"

I gave him the number of the Alaska Teacher's Placement Office at the University of Alaska–Fairbanks.

"I'm attending the job placement fair up there in two weeks."

He raised a concerned eyebrow. My words had the desired effect. Nothing like a rival to make us fully appreciate the object of our desire. We shook hands and parted company. To this day I can't decide if Dr. Walls offered me the position in the village of Nyotek as a reward for my perseverance or as a punishment for my temer- ity in dating his daughter and waking him from a sound sleep.

Two weeks later I walked into Bob Egan's office to see what districts were interviewing that day, and was met with a happy scream from his secretary.

"Stephen! There's an important message for you from the Kenai Peninsula School District! A Dr. Walls wants you to call him right away."

I had had eight interviews in the six days I'd been in Fairbanks, for openings in remote villages like Angoon and Barrow. What was worse, I was fairly certain of receiving an offer from one of these forlorn outposts, an offer which, despite my misgivings, I feared I would accept. I was looking at two years of hard time in the remotest reaches of the interior. Then over the phone Dr. Walls broke the good news to me. He had gone to the board with his recommendation that I be hired to teach in the Athabascan village of Nyotek. The board had given its approval. Did I want the job?

It was a "no-brainer." Without a moment's hesitation, I accepted, never knowing what I had just committed myself to, what I was getting into, or all the difficulties that were in store for me.

"Good. Can you be here to sign the contract by the twenty-first?"

"Of June?"

"Yes!"

The same date as my birthday! My luck was still holding. I assured him I would be there. The office was abuzz with the word one of their recruits had landed a position with the Kenai Peninsula School District, an almost unheard of occurrence. Congratulations were offered all around, from Bob and his secretaries, from his partner, Steve, and from the other teachers with whom I had formed a unique bond during that week.

After the initial euphoria wore off, reality set in and thoughts of an entirely different nature disturbed my peace of mind. Could I handle the harsh conditions that came with my new home— the isolation, the loneliness, the racial tensions? Could I handle the regimentation of work after all these months of freedom? On the one hand, I felt I was embarking on a grand new adventure, that for me life (or at least my professional life) was just beginning. On the other hand, I feared I was making a big mistake, as if I'd just joined the army or the peace corps, had irreversibly committed myself to a course I might come to regret, and soon. Will these students accept me?

And so my fate, for better or worse, had been sealed. I was off to teach in the remote village of Nyotek, population 360 Athabascan Indians, located on the deserted western sore of the Cook Inlet, a forty-five minute flight by bush plane from Anchorage. It wasn't Anchorage, and it wasn't Homer or Kenai or Soldotna or the Matanuska Valley; but neither was it the Pribiloffs or the Aleutians, Barrow, or Nome. Moreover, it was close enough to Anchorage to get away when the need rose, and it was in one of the most desirable regions of the state: one whose winters were "moderate" by Alaskan standards. Instead of fifty below zero, the average winter temperature was seven degrees above zero.

"Hell, I experienced worse than that in Jackson Hole!"

As luck would have it, I was also bound for the very village that my Hawaiian friend, Linda, had once taught in. If I recalled correctly, hadn't she given birth to little Holly in Nyotek? "Won't she be surprised to hear this." I hadn't been planning to contact her, but now I couldn't resist. Her old Alaskan home was just down the road from Soldotna, in Kasilof.

She and I had simply changed places. Funny, that I would travel all these thousands of miles only to end up teaching in the very same Indian village she had once taught in. I didn't realize at the time just how much my friendship with Linda would pave the way for me in Nyotek. My luck was still holding. And I prayed it would hold awhile longer.

Before leaving Fairbanks, I attended the Midnight Sun Writer's Conference where I was able to meet and speak with the poet William Stafford and with the Native American writers Geary Hobson and James Welch, all of whose works would come to play a part in my own borderland pedagogy, along with the works of Jack London and Farley Mowat, which I'd read for companionship on my travels to and across Alaska. In the arduous and challenging months ahead I would be grateful for this serendipitous encounter with these writers and teachers.

Now that I knew the name of the village, Nyotek, in which I would be teaching, I began asking anyone and everyone at the job fair and writer's conference about it. Bob introduced me to a group of Alaskan teachers conducting a workshop on books to teach in the bush. I found myself in a veritable nest of bush teachers: a free-spirited, iconoclastic group whose ideas were as bold as they were unconventional. I asked each of them if they could recommend books to use, especially pertaining to native cultures. I was encouraged by their responses about Nyotek.

"What's the scenery like?"

"Oh, you know. Forests, hills, mountains."

"It's not flat. Be thankful for that."

"And not too cold either. That's the advantage of being on the coast instead of in the interior."

"Do you know what you're getting into?"

"What do you mean?"

"Well, Nyotek is probably the wealthiest native village in Alaska. Oil was discovered there a few years ago. The natives struck a deal with the oil companies. They have a brand new high school. They're living in modern redwood homes. They've taken a lot of criticism from other villages for selling out, for betraying their own people. In the arena of native politics, Nyotek is somewhat of a loose cannon."

"Have you had any cross-cultural experience?"

I nodded. "My teacher training in Hawaii was mostly cross-cultural."

"Good. That should help ease the culture shock a little. Most native students in high school will have about a fifth grade reading ability. I'd get there a month early just to get used to living in a village."

"And so you'll have time to order the books you want, and any other supplies you might need."

"I want to use books they can relate to, books about Alaska and other native peoples."

"An interesting idea."

"I think it's a good idea. In my village we started this project where we sent the native kids into the village to talk to the old people and ask them for stories, which they wrote down in their journals. Then we made a play out of them that we performed at Christmas for the village. We made recordings of Eskimo ceremonies, filmed them."

I too was anxious to gather and record the myths, legends, songs, and lore of Nyotek. In time, I would be brought face-to-face with the ethical implications of my own fetishization of the authentic native. At the moment I had more immediate concerns, however.

"You better request any films you want now, if you want them by spring."

I was starting to get excited, was feeling a little more confident: a pedagogical plan was beginning to take shape in my mind. It would gestate over the next three years, emerging one feature at a time, a process as laborious as it was painful. And this chance encounter with these veteran bush teachers was critical to its conception insofar as they sewed the seeds of an alternative indigenous pedagogy in my mind. I bathed in their lore and their knowledge, intent on imbibing as much of it as I could in the brief period we had together. Seeing the bold, experimental things other bush teachers were doing in their villages, as well as the agency they enjoyed implementing their ideas, encouraged me to adopt a similar experimental approach, one that was willing to try radical new approaches in order to engage the interests of borderland students, one that was willing to literally "throw out the book." At first I would rely on what was familiar to me, instead of what was right for them. I would follow in the pedagogical footsteps of my predecessors until I got my own bearings as a bush teacher, until I got a feel for the lay of the land.

"I had to do my student teaching in the bush, under the eye of this little old lady, this old-fashioned school marm, who tried to teach 'em grammar. All remedial stuff. Bored 'em to tears. And she taught it with missionary zeal. But they have no use for it whatsoever. Few, if any, of them will ever leave the village to go to college."

This bit of unsolicited intelligence was disquieting insofar as a college prep approach to teaching comprised the foundation of my current pedagogy. "Maybe it'll be different in the village I'm going to."

That day I attended a workshop by the Native American writer, Geary Hobson, who had edited the definitive collection of Native American poetry, *The Remembered Earth*, which I would use in my college course in Native American studies years later. My gaze took in the cowboy boots, the long silky hair, the row of pens in the pocket of his denim shirt, the chiseled, pock-marked face, as thin as his nose, the high cheekbones, the eyebrows like grey stickers.

He addressed us in a deep, soft-spoken voice.

"A little current within language . . . the words nudge each other along in a sort of key signature . . . so far, I sound pretty brilliant. I think I'll quit while I'm ahead. When doing poetry, nothing is too slight. I'm thinking of commas, syllables. Keats' letters are some of the most wonderful things I know of."

This set me to wondering if there might be some way of fusing the Great Books with non-canonical, native-voiced works. After all, here was a Native American writer who drew inspiration from the poetry of a dead, white, male canonized in English. Might there be others who had something to say to the native mind?

Geary's voice was still sending its soft pulse through the classroom.

"Once the pages are done rattling, I begin. . . . There's a difference between ambiguity and letting something resonate from the page. Alaska is a good place for the writer. The myth of the frontier is disappearing. It's a place today where many elements of the contemporary world are coming together. A pulsation of boom and bust against a background of eternity. There's a Yupik song that goes, "You who live amidst the stars, the caribou is far away. The leader is dying. Come down and help us.""

He continued to elaborate on the unique challenge Alaska poses to the writer.

"Alaska writing naturally has to do with nature. But you can't just look at the mountains and think that's enough. True, Alaska is a good laboratory for studying Nature. But anywhere there's humans there's a little of the same struggle seen 'round the world. The same human drama unfolds here as other places. Individuals struggling to carve out an existence in a harsh land. Native peoples struggling to protect their life-ways from the encroachments of an invading culture. Sometimes, the best way to write about Alaska is to get away from it. A great burden is removed. I'm too conscious about it when I'm here. There's a tendency among Alaskans, to which writers fall victim, to overromanticize Nature, the great myth of the Frontier, to provide what remains of it to those for whom it has disappeared. And we are trapped by this writing tradition. Editors reject manuscripts that don't speak to this mythic Alaska, that don't write about this 'moose culture,' as I call it."

The room broke out in laughter.

"Very few Alaskans have even tasted the frontier lifestyle. It's increasingly difficult to breakout of this mythic tradition and write something new when it's what the readers expect, what the editors demand. I think there's a tremendous story taking place in Alaska. You can sense the vitality, the variety of viewpoints and lifestyles here. It's an ideal situation for a writer because the field is wide open. It's waiting for someone like Michener to come along and tell the Alaska story. But even Michener is about myth-making, to a certain extent."

Jack Cady was the next to speak about writing and Alaska.

"I like the way words run over the page. I have this vision of mustangs scattering over the sage, kicking up dust."

Afterward, I approached Geary Hobson, seeking the titles of works I might use in my classroom. He suggested, *When the Legends Die* (Ute), *Turkey Brother* (Iroquois) and two by a fellow Native American and writing conference participant, James Welch: *Blood in the Snow* and *Death of Jim Loney*. I vowed to buy and read them before arriving in the village.

On June 21st (my birthday), I signed my first contract as a teacher. I spent fifteen minutes signing forms in the office of the secretary, Betsy: oath of office, w-4, life, medical, dental, and optical insurance, retirement, and method of payment. Betsy greeted and treated me as if I was one of the family. I was quietly very happy, for it appeared that at last I had freed myself from the ogre of poverty who had been hounding my heels since my undergraduate days at University of California at Santa Barbara. I could go to the dentist for the first time in seven years, pay off some old debts, including my student loans, and if I chose, retire in twenty years at fifty percent of my salary.

I shuddered at the burden placed on me, of teaching native children, and wondered if I'd measure up to that burden, if I'd hold up under it. I looked at the calendar and saw only one week off for Christmas, three days for Easter, and only three holidays in the five months between January and May and wondered: "Can I take it? Nine months in the bush? Can I really teach English? Under these conditions? Have I gotten in over my head? Will the Indian children and I get along?" It was all looming so large in my immediate future, I shuddered to think about it.

I plucked up the nerve and asked Betsy if it might be possible to receive an advance on my first check to meet the expenses of relocating to the bush: clothes, several months of groceries, a Coleman stove for power outages, etc. She steered me to the Alaska School Employees Credit Union where I was able to open an account and secure an advance of $500, which I could repay through payroll deductions over a sixth-month period. The friendly loan officer extended this credit despite the fact I had no cash, no credit cards, no bank account, and no assets, not even a car. He looked at me after reading my application, and with a smile on his face and a note of disbelief in his voice asked, "Don't you own anything?"

"Well, I don't own any land or a car, if that's what you mean."

"Do you have any personal belongings?"

"Well, yes. A dog. And a backpack."

His smile broadened.

"I realize I'm a poor risk."

"No. I don't think you're a poor risk at all."

I showed him a copy of the contract I had just signed that morning. I couldn't bring myself to look at him while he was reading the list of my assets, liabilities, and net worth. The column of zeros was embarrassingly long.

"Well, it looks like you're about to go from the outhouse to the penthouse!"

"Yes, my own little penthouse on the tundra."

And so I joined the little colony of old high school friends who had come north. By sheer coincidence, an old girlfriend, Cherie, was living with her mother in Anchorage. She too had been part of the circle of old friends that included Chuck, Norm, Rosso and his cousin, Ron. Cherie and her mother were kind enough to take me in, allowing me to use their house as a base camp to mount my expedition into the Alaskan bush. They also threw a going away party in my honor on the eve of my flight into the Alaskan interior. There, our little colony assembled, marveling at the strange congruence of our fates, which had brought us separately to this land four thousand miles and ten years removed from our high school. Only one disquieting note was sounded at this farewell party by Senator Sackeen, for whom Cherie's mom worked as an administrative assistant. Part Athabascan himself, when he heard I was headed to the village of Nyotek, he merely tilted his head toward the kitchen ceiling and laughed.

"Good luck!"

I received my first glimpse of Nyotek through the wing struts of Jimmy St. Claire's bush plane. The plane was loaded with my belongings, several months worth of groceries, and my pet dog, Misty, whom I had had shipped north to ease the loneliness and isolation of my new home, so much so in fact that Jimmy had asked me to hop out of the passenger seat and lift the tail off the runway so he could start taxiing.

As if guessing my fears, he was quick to reassure me.

"Don't worry. This little bird has a better thrust-to-weight ratio than any plane flying out of Anchorage."

Though diminutive, Jimmy was as full of pluck as a duck on the wing. He was attired in his habitual uniform: mechanic's overalls and a leather flying cap with earflaps, circa World War II. Through the Cessna's windshield I watched with wide-open eyes the unfamiliar, unearthly, and limitless landscape below. The shadow of Jimmy's Cessna moved slowly if steadily across this monolithic place like a mosquito crawling upon the gray, monochromatic skin of an elephant. The waters of the Cook Inlet, which we quickly crossed, were likewise gray, cleaved here and there by the rounded backs of beluga whales, as if by white porpoises, and torn into a dozen, contesting currents by the notorious bore tides.

I lifted my gaze to the landscape framed in Jimmy's bug-smeared windshield, toward which we were racing at 200 miles per hour. A lake-filled, forested, table-land trapped between the sea and the buttress of the Alaska range, and curving southward for as far as I could see, for the entire length of the Cook Inlet, without a sign of habitation. Jimmy kept up a steady chatter pertaining to the features of the landscape and the wildlife he'd sighted on recent trips. My attention, however, was riveted to the lonely white steeple of a Russian orthodox church that was the first sign of civilization on this side of the Cook Inlet, and the first evidence of the village toward which I was heading. Jimmy homed in on this landmark like a whaler navigating toward a lighthouse. At such moments, time passes all too quickly. I found myself wishing the flight would last another hour, would in fact go on forever. The final grains in the hourglass of my pre-bush teacher life were slipping away, and I found myself simultaneously resisting the inevitable and nerving myself to it.

The features of the village itself began to appear, delineated from the trackless forest and the blond bluffs that encompassed it. The images that appeared below me did not in the least conform to my preconceived notions of an Athabascan Indian village: prefabricated, cookie-cutter, tract homes lined a series of gravel streets that looped upon themselves like gray intestines; through a fissure in the birch canopy I caught a glimpse of redwood rooftops circled in a cul-de-sac. Each house was complemented by a miniature cabin from which arose columns of blue woodsmoke. As Jimmy pointed out, these were the "smokehouses" for curing salmon. The last of three silver salmon runs, beginning in May and continuing through August, had just ended. Strips of nutritious red flesh hung from drying racks, curing in the sun. The seasonal rhythms of these people, as I was to discover shortly, were intimately yoked to the movements of two animals: the salmon and the moose. Life in this corner of the Alaskan bush was organized around the behavioral patterns of these indigenous species. If activity in the winter was severely depressed, in the summer it reached manic dimensions, reaching its climax in late August and early September with the last salmon run, the autumn moose hunt, and the onset of the short-lived berry-picking season. My arrival, as well as the commencement of the academic year, coincided with this feverish communal activity, and to a certain extent was overshadowed by it. As we banked over the village, I saw that it was dominated by two structures: the steeple of the Russian Orthodox church and the blue cinderblock of E. L. Elmendorf School. The church occupied the only hill while the school was situated in the geographic center of the village, as incongruously as if an industrial warehouse had been built in the middle of a rural neighborhood. These two edifices of the dominant Euro-American culture reinscribed the asymmetrical power relations between the whites and the Athabascans, reserving the heights and the center for the colonizer while relegating the indigene to the geographic margins of his or her own "home."

As we straightened out for our final approach to the runway, we flew right over the little cemetery that occupied a grassy slope adjacent to the village. The wrought-iron fences, large tombstones, and fresh bouquets all bore witness to the influence of the Russian Orthodox church in this region, an influence that was also reflected in the last names of the Athabascans and the place-names that designated many features of their homeland. I would soon have reason to visit this cemetery, but until that occasion the church stood like a lonely, abandoned lighthouse atop its promontory, functioning more as a landmark than anything else, a visual guide for bush pilots to navigate by.

The gravel airstrip slashed through the birch forest like a thousand-yard scar. A minute later the wheels of the Cessna 110 touched down with a twin puff of dust. If one journey had ended, another had just begun. I stood beside my dog and duffel bags awaiting the arrival of the principal in the school's black van, watching the yellow bush plane disappear into the sub-arctic sky, its mosquito-like drone giving way at last to a disquieting silence. The only other place I have heard such ear-ringing quietude was the western rim of the Grand Canyon. My arrival from the sky commanded all the attention of a cottonwood leaf falling in a forest. Then my eyes caught the words spray-painted onto a weather-beaten, lopsided tool-shed that was the only structure on the gravel runway.

"Welcome to the Nyotek Hilton! Rezervation required."

This "sign" was significant for a number of reasons: it showed that humor was alive and kicking in the Alaskan bush, for what could be more comical than the comparison of a toolshed on its last legs to a Hilton hotel? Yet, this "sign" resonated with other, less innocent meanings. The phrase, "rezervation required," puns on the oppressive, if historical fact that for Athabascans, as for all Native Americans, a "rezervation" is still "required," thereby calling the colonizer's attention to the ongoing injustice of their political plight. Further, the phrase playfully subverts and inverts the asymmetrical power relations of the conlonizer-colonized dynamic (which historically has marginalized the Other) by marginalizing the colonizer, for whom a "reservation" is "required" on the rezervation. This sign evidences the ubiquitous and critical role that various tropes of resistance play in the borderland "contact zone": irony, parody, satire, sly civility, and mimicry are just a few of the tropes the Other deploys to answer colonialism back in its own tongue.

This seemingly insignificant and innocent "sign," when "read" in its ambivalent entirety, is therefore a perfect trope for the ambivalent, in-between existence of the Other in the bicultural borderlands: an existence that is conditioned by the tensions between a dominant Euro-American culture and an indigenous subculture. This "sign," like Native American identity itself, was a sliding signifier, as slippery as a salmon in the hand, resisting my attempts to grasp it with any certainty. As such, it was an apt introduction to the bicultural, in-between, careers of the Athabascans, and of my students in particular, a perfect threshold sign marking my arrival in the land of the indigene, and the beginning of my career as a bush teacher.

2

Calibans of the Contact Zone
Resistance and Marginality in the Borderlands

Where there is power, there is resistance.

—Foucault 93

Alienation in school is the number one problem, depressing academic performance and elevating student resistance.

—Shor 14

My first encounters with the land, the Athabascans, and the students consisted of a series of shocks. I have already described some of the effects of my initial encounter with the Alaskan landscape. No less shocking was my first contact with the Athabascan culture. Indeed, as Lewis and Jungman observe, "the barriers that cultural differences pose may be more formidable than those presented by even the harshest physical environment" (*On Being Foreign* xi). Even such a common occurrence as a greeting on the street underscored these cultural differences. For example, instead of returning my friendly salutations, many Athabascans averted their eyes. This I mistook for incivility, if not an indirect form of hostility. This "sign" was the cause of some bewilderment and resentment on my part; however, what I mistook for impoliteness was in reality a sign of politeness. In averting their eyes from mine, in looking to the gravel at their feet, many of my new hosts were merely following a traditional custom that considered it impolite to look any stranger directly in the eyes, the precise opposite of the customs governing behavior between strangers in Euro-American culture. I say "many" because this particular "sign" is coded with other, more ambiguous meanings. For others, averting the eyes from those of a white stranger evinced their "wary mistrust" of the Outsider who has come into their midst bearing the gifts of civilization: literacy, religion, technology, and all the other trappings of a Euro-American culture whose dominance implies the extinction of their own subsistence lifestyle. Their aloof skepticism of the well-meaning outsider reprises the attitude of Chinese immigrants toward whites in San Francisco in the nineteenth century, as Rodanzo Adams observes:

> Doubtless there are in San Francisco white men and women who are well known to some of the Chinese and who are trusted, but the normal attitude of the Chinese toward an unintroduced white stranger with a friendly manner is one of distrust. (319)

The shock of this realization was the shock of recognition: of seeing myself through the eyes of my hosts instead of through my own. The two images were not the same, and to a significant degree were mutually opposed to one another. If, on the one hand, I saw myself and my mission in a favorable light, as fostering academic literacy among Athabascan children, many of my hosts had a less charitable view of that mission. These initial meetings on the gravel roads of Nyotek were the first in a series of encounters that underscored this disconnect between these two views of myself and my mission. This narrative is largely an account of the effort to reconcile those conflicting perceptions. In the final analysis, the greetings we "signed" to one another were as coded with ambiguities as the sign I encountered at the airstrip.

I mention these initial encounters to underscore the cultural misperceptions that problematize relations between colonizer and colonized, and to illustrate as well the necessity for the bush teacher to educate himself or herself to the "signs" of the Other's culture in the quest for a purer cross-cultural communication, for a more accurate translation of meaning across cultures. These encounters manifest the inherent difficulties of negotiating this cross-cultural divide, where signals get crossed, greetings get mistaken for insults, and "signs" mistaken for "wonders." As a result of these misperceptions, the gulf separating me from my Athabascan hosts seemed as deep as that dividing the two shores of the Cook Inlet, the one as "civilized" as the other was "wild." Moreover, these misperceptions, as Lewis and Jungman observe, "occur most frequently during the [initial] phase of the cross-cultural experience" and are due largely to the "sojourner's inability to understand the context of events" (42). Consequently, the cross-cultural traveler "is likely not to consider how he appears to others during this period, primarily because he is so deeply involved as a spectator of all that is going on around him that he has difficulty imagining that he himself is the spectacle" (41).

Other encounters with the Athabascans were less ambiguous, though none the less shocking for all that. While walking on the beach one day shortly after my arrival, an old native pulled a ten-pound silver salmon from his set-net and made a gift of it to me, holding it up by the tail with a grin. Without saying a word, he laid it across my outstretched hands, offering yet another "sign" of the multiple positions the Athabascan assumes relative to the outsider.

Initially, my morale suffered not only as a consequence of my ambivalent reception by some of the Athabascans, but as a consequence of the living conditions I encountered. They were everything Bob Egan had said they would be, if not more so. Standing on the bluffs of the far shore of the Cook Inlet, gazing across its formidable expanse to the lights of the Kenai Peninsula kindled a sense of isolation, loneliness, and desolation which at times overwhelmed my spirits. This geographical isolation was compounded by the social marginalization I experienced as a white bush teacher living on an Indian reservation. Cabin fever, racial tension, and loneliness all wrecked havoc on my morale. There was little to relieve the routine of teaching: no malls, no restaurants, no cinema. Just the white steeple of the Russian Orthodox Church dominating the village from the height of a lonely, windswept hill: a trope for my own incongruous solitude.

But things could have been worse, as they were for my colleagues who accepted positions in the Pribiloffs and Aleutians. At least I had regular mail service, central heating, and running water, whereas they were reduced to using outhouses and honey-buckets. At least I could fly out for Christmas, whereas they enjoyed no such luxury. And when the hardships of the bush became too much to bear, Anchorage was only a forty-five-minute flight away.

My initial encounters with the students were no less shocking than those with the Alaskan landscape and the Athabascan culture. Problems occurred which no teacher-training program situated in the Lower Forty-eight could possibly anticipate. I arrived at school one morning to find Alvin crying because a grizzly bear had killed his pet moose. I entered the teacher's lounge one morning to find a female colleague in tears because she had been chased by a grizzly on her way to school. She accidentally startled it while passing a blueberry patch. Like their parents, many students chewed homemade snuff, which they made by "cutting" regular chewing tobacco with an ear-shaped fungus found on the trunks of birch trees. Throughout class there was a steady stream of students to and from the sink, into which the black juice was expectorated.

Not 5 minutes into my first class, an Athabascan girl of mixed-race decent, Erin, stood up and demanded to know "why we should listen to anything you say. You'll just be gone in two years anyway." When I told her to sit down, she gave me a one-fingered salute and left the room before I could send her to the office. That first semester I also lost three-fifths of my journalism/publications course when Doris, Debbie, and Veronica became pregnant and dropped out of school. I also almost lost my enthusiasm for teaching period. As initiations go, mine was fairly typical; once passed, however, it conferred membership into a classroom community more endearing than any I've known in my ensuing career.

Seasonal absenteeism was another problem. The commencement of the school year coincided with the fall moose-hunting season. One morning I arrived to find an unusual number of empty seats. Many parents in the village and timber camp removed their children from school to assist with the annual moose hunt, on which every family depended to supplement their diet. Moose was the primary source of meat in the diets of Athabascans and whites alike. For centuries, moose hunting had been an integral part of the Athabascan's subsistence lifestyle. I will revisit the cultural conflicts that were associated with moose hunting, and their implications for borderland pedagogy, in the last chapter. For three weeks in September schooling took a back seat to these subsistence activities, as it did at the end of the school year which was foreshortened to mid-May to accommodate the Athabascans' subsistence salmon fishing activities. We were therefore encouraged by the principal to teach through these periods by showing films, playing games, taking field trips, or otherwise delaying instruction until the majority of students returned to class.

Another problem unique to this pedagogical situation was the configuration of the classes inasmuch as two grade levels were combined into a single class due to the small numbers of students. The entire K through 12 population varied from 88 to 112 during my three years, of which anywhere from 35 to 58 were in grades 7 through 12. Thus, I found myself teaching classes in which grades 7 to 8, 9 to 10, and 11 to 12 were combined. This presented some unique problems, for not only must I devise plans for a broader range of abilities, but those plans had to be devised on a two-year basis so that this year's seventh graders would not have the same material next year as eighth graders. The acquisition of literacy can be adversely affected by pedagogical exigencies peculiar to the borderland classroom, and to the reservation classroom in particular. Lame Deer offers a compelling explanation for the elementary reading levels of many Native Americans of his generation, who read at the third grade level for the simple reason that "the Government teachers were all third grade teachers":

> They taught up to this grade and that was the highest. I stayed in that goddamn third grade for six years. There wasn't any other. The Indian people of my generation will tell you that it was the same at the other schools all over the reservations. Year after year the same grade over again. (24)

The teaching load posed other problems. Though hired as a language arts/history specialist, I wound up teaching as a generalist that first year in the bush. As a result, I was assigned six different courses, half of which I had no formal training in, which meant six separate "preps." Though the secondary school only served fifty-five students, it offered a curriculum similar to a school in Anchorage serving twelve hundred students. Thus, my first year I found myself teaching English, history, algebra, arts and crafts, journalism, and yearbook. This not only tested the limits of my ability, but of my sanity.

Yet, what initially appeared to be one of the greatest problems of this pedagogical situation turned out to be its greatest blessing. This multi-disciplinary course load allowed me to grow as a teacher in unexpected directions and opened avenues for inventive approaches to borderland pedagogy that might have remained unexplored had I not been placed in this unique, if initially overwhelming, situation. As a consequence of this arrangement I was perfectly situated to implement an innovative, interdisciplinary course of instruction, of which I will have more to say in the second half of this work.

Instruction was frequently impacted by tragedies unique to this situation and that claimed the lives of the young in inordinate numbers. On two occasions the village-timber camp community was jolted by plane crashes, one of which claimed the lives of the well-loved janitor, his wife, and his niece, a popular student in the fourth grade, to whom we dedicated that year's annual. Kitty, the equally beloved secretary, was tragically killed by her own son, also one of my students, whose gun accidentally discharged while jumping out of their pickup truck during a moose hunt. In these remote borderlands, death assumed a guise as freakish as it was violent. A student drowned when he fell through a frozen lake one spring while checking his traplines. Another was seriously injured in a high-speed snowmobile crash. Another was killed in Anchorage while driving under the influence of alcohol. Alvin was buried alive in a mudslide while walking home from the bus stop one day, and barely dug out in time by his schoolmates. Many native students were still grieving over the death of a well-liked senior who had committed suicide the previous year. Others still felt the loss of friends who had died from drug overdoses. The former president of the tribal council, and the husband of my landlady, died tragically when he was trapped on the roof of a burning hotel in Anchorage. The principal would later pull an Athabascan woman from a burning trailer, saving her life. In a community of 360 souls, where everyone is a relative of everyone else, a death has a more pronounced impact than it might in a community whose members are not bound by ties of kinship. At times, it seemed as if a cloud of misfortune hovered over this small Athabascan village.

The grief and absenteeism generated by these tragedies also had an adverse effect on classroom performance, imposing upon the bush teacher a special obligation to be aware of which students were suffering more acutely as a consequence of kinship ties to the deceased, and to account for this in his or her pedagogy, whose aim at such times had more to do with healing than with the acquisition of literacy. At such times, and in such a setting, the borderland teacher facilitates the educational process by helping the healing process, for which he or she is amply rewarded when the smiles reappear on a young face like sparkles of sunshine upon the snow.

Resistance and Marginality in the Borderland Classroom

These problems, diverse as they might be, paled in comparison with the most ubiquitous problems: those associated with the adverse affects of acculturation and deracination, with what Irving Howe terms the "tensions of biculturalism" (110), with what Edward Said calls the "mutilations of exile (51)." The ferocity of the processes of deracination and quasiassimilation left the Athabascan students occupying a variety of subject positions relative to the dominant culture and the indigenous subculture, each enacting its own resistance. Whereas some identified more closely with the dominant, Euro-American culture, others identified more closely with the Athabascan subculture. Moreover, there were differences among students within each of these groups, some manifesting hostile attitudes toward the culture they did not identify with, whether this was the indigenous subculture or the dominant Euro-American culture. In between these two polarities of identification was yet another group of students who identified closely with neither culture, who were alienated from both, drifting in an acultural limbo, the students who today would be labeled most "at risk," who evinced a good deal of apathy, confusion, ambivalence, introversion, or nihilism within the classroom, as well as self-destructive behavior outside it: alcoholism, vandalism, drug abuse, and suicide, to name a few.

Before proceeding with this discussion of the group dynamics in this borderland classroom, I want to address the ethical implications associated with any effort to categorize, taxonomize, or ontologically colonize the Other. I am not proffering these distinctions in an effort to essentialize personality traits in the bicultural borderlands, or to reduce the Other to a series of exotic types that merely reinscribe the dehumanizing signifying practices of those who have historically colonized him or her. If my experience in the bicultural borderlands of Alaska has shown me anything, it is that students position and reposition themselves in a variety of ways relative to the dominant and to the indigenous culture, that there are resistances peculiar to these various subject positions, and that there is often movement among these hybrid identities. It is unethical to speak of these categories of hybrid identities (in absolute or relative terms) if the intent or the effect is to reinscribe dehumanizing and colonizing practices of signification. It is altogether useful to speak of them, however, if they generate a deeper awareness of the adverse effects of oppression, not the least of which is the production of an alienated, fragmented, or conflicted indigenous personality, in order to eliminate and heal the historical, psychological, economical, and material effects of oppression. The bicultural identities I observe are not located within categories whose boundaries are fixed and stable, but subject to blurring, hybridization, and transgression by subjects that are themselves unstable, fluid, shifting, and multiple. Nevertheless, there are characteristics of personality that distinguish Mike from David, Erin from Velma and Peter, and which reinforce the assertion that the Native American Other is not unitary but multiple, not one Other but many, not the Same but itself enriched by Difference.

Although the personality of every student bore evidence of the adverse effects of marginalization, in some those effects were moderate, in others they were extreme. But whether extreme or moderate, these multiple effects of biculturalism problematized pedagogy on a daily basis. Alvin might come to school crying over the pet moose killed by a grizzly bear, or students might not come to school at all because of their subsistence fishing and hunting activities, but these problems were ephemeral and resolved themselves. More difficult to perceive were the day-to-day manifestations of bicultural marginalization that so profoundly influenced the group dynamics of this borderland classroom, as well as the classroom performance of these students, and which ultimately forced me to reexamine the goals, assumptions, methodology, practicality, and morality of the pedagogy of assimilation or "initiation" that I practiced.

Alaska has been described as a place of extremes. Geographically, it is situated at the extreme ends of the North American continent. Culturally, it is situated at the extreme ends of Empire. Temperatures, likewise, can range from one extreme to the other, from ninety degrees Fahrenheit in Fairbanks in June to seventy below zero in Barrow in December. Daylight similarly fluctuates between extremes, lasting until 3:00 a.m. in the summer, no longer than the length of a composition class in winter. It should come as no great surprise then that the behaviors, discourses, and personalities of native students in these bicultural borderlands should exhibit extreme traits: ranging from hostility and nihilism on the one hand to apathy and ambivalence, confusion and withdrawal on the other. When marginalized students cross the threshold into the classroom they are experiencing a violent rupture with their home culture and an equally violent "initiation" into the dominant culture. Feelings of shock, uncertainty, insecurity, alienation, confusion, and homesickness are the norm.

To reiterate, I am not proffering these observations in support of essentialist claims that presume distinctions that are absolute, rigid, and reductive. Rather, the students merely displayed tendencies to identify more closely with one culture or the other, tendencies which were themselves characterized by differences, and which were not completely free of identifications with the opposite culture. Perhaps it would be more accurate to suggest that there was a dominant tendency to identify with one culture, and a lesser countertendency toward identification with the opposite culture, and that this dynamic resolved itself into a multiplicity of subject positions across cultures. These divided allegiances produced tensions in the bicultural student which in turn produced a range of effects, similar to the frictions produced by the dynamics of plate tectonics, generated by the violent process of subduction in which one continental plate slides under another, producing faultlines that destabilize the earth in violent quakes.

What I was confronted with was not one Other, but many Others, each enacting his or her own resistance, enunciating a discourse, exhibiting behaviors, and manifesting personality traits peculiar to itself, all manifesting to one degree or another the ill-effects of bicultural marginalization. Further, I wish to assert that these subject positions were less stable in some instances than in others, allowing for movement between them, as students positioned and repositioned themselves along this continuum of hybrid identities. Thus, I want to posit this range of bicultural identities as a continuum that allows for shadings and gradations and indeterminacy, not as a line in which a limited number of distinct positions are held always and forever, as though they "signed" a set of finite numbers between the polar extremes of absolute identity with one culture or the other. The point I want to make is that the processes of acculturation, deracination, and reculturation affected these students in different ways, producing myriad adverse effects that call into question the practicality and morality of a pedagogy that itself reproduces these effects, albeit often unwittingly, and that orients itself toward one goal: initiation into the dominant culture, often assuming that such assimilation is consonant with the interests, well-being, and needs of the native student.

In the following section I want to examine this heteroglossia of hybrid identities, and the resistances associated with the multiple subject positions assumed by Athabascan students relative to the dominant culture and the indigenous subculture. I also wish to assert that in order to more effectively teach in such a bicultural borderland milieu where the processes of acculturation, deracination, and reculturation exert a strong influence upon personality, behavior, discourse, and performance in the classroom, it behooves the practitioner to acquaint himself or herself with those diverse effects. Effective pedagogy in such a setting is a function, to a certain extent, of the practitioner's ability to assess where in this spectrum of hybrid identities any given student may be at any given period in their bicultural careers. Hence attitudes about the two cultures are subject to change, and indeed such evolution of consciousness is one sign of an active learning environment, if one defines such an environment as a space where self-reflexive inquiry into diverse aspects of the learner's lived reality can freely and frequently occur.

Before proceeding further, I want to clarify a point: these subject positions are not always freely chosen by the borderland learner, but are often the outcomes determined by the experience of biculturalism itself. If the violence of deracination had effected a rupture between many of these students and their Athabascan subculture, launching them on a journey toward the dominant culture, then the violence of discrimination in that culture had turned them back at its gates, abandoning them to an acultural wilderness of alienation, confusion, conflict, ambiguity, and hostility—a cultural limbo or no-man's land, a deculturized contact zone outside the boundaries of either culture.

The Resistance of Acculturation and Reculturation

Resistance in this borderland classroom, as in the village, assumed many forms. Some students, such as Mark, resisted instruction in the Great Books of the canon, in the master narratives of American history, in the thesis-driven theme, in the scientific mode of inquiry, in the academic codes of standard English, and in anything that served an assimilationist purpose because they feared that by learning such things they would not be Athabascan anymore. The acquisition of literacy threatened their solidarity with the Athabascan subculture, the loss of which was too steep a price to pay for mastering the academic codes of the dominant culture. Mark's resistance to the dominant culture was sometimes enacted through a legitimate discourse of "sly civility" and the tropes associated with it: parody, satire, irony, and mimicry (Bhabha 79). For example, discovering in *Black Elk Speaks* that the Lakota word for white man was "Wasichu," Mark began greeting me in front of the class with a "Hi, Mr. Wasichu." This was accompanied by a good-natured laugh and the traditional Athabascan disclaimer signifying no offense had been meant: "I jokes." Thus, Mark's resistance was enacted from within the ambit of colonialism through a double-speaking "antic disposition" that veiled resistance while enacting it, in which the cloak of civility concealed the satiric dagger of resistance. It therefore comprised one of the milder forms that resistance assumed in this borderland classroom in contradistinction to the more openly hostile, extreme resistances enunciated by some of his Athabascan peers.

At the opposite end of the bicultural spectrum from Mark was David, who identified more strongly with the dominant culture and who resisted any instruction foregrounding the recuperation of his ancestral culture for the simple reason that, unlike Mark, he didn't want to be Athabascan anymore. Thus, he not only refused to participate in the bilingual education program, but in the Foxfire program as well, which was oriented toward the recuperation of traditional Athabascan culture. Similarly, when the focus in reading shifted from the Great Books of the Western canon to narratives from the borderlands such as Black Elk's, David voiced his opposition by demanding to know, "Why do we have to read this junk?" I will revisit the implications of David's resistance in Chapter 6.

David's alienation from his peers was the by-product of his difference from them. Unlike most of them, he was an Athabascan of mixed-race decent who had left the reservation to be educated in Anchorage. Disillusioned by the discrimination he encountered there, he returned to the village for his senior year, carrying as it were a chip on either shoulder against both cultures. The marginalization he experienced in Anchorage was one factor influencing his refusal to pursue postsecondary education, this despite a 4.0 grade point average (g.p.a.). He had not anticipated, nor had he discovered a way to cope with, the effects of culture shock, not the least of which was the discrimination he experienced in the metropolis. College often engenders ambivalent attitudes in some bicultural students: if on the one hand, it beckons with the promises of the American materialist dream, then on the other it threatens the student with marginalization, isolation, alienation, and deracination, with loss of identity, family, friends, and home. Sojourners in the dominant culture, like David, are victimized by the unequal code of race relations that makes difference instead of merit the determining factor in their bicultural odyssey. Thus, their effort to assimilate never progresses beyond the spectator phase to a fuller accommodation with the dominant culture.

When David returned to the village for his senior year, he held himself aloof from his peers, Athabascan as well as white, sitting alone along a wall, manifesting an almost narcissistic alienation. His estrangement was, in my opinion, the by-product of several differences: his strong identification with Euro-American culture, his mixed-race heritage, his senior status, his 4.0 g.p.a, his superior athletic prowess (he was captain of the basketball team), and his command of standard English. Like Maya Angelou's narrator in the beginning of *Caged Bird*, he wanted to be white, and if not white, then like white: "I was going to look like one of the sweet little white girls who were everybody's dream of what was right with the world" (1). David's open hostility toward his native culture was all the more ironic given his father's role as the foremost "gatekeeper" of Athabascan lore in the village, a role that was recognized when he was chosen as the instructor of Dena'ina and as the consultant for the Foxfire project. His rejection of the Athabascan culture exemplifies the careers of many bicultural students who are anxious to escape the control of ancestral groups. This is evidenced not only in the careers of Native American students, but in the experience of the descendants of immigrant groups, as documented by Amy Tan in *The Joy Luck Club*, and by Irving Howe, who notes that Jewish immigrants to America came to view their traditions as "alien" and to "unconsciously resent and despise those traditions" (Living 110). Adams echoes these findings in his observations of Asian immigrants to Hawaii, noting that "in the second and third generation the tendency is toward emancipation from the control of both ancestral groups":

> Needless to say, these changes are accompanied by a certain amount of conflict within the family, the older people standing more for the maintenance of traditional ways and the young contending for the right of choice—for a family organization of less solidarity and one more in harmony with an American outlook. (294)

The resistances enacted by Mark and David not only made me aware of the tensions in the student population, but of the generational tensions in some Athabascan families. So strong was David's renunciation of his native culture that he refused to say a word to his own father. Was this rift with his father so violent that it precipitated the rift with his ancestral culture? Whatever its causes, David's apostasy from the Athabascan subculture typified the cultural drift of many students, and was the cause of growing concerns among the elders, who tried to combat it in a number of ways: first, by reviving ancestral traditions like the potlatch and the beluga whale hunt; second, by infiltrating the curriculum with courses foregrounding the recuperation of the Athabascan culture, including instruction in Dena'ina. These elders, working in conjunction with the tribal council, successfully lobbied the school board to institute a number of changes in the curriculum. Not only did they recolonize the bilingual education program with instruction in Dena'ina, the Athabascan's mother tongue, but they re-colonized the home economics classroom with instruction in skin sewing and native recipes, and physical education with competitions in the "native olympics": a series of activities that privileged the recovery of traditional Athabascan games, such as the "jump and kick" in which the contestant leapt high in the air to kick a dangling ball with one or both feet. They were also successful integrating the Foxfire project into the curriculum, thereby influencing instruction across a variety of elective courses (Chapter 5).

The school and the Athabascan students became a strategic site of this cross-cultural contestation. The proponents of either culture realized that the allegiance of the younger generation was essential for the reproduction of their respective culture, and that the school was a critical site for winning this allegiance. Ties to the ancestral culture are weakened, if not severed altogether, by schooling, "as children and grandchildren acquire an adequate command of the English language, as they acquire a better economic status, and as their education fits them for participation in the social life of the larger community" (Adams 294). If students like David continued to ignore or otherwise abandon their native culture in increasing numbers, then the only thing standing between that culture and extinction was Time. Once the last of the elders who knew the old ways passed away, there would be no means of perpetuating those ways. As Kathleen Mullen Sands asserts in "American Indian Autobiography," these traditional lifeways "are in danger of being lost to the future because they are always just one generation from extinction" (qtd. in Allen 56). The urgency and anguish of the Athabascan elders is captured by the poet northSun in "what gramma said late at nite":

> gramma thinks about her grandchildren\ they're losing the
> ways\ don't know how to talk Indian\ don't understand me
> when\ I ask for tobacco don't know how to skin rabbit\ sad
> sad\ they're losing the ways. (qtd. in Allen 118)

Elders like Max and Nellie are sustained by the hope that for every David who is lost to the dominant culture and for every Hank who is lost to the ravages of bicultural alienation, who falls victim to suicide, drug overdose, alcoholism, or incarceration, there will be a Mark who is interested in the ways of his ancestors, who might identify on the superficial level of technology with the dominant culture (buying its snow mobiles, its high-powered rifles, its boomboxes and its televisions), but who identities on the deeper level of spirituality and mores with his native culture. And it is around their native spirituality that the Athabascans have drawn their circle in the sand, determined to defend it's vitality, to safeguard its integrity, to form a protective shield of knowledge and teaching about this lore, against those who would see it suppressed, appropriated, or forgotten. And this struggle they are willing to wage by whatever means necessary, for it is a critical component of Native American resistance struggle, even to the point of infiltrating the reservation schools that have traditionally served as vehicles of assimilation into the dominant culture. The Athabascans of Nyotek succeeded in prying that door ajar, in infiltrating the curriculum through the bilingual and Foxfire programs, as a means of insuring the survival of that which they held dearest: their own native lifeways.

This was a significant, if small, victory after the devastating losses of the Alaska Native Lands Claims Settlement (ANLCS), of which I will have more to say in the final chapter, a victory that signified a watershed in local relations between the colonizer and the colonized, a turning point, perhaps even a new dawn. When I arrived in the village the curriculum was beginning to reflect this hybridized character, this tug-of-war between dominant culture and native subculture for the allegiance of the students. The Athabascans were finally beginning to wage their struggle on the colonizer's terrain, within the very institutions used to accelerate the genocide of their own culture. The Athabascan students, no matter what their position relative to the dominant culture and the indigenous subculture, were the site of a fierce contestation between these two cultures. If teachers like myself recruited them into the dominant culture with evangelical zeal, preaching the advantages of a college education, then elders like Max and radical activists like David

Standmark, the tribal council president, were just as evangelical in their recruitment efforts regarding the traditional and contemporary aspects of Athabascan culture. All were vying for the allegiance of these students, whose personalities manifested the effects of this cross-cultural conflict: confusion, ambivalence, apathy, and resentment. Mark and David represented the polarities of resistance enunciated in the classroom, not only in kind but in degree. Whereas Mark's resistance stemmed from his close affinity with the Athabascan culture, David's resistance was the by-product of his renunciation of that culture and close identification with Euro-American culture. Although both students manifested the effects of marginalization, in Mark's case those effects were more benign, whereas with David they produced more extreme traits. These were not, however, the only forms that resistance assumed in the classroom.

Erin's Revolt

There were not only differences between these two groups, but within them. Erin, like Mark, identified more strongly with her Athabascan culture. Whereas Mark identified more strongly with the traditional elements of his ancestral culture, Erin identified more closely with its contemporary aspects, including her people's resistance struggle against neocolonialism. She shared David's contempt for orthodox Athabascan culture, but for a different reason. If he rejected those traditions because they were an impediment to assimilation, Erin renounced them because they had been too complicit in the process of colonization. Unlike David, Erin's rejection of Athabascan traditions was surpassed only by her hostility toward the dominant culture, whose marginalizing racism she had experienced in Anchorage, where she, like David, had been schooled for a period. In the classroom her resistance was enacted through an illegitimate discourse of back talk and the tropes associated with it: profanity, name-calling, obscene gestures. She rejected anything that reinscribed the traditional stereotype of the Indian-as-craftsperson, surrounded by beads and feathers, skins and drums, while embracing subject positions that broke with that tradition: the Athabascan-as-activist, for example. She wasted no time voicing her hostility toward the colonizer, as incarnated in a white male bush teacher. Five minutes into my teaching career, I was confronted by the angry insurrection of this fifteen-year-old Athabascan girl who rose from her seat in defiance of my authority.

"Why should we listen to anything you say? You'll just be gone in two years anyway. Just like all the other teachers they send over here."

I was taken aback by the hostile, confrontational tone in her voice, by this completely unexpected challenge to, if not outright rejection of, my authority. I had anticipated some resistance, but not this soon, nor this blunt. I had assumed that such resistance, at least initially, would assume more covert forms, that my pedagogical honeymoon would last longer than five minutes.

I heard a collective gasp of disbelief and a few titters of approval. When I recovered from my initial shock and embarrassment, I reacted to this unexpected challenge to my authority by becoming more authoritarian.

"Would you please sit down?"

"Fuck you, Mr. Brown."

Talk about "unsolicited oppositional discourse"! (Pratt 39).

Events quickly deteriorated in an escalating cycle of discipline and disobedience: she gave me a "one-fingered salute;" I banished her to the principal's office; she "cut" school; when this was brought to my attention, I notified the principal who responded by "suspending" her for five days.

Erin's resistance can be comprehended, at least partially, within the context of colonizer-colonized relations insofar as it reinscribes the insurrections of the colonized Other across a broad range of topoi, extending from Ireland to Algeria, from Polynesia to Palestine. Thus, the escalating cycle of discipline and disobedience that drives the teacher-student dynamic in this situation reinscribes on a microcosmic scale the macrocosmic dynamic of "European power and native insurrection" wherein colonial oppression begets indigenous resistance which in turn intensifies the efforts to repress that resistance" (Parry 44). Such resistance, as Seamus Deane observes, only "aggravates the ferocity of the process of subjugation" (12).

Erin's resistance underscored, as well, her refusal to accept stereotypes of the Athabascan female as passive, silent, and spoken to, positing in its place a native subject that is active, dissonant, and speaking out, reinscribing the reluctance of the Irish "to yield to caricatures of themselves as barbarous or uncivilized" (13). Erin's insurrection may thus be seen as the by-product of an anticoloniz-ing resolve to resist the closure of subject positions deemed "ille-gitimate" by the colonizer, as the product of a decolonizing determination to occupy those forbidden topoi of indigenous iden-tity, to inhabit those illegitimate spaces of Athabascan subjectivity, to territorialize those subversive terrains of the "bad" Other that the colonizer has condemned to silence. Parry writes,

> The outcome of this agonistic exchange, in which those ad-dressed challenge their interlocaturs, is that the hegemonic discourse, forged in the process of disobedience and combat, occupying new, never colonized and "utopian" territory, and prefiguring other relationships, values, and aspirations, is enunciated. (43–44)

The significance of Erin's revolt is that it subverted the stereo-type of the passive, silent Athabascan female so rigidly adhered to by some of her peers, while establishing other subject positions. If pedagogy attempted to close off or limit the number of native sub-ject positions through a unitary discourse of domination, Erin's insurrection resisted that attempt to close off these other, "illegiti-mate," "utopian," "never colonized," or postcolonized subject posi-tions. If traditional borderland pedagogy privileged the silent, obedient, good Other, then Erin's revolt by contrast foregrounded the carnivalesque insurrection of the loud, disobedient, "bad" Other. Through a discourse of disobedience, profanity, "back talk," and obscene gestures, she resisted conscription into the stereotype, using her marginalization within the classroom as a site from which to enact liberatory resistance, to regain a more active, speaking sub-ject position. Moreover, her discourse of disobedience, and its ten-dency to foreground profane words and gestures, reinscribed the array of resistant tropes used by the native writer to enact similar resistance in the realm of aesthetics: irony, parody, satire, allegory, and magical realism, a point I will develop at greater length in Chapter 6. Because the Athabascans had yet to evolve a body of literature that might serve as a vehicle of resistance, resistance on the reservation assumed the form of nonaesthetic, linguistic insur-rections. Thus, language becomes a tool with which to subvert "the discursive conditions of domination," including a pedagogy, which attempts to subsume, or otherwise silence the voice of the indigene (Bhabha 154). Erin's revolt would also seem to call into question Spivak's contention that the subaltern can't speak as long as he or she must speak in the tongue of the oppressor. Ashcroft, Griffiths, and Tiffen define the subaltern as "those who are never taken into account" (8). The autonomy that such discourse suggests lends weight to Bhabha's contrary assertion that the subaltern can speak effectively by using the discourse of the colonizer to leverage a measure of autonomy through such discursive strategies as "sly civility" and "mimicry." While acknowledging that subaltern speech "is in some sense conditioned upon the dominant discourse," Bhabha nevertheless asserts that through such tropes as mimicry, sly civility, allegory, irony, and parody, subaltern discourse "subverts and menaces the authority within which it necessarily comes into being" (qtd. in Griffiths 75). As Sharpe attests, "in words such as 'refusal,' 'subversion,' and 'intervention,' Bhabha ascribes a more active agency to the colonized than does Spivak" (145). Alter/native subject positions, such as that enunciated by Erin, are some of "the most powerful weapons within the arsenal of the subaltern subject" inasmuch as they are not "founded in the closed and limited construction of a pure, authentic sign" [the good Other] but in endless and excessive transformation of the subject positions possible within the hybridized" (Griffiths 241). What is required, therefore, is a borderland pedagogy that foregrounds these differences, that privileges a multiplicity of subaltern subject positions, each enunciating its own resistance, as opposed to a pedagogy that reduces all Others to The Other by privileging the stereotype of the silent, obedient, and passive native as the one and only authentic native, that marginalizes the bad Other, and all the signs by which it is known, while recognizing and rewarding the good Other.

To what extent was Erin's resistance the result of her gender and her mixed-race ancestry? As Spivak argues, "If in the context of colonial production, the subaltern has no history and cannot speak, the subaltern as female is even more deeply in shadow" (287), and the subaltern as mixed-race female is more deeply in shadow still. As a female, Erin was regarded as Other by males; as an Athabascan she was regarded as Other by whites; and as a mixed-race native she was regarded as Other by her full-blooded peers. She was, as Edward Said asserts, "an exile among exiles" (51). What effect did Erin's mixed-race heritage, and the marginalization it produced, have on the extreme behavior she manifested in the classroom? Adams' observations suggest a strong correlation between mixed-race marginalization and extreme personality traits: "the code of race relations tends to make racial status" a determining factor, "hence the position of the mixed bloods is such as to result in the development of the more extreme types of marginal behavior" (291). As Erin's revolt suggests, the silence of the subaltern is not as absolute as Spivak implies; but neither is the resistance enacted by the Other as autonomous as some would imply. The victories that are won are pyrrhic insofar as they are gained through the contaminating tongue of the colonizer. Argues Derek Walcott in "The Muse of History,"

> [T]hey must abuse master or hero in his own language, and this implies self-deceit. Their view of Caliban is of the enraged pupil. They cannot separate the rage of Caliban from the beauty of his speech when the speeches of Caliban are equal in their power to those of his tutor. The language of the torturer mastered by the victim. This is viewed as servitude, not victory. (qtd. in Ashcroft 371)

Is it any wonder then that language becomes the conduit through which the Other expresses the Self? Denied social contacts, not only within the dominant culture but within the indigenous subculture, is it any wonder that language becomes a refuge for identity, a rhetorical homeland for the double displacement of the mixed-raced Other, a linguistic crawl space that provides the marginalized native a "safe house," a "shelter from the legacy of oppression" and the "mutilations of exile." Home for Erin, as it is for Laura, the protagonist of "Temps Perdi," "is a language like 'a carib skin,' a mosquito net of language that protects and confines the writer" (Rhys, qtd. in Wilson 71). If borderland pedagogy seeks to be truly student-centered in practice and in theory, it must somehow make room for the diverse subject positions students assume relative to the dominant culture and indigenous subculture, must somehow find a way of making room in the classroom not only for the voices of those desiring assimilation, but for the disruptive, anticolonizing voices of those seeking only to be different, to be themselves, to be Athabascan. Pedagogy in the borderlands has traditionally been about power whereas it needs to become about possibilities; more precisely, it needs to empower the native student by foregrounding the possibilities available to him and her, by privileging alter/natives that are contestatory, participatory, and liberatory.

The Passive Resistance of Bicultural Alienation

> But one may fail because of overwhelming circumstances . . . and, at the worst, the defeated may fall to a level where effort ceases. (Adams 278)

The largest group of Athabascan students positioned themselves somewhere between these two poles, identifying closely with neither the indigenous subculture nor the dominant culture. This is not to imply that their situation was the result of choices freely arrived at; rather, their displacement was determined by the adverse effects of deracination and assimilation. They were the victims of a dual alienation that left them without any identity, without a home in either the physical or the psychic sense. They suffered the debilitating effects of an Athabascan diaspora rendered all the more ironic by the fact that it was played out on the very landscape that was once theirs, within sight and sound of the very peaks and coastlines, lakes and woods with which their very identity as a people had once been inseparable. Lewis and Jungman write,

> At some point during this process, however, there seems to occur a kind of crisis of personality, or identity, a period when the individual feels poised precariously over the abyss that seems to separate the two cultures. . . . It is at this point that all life can seem artificial and pointless. (xix)

For many weeks when I looked out from the lectern all I saw of these native students was the tops of their heads, which were bowed in seeming contemplation of their desktops, but which were in reality filled with paralyzing thoughts of their own inadequacies as writers, readers, and speakers of standard English. For weeks at a time I neither heard their voices nor saw their faces. Like the

immigrants of whom Adams writes, they too were seemingly overwhelmed by their singular circumstances. They appeared to be
paralyzed by the debilitating effects of deracination and marginalization that had bleached their subculture out of them while
denying them full membership in the dominant culture, and this
produced a bicultural alienation that was evidenced by a myriad of
debilitating effects: confusion, apathy, ambivalence, anger, nihilism, shame, and silence, to name just a few.

All were seemingly overwhelmed into silence by a collective awareness of their academic inadequacies: of their thick native accents, of
their poor command of standard English, of its written and spoken
codes, of their inability to process the Word as written in Academic
English, of their illegible penmanship, poor spelling, fifth-grade reading level, of their "deficient" comprehension skills and their "poor"
aptitude on tests. Every time they opened their mouths to speak,
these "inadequacies" were exposed. Therefore, if given the choice,
they remained silent. Silence was the shroud that concealed a paralyzing awareness of their own "deficiencies," the operatic mask that
hid their intellectual "shortcomings." For these Athabascan students,
schooling meant a painful encounter with these realities on a weekly,
daily, and hourly basis. Schooling, therefore, intensified their need
to escape such a painful, self-conscious "reality check" through a
variety of self-destructive behaviors: absenteeism, alcoholism, drug
abuse, even suicide in extreme cases. The preponderance of small
tombstones on the hillside south of the reservation was a poignant
reminder of the lives that had come to an end as tragic as it was
premature. They were overwhelmed by the circumstances of their
alienation, by the jibes of their Athabascan classmates, by the racial
slurs of the white timber camp students, by the reproaches of some
teachers who regarded them as so much "dead wood" in the classroom, and finally by circumstances beyond their control. Given all
of this, is it any wonder that these students "fall to a level where
effort ceases"? Paulo Freire provides a compelling portrait of the
alienated borderland learner, whose development is arrested by the
intractable nature of the conflict that divides not only his loyalties
but his soul:

> The oppressed suffer from the duality which has established
> itself in their inmost being. They discover that without free-
> dom they cannot exist authentically. . . . they are at one and

the same time themselves and the oppressor whose consciousness they have internalized. The conflict lies in the choice
between being wholly themselves or being divided; between
ejecting the oppressor within or not ejecting him; between
human solidarity or alienation; between following prescrip-
tions or having choices; between being spectators or actors . . .
between speaking out or being silent, castrated in their power
to create and recreate, in their power to transform the world.
This is the tragic dilemma of the oppressed which education
must take into account. (32–33)

These silent students, whose presence was in reality an absence,
who were in reality "absent" from the learning process even when
"present," manifested their difference from their more acculturated
peers not only in spelling and penmanship, in reading and writing,
but in dress, discourse, and behavior as well. As with many of their
Athabascan classmates, the process of deracination had left them
alienated from their indigenous subculture. Unlike most of their
peers, however, the complementary process of acculturation had
been arrested at a more superficial stage. If they had assimilated
the dominant culture's technologies (its two-thousand-dollar snow-
mobiles, its two-hundred-dollar boomboxes, its chainsaws and high-
powered rifles) they had not assimilated its modes of dress or speech.
In contradistinction to their classmates, who wore Brittanias, Dock-
ers and Nikes, and who spoke standard English with little or no
Athabascan accent, these students dressed in the same monochromatic, functional uniform as the older generation of Athabascans:
heavy work boots, woolen work shirts, and jeans. They tended to
drop out of school in greater numbers and to engage in nihilistic
patterns of behavior: in crime sprees, drinking binges, and drug
overdoses. Observes Adams, "more than the others they are found
in the prisons and jails and in an exceptionally high degree they
depend on the agencies of charity" (290). The aborted careers of
this group are what produce the negative stereotype of the dumb,
lazy, good-for-nuthin' "injun," whose marginalization is mistakenly
assumed to be the inevitable result of these traits when in reality
it is the cause of them.

Traditionally, subcultures like the Athabascan's exerted a great
degree of "moral control" over its members. When that culture is
suppressed, when it is "bleached out" of its members through the

dual processes of deracination and quasiacculturation into the dominant culture, those controls disappear, producing a "decadence of special group morale," one of whose by-products is an "increase in anti-social conduct" (Adams 305). These are the students that have been labeled the most "at risk," the most likely to "fail," or drop out. They are left to dwell on the fringes of both cultures, on the extreme margins of the contact zone where presence mutates into eternal absence and agency degenerates into apathy. They comprise the borderland classroom's counterpart to the silent majority for whom the silence of the Far North constitutes a bitterly ironic backdrop to their own cultural silencing. Lacking membership in either culture, they are abandoned to the open orphanage of their bicultural alienation—like the students shipwrecked on the shores of an acultural island in *Lord of the Flies*—a fitting trope for the dehumanizing effects of marginalization among teenagers reduced to the most atavistic struggle for survival.

Is it any wonder that such circumstances produce what we would term "abnormal," "anti-social," or "nihilistic" behavior? Such students have been cast off by both cultures, inhabiting an island of exile within the contact zone—a veritable wilderness of alienation that poses challenges to survival most are ill-equipped to confront, much less surmount. Is it any wonder then that so many succumb to the "beast" of drug or alcohol addiction in order to escape the even darker "beast" of isolation, an isolation made all the more unbearable given their communal heritage? Lacking a language to describe their oppressive experience, to name their world, is it any wonder that they remain silent, that they are held captive in silence because they lack the "signs" for making such a confusing world intelligible to themselves, much less to anyone else? And if they are ever to escape this island of isolation in the heart of their native darkness they must do what the boys in *Flies* did: discover a means for signaling their presence to the world. This is what pedagogy can, and must do, for borderland learners: give them the means of signing themselves into existence, of signing their presence to the world, so that each might sing the song of a native self. As Maya Angelou observes, the caged bird sings with a freedom it doesn't possess, sings of the freedom it has never known, and in singing surmounts its captivity. Here is an audience of captives whose captivity teachers unwittingly prolong and intensify by prolonging and intensifying their bicultural alienation through a pedagogy of assimilation predicated on the concomitant process of cultural genocide. Canonical texts like *Flies* and noncanonical works like *Caged Bird* can provide borderland students with a language for enunciating their exilic careers, with the signs that enable them to sing the song of themselves.

Unlike their noisier, more assimilated classmates, these students spoke rarely, if at all, in the classroom. Of the multiple discourses enunciated by native students within the classroom, theirs was the most marginalized for the simple reason it was rarely if ever heard. Within the classroom, the self-conscious silence of these students was a poignant counterpoint to the unsolicited speech of their peers: to Mark's lore of the Athabascans, to David's resistance to that lore, to Erin's counterhegemonic insurrections.

At first I assumed they were merely shy or behaving in accordance with Athabascan customs that mandated indirectness in the presence of a white stranger. However, when their silence persisted through the autumn and into the winter I began to wonder if it might be the by-product of a deeper "block," of a more paralyzing check on their spirits—the result, for example, of a debilitating sense of shame, arising from a self-conscious conviction of their own academic inadequacies of the type so eloquently described by Angelou in *Caged Bird*: "If growing up is painful for the Southern Black girl, being aware of her displacement is the rust on the razor that threatens the throat" (3). Like Angelou's narrator, these students had imposed silence upon themselves as a means of coping with the traumatic effects of their own difference, with the amputations of deracination and the mutilations of marginalization, with the "otherness" of their Otherness. The trauma-induced muteness of Angelou's narrator is an apt trope for the cultural silencing of these students, and thus a useful text to "read" in such a topos. Thus, noncanonical as well as canonical texts comprise useful vehicles for conducting an inquiry into the debilitating effects of marginalization, deracination, and acculturation.

Learning how to interpret their silence is a critical lesson for the practitioner whose own attitude toward, and understanding of, the seeming "apathy" or "indifference" of these students must itself undergo a transformation if meaningful interaction and active learning are to occur; that is, if the passive absence of such students is be transformed into an active presence. Learning how to "read" their silence is the first step to liberating the voices caged within it, to transforming the winter of their silent discontent into a spring chorus of reemergence.

Though marginalized to the point of invisibility within the class-room, the conduct of these students was not in the least disruptive. Indeed, it was almost as if they would do anything so as not to be noticed, as if their overriding aim was to blend into the walls and the desks, was to disappear, to escape from this confined space of academic mirrors that was forever confronting them with unpleas-ant images of their own inadequacies as learners. Their silence was a form of disappearing from an oppressive situation, a guise of invisibility they assumed in order to survive in a hostile, threaten-ing environment. The attendance sheet might indicate that these students were "present" on a daily basis, but they were present in name only.

When they did speak English, it was with the thick, glottal accents of Dena'ina, their mother tongue. Thus, speech itself intensified their sense of difference, impeding their assimilation inasmuch as the freedom to form social relations in the dominant culture is impaired by any difference, whether in complexion or accent, as the result of a code of race relations that privileges "sameness" and marginalizes "difference." As Adams asserts, "lan-guage deficiencies tend to limit social contact and the lack of con-tact means the lack of opportunity for acculturation" (284). These students, consequently, become ghettoized within their own cul-ture, and particularly within the classroom, where "sameness" or approximation to an American ideal, to norms and standard codes of speech, dress, behavior, is the harsh measuring stick to which all students are held—the great "ruler" by which all are measured. Those who don't measure up to the codes of "sameness" are found wanting, and thus marginalized, by natives as well as whites, by students as well as teachers.

For Joey, Hank, Velma, and Pete, coming to class entailed a painful encounter with their own "shortcomings" relative to the putative "norms." For them it was a demoralizing "reality-check" that operates as a check on their self-esteem, as if their personali-ties were being graded by teachers and even worse by their peers, native as well as white, and given a big, black "check" mark, connoting failure not just on a grammatical exam, on a composition quiz, or on a reading comprehension test, but on the more totalizing plane of personality and acculturation. They have not only "failed" the test of penmanship, grammar, and reading, but even worse they have failed the test of "assimilation" that their peers have passed with flying colors. And of this they are reminded every time they cross the academic threshold with its rigid and ubiquitous standards of measurement. For these students, entering a reservation classroom entails as much culture shock as Ellis Island entailed for European immigrants a century ago.

It behooves the borderland practitioner to learn how to "walk in the moccasins" of these students, to see the experience of schooling from their perspective, to open his or her eyes to the mutilations of marginalization these students are experiencing on a daily basis. Every waking moment in class is for these students a harsh reminder that they do not "measure up" to the colonizer's standards of "sameness" across a broad spectrum of criteria. The pejorative terms used to describe these students by teachers ("dead wood") reinforces the perception that not only have they "fallen to a level where effort ceases," but that their teachers' misperceptions about them have fallen to a similar level. Believing such students to be beyond academic redemption, their teachers cease to make the effort to reach them, much less to understand the causes of their alienation, apathy, ambivalence, confusion, and conflict. The apathy that is the primary effect of a traditional pedagogy becomes the goal of it as well: "I don't care if they fail, as long as they don't disrupt the class while failing." The problem, in short, is assumed to lie with the student and not with a pedagogy that fails to take any account of their lived realities, or to manifest any interest in exploring useful alter/natives designed to counter the adverse effects of bicultural marginalization. Instead, these students are seen as hereditarily defective: their extreme alienation is viewed in a similar light as the "knots" that ruin a piece of kindling, that thwart the attempt to build a fire from it, that refuses to "ignite," or that once ignited refuses to burn evenly, like "good" pieces of wood, producing instead a violent explosion of sparks, as for example when Joey's short fuse went off, producing a disruptive, profanity-laced outburst directed at his teacher or at one of his classmates. This eruption was all the more violent because of the months-long silence that had preceded it. As Lame Deer observes, "We are lousy raw material from which to form a capitalist. We could do it easily, but then we would stop being Indians" (35).

To the eye untutored in the underlying causes of these effects, as was I when I first arrived in the village, the behavior, personalities, and discourse of these students seems to validate the negative stereotype of the "bad" Other: of the stupid, slow, lazy, drunken, nihilistic, good-for-nuthin' injun. Those who subscribe to this stereotype commit the egregious error of mistaking the effects of marginalization for its causes. As Adams contends, these students fail not from any inherent defect in their character or in their heredity, but simply from "overwhelming circumstances" that reduce them to a state "where effort ceases" (278). The apathy induced by their oppression is often mistaken by the colonizer as an inherent docility, when in reality it is an outward manifestation of an extreme fatalism sired by the emasculating effects of their colonization. Again, Freire's observations are to the point:

> They nearly always express fatalistic attitudes toward their situation. When superficially analyzed, this fatalism is sometimes interpreted as a docility that is a trait of national character. Fatalism in the guise of docility is the fruit of an historical or social situation, not an essential characteristic of a people's behavior. It is almost always related to the power of destiny or fate or fortune. (47–48)

This fatalism manifests itself as well in their reluctance to join the resistance struggle of their people outside the classroom, and of their peers inside it. As Freire observes, "as long as their ambiguity persists, the oppressed are reluctant to resist, and totally lack confidence in themselves. They have a diffuse, magical belief in the invulnerability and power of the oppressor" (50).

Thus, the negative effects associated with their cultural disorganization (apathy, confusion, ambivalence, nihilism, shame, alienation, withdrawal, docility, low self-esteem, drug-abuse, alcoholism, crime-sprees) are the direct result of their marginalization, not the causes of it. How can such students manifest the traits privileged by the dominant culture (initiative, resourcefulness, ambition) if never given the opportunity in the culture at large to practice them? What worth do these traits have if they are never to be utilized?

Yet, these students are represented by whites as if the reverse was true: the apathy and nihilism generated by their exclusion from the dominant culture are posited as the cause of that exclusion. As Freire attests, "By his accusation the colonizer establishes the colonized as being lazy. He decides the laziness is constitutional in the very nature of the colonized" (136n). Thus, the personality traits produced by his or her marginalization are assumed to be proof positive that the native inherently and hereditarily lacks the "right stuff" for full participation in the American materialist dream. Hereditary differences in skin color are augmented by a host of other differences in personality traits, which are erroneously assumed to be hereditary as well. The colonizer's racial intolerance thus produces the very traits that the colonizer then uses in order to rationalize his or her racial intolerance of the native. This cause-effect relationship between discrimination and personality development is then inverted by the colonizer to justify the further oppression of the native. Observes Adams, "In many cases the inferiority of social status contributes to the development of personality traits that tend to justify the exclusion of hybrids from the society of the race of 'superior' status" (310). Freire similarly observes that the "professionals, in order to justify their failure, say that the members of the invaded group are 'inferior' because they are 'ingrates,' 'shiftless,' 'diseased,' or of 'mixed blood'" (154). Pete, Velma, Joey, and Hank had been reduced to a state of apathy in the classroom by the process of deracination without acculturation, by the irrelevancy of a college-prep curriculum to their lived realities and future plans, and by the standards of measurement associated with that curriculum which were forever exposing their "deficiencies." Their classroom apathy was compounded by the alcohol they drank, the drugs they consumed, and the snuff they chewed to cope with the confusions, contradictions, and ambiguities of their bicultural, or rather acultural, existence.

Their assimilation was impeded by other factors as well: by the great disparity between their indigenous subculture and the dominant Euro-American culture. This also reinforces negative stereotypes of the native. "If there is a great disparity of cultures," as Adams observes, "the people will advance slowly and they will seem to be stupid, and no matter whether it is true or not, they will be considered to have innate inferiority or biological inheritance"(254). Acculturation is thus slowed by the great abyss between the two cultures, making the native appear to be slow-witted, which in turn is seized upon by whites to further justify his or her marginalization. As Adams notes, "the inter-mediate status conditions their personality traits in such a way as to justify the status they actually have" (238).

With little or no opportunity to exercise the traits privileged in the Euro-American culture, many native students cease cultivating them. Two factors made the acquisition of such traits, and of literacy itself, irrelevant to their lived realties: the unequal code of race relations that denied them full access to the dominant culture and the cash allotments they received from various transnational corporations and government agencies for the rights to the natural resources on their land, if not to the land itself. These monthly cash payments were like an opiate the dominant culture administered to the natives to dull the pain of their bicultural alienation, to repress the impulse to insurrection, to perpetuate the status quo. Thus, the various neocolonial apparatuses of the dominant culture, including schools, corporations, and churches, succeeded in addicting the native to a cash-based economy while denying him or her full and equal participation in that economy—an addiction that sounded the death-knell of their own subsistence lifestyle. Cash, of which these corporations and government subsidized institutions had plenty, was no less a destructive agent than the alcohol they drank and the drugs they consumed, with respect to its corrosive impact on their subsistence lifestyle. This further reinforced the negative stereotype of the "lazy injun' on the dole," again as if it was a cause, instead of an effect of an inability to freely form social contacts in the dominant culture.

Other personality traits that reinforce the colonizer's negative stereotype of the native are derivative of the subculture. Individual competition for material gain, whether in the form of a raise at work or a grade in class, conflicts with the communal ideology of the Athabascan. Like their Hawaiian counterparts, an Athabascan "cannot make even a start toward economic competence because if he accumulates some property his moral standards compel him to share it with his needy relatives and friends" (Adams 244). The situation is compounded by the disparity between each culture's definition of "family." The Athabascan traditionally has no conception of the term "nuclear family." For the Athabascan, the family includes all relatives, and to a certain extent, every member of the tribe, making it an extended family. This has important implications, for status in such a community is not based on individual material gain, as in Euro-American culture; indeed, it is a function of the precise opposite: of the individual's tendency to share the wealth with other members of the community. This communal code of living was still in evidence in the village, not only in the extended families to which my students belonged, but in the preservation of such traditions as the potlatch, or giveaway, which was held on an annual basis in the school gymnasium.

Not surprisingly, the effects engendered by these "tensions of biculturalism," the great disparity between the codes privileged in the two cultures, negatively affected their acquisition of literacy. As Michael Holzman affirms in "Writing as Social Action," "the contrast between the culture of the school and that of the community creates an interference pattern . . . more and more successfully blocking the communication, the teaching and learning, of skills and knowledge" (164–65). For these students, the disparity between cultures often proves too great to overcome. Already faced with a difficult task in negotiating this cultural disjunction, they are now told they are too slow to manage the transition, that they lack the requisite intelligence to fully assimilate into the dominant culture. Once again, they are victimized by assumptions that misconstrue effects for causes, victimized by a bicultural catch 22.

Metaphorically speaking, these "inherent" traits (slowness, lethargy, stupidity) are the "negative" image of the personality traits produced in the colonizer (initiative, ambition, resourcefulness) by his or her legitimate social status and full assimilation. In other words, the agency manifested by Euro-Americans relative to the native Other produces all the attributes they manifest. The ability to freely form social contacts, to attain goals, the "zest for power, initiative, resourcefulness come with the exercise of authority," even as apathy, indolence, and nihilistic behavior are generated by the denial of authority (249). Of what use to the Other is a zest for power that has no realistic chance of ever being actualized? Of what practical value is ambition if the Other is denied access to the dominant culture as a consequence of an asymmetrical code of race relations that isolates and devalues difference? Of what practical value to the Athabascan is a postsecondary education if he or she is denied access to the marketplace beyond the academy because of discriminatory hiring practices? Of what practical value to the native are initiative and ingenuity, if these likewise are destined to die on their indigenous vine? Of what worth is a facility for forming social relations in the dominant culture, if the native is denied the equal opportunity for doing so? These dominant traits of the Euro-American personality perish in the harsh context of alienation, marginalization, and discrimination. For the native Other these attributes have negative survival value. Adams describes their predicament with succinct eloquence: "Without authority, they manifest those traits dictated by the situation: apathy, indolence, a sense of inferiority, and these effects are pointed to by those in authority as the cause of their condition when they are in fact the effect of it" (249).

Now descendants of European immigrants might very well assert that their ancestors overcame similar discriminatory practices though initiative, ambition, hard work, and ingenuity. However, a critical difference distinguishes the careers of these immigrants from their Native American counterparts, and it is this: the disjunction between the two cultures was not nearly as great for the European immigrant as it for the Native American. European immigrants were coming from a culture that similarly privileged a cash-based economy, an individualistic work ethic. They already possessed many of the attributes that favored assimilation into the dominant culture because they had the opportunity to exercise these traits in their home culture. Thus, the degree of cross-cultural disparity was nowhere near as severe for these immigrants as it is for the Native American, and as Adams research shows, one of the primary factors affecting the rate of assimilation is the degree of difference between the two cultures.

The violence of the effects produced by this dual alienation, by this fragmenting of the native personality, has induced Rodanzo Adams and Patrick Colm Hogan to describe the end result as a state of "cultural disorganization" or "cultural disintegration" respectively (277, 88). Hogan writes, cultural disintegration involves a sense of alienation from all cultures, being "no longer at ease" (in Chinua Achebe's phrase) in any culture, finding a home neither in indigenous tradition nor in Europeanization. Clearly, alienation is not in itself an experience one chooses to have; it is rather an inability to enact any choice . . . frequently associated with emotional and mental disintegration. (88)

In contradistinction to Mark, David, or Erin, who identified more strongly with one or the other culture, these students identified strongly with neither culture. Lacking a culture that conferred membership, they comprised as it were a community unto themselves: a community of exiles among exiles. Hogan's comments are instructive not only because they provide a working definition for "cultural disintegration," but because they underscore the determined nature of such experience—an experience that is not the result of free choice, but of "overwhelming circumstances."

The experience of bicultural alienation for such students is a difficult one. As Adams affirms, "their lot is a hard one, for they are marginal not only in respect to their positions in relations to two peoples and two cultures, but also in respect to their personality traits":

Owing loyalty to two peoples and to more or less conflicting organizations of customs and standards, the marginal man [and woman] does not yield full allegiance to either. . . . The conflict inherent in this situation gives rise to inner conflict and behavior tends to be disorganized. (277)

In their silent passivity and dual alienation from dominant culture and indigenous subculture, Hank, Joey, Pete, and Velma resembled Tayo, the protagonist in Leslie Silko's *Ceremony*, of whom Paul Gunn Allen says, "invisible and stilled, like an embryo, he floats, helpless and voiceless, on the current of duality, his being torn by grief and anger" (128). The double alienation of these borderland learners also reminded me of the ptarmigan, an indigenous game bird, whose autumn plumage became a motley mixture of brown and white, of summer and winter markings—a half molted condition that left them ill-adapted to the colors of either season, to either the brown leaves of a dying summer or to the white snows of the impending winter. Trinh Minh-ha succinctly voices the bicultural alienation experienced by students like Velma: "Not quite the Same, not quite the Other, she stands in the undetermined threshold place where she constantly drifts in and out" (218). The conflicted topos that Velma and her peers occupy "is the perilous territory of not-belonging. This is where in primitive times, people were banished, and where in the modern era, aggregates of humanity loiter as refugees and displaced persons" (Said 51). Freire's analysis of the effects of colonization upon the Other reinscribes the observations of Silko, Gunn-Allen, Minh-Ha, and Said insofar as it also attests to the dual, conflicted world that the oppressed inherits:

> There is also an unnatural living death: life which is denied its fullness. Oppression dualizes the "I" of the oppressed. Thereby making him ambiguous, emotionally unstable, and fearful of freedom. Part of the oppressed "I" is located in the reality to which he adheres; part is located outside himself, in the mysterious forces which he regards as responsible for a reality about which he can do nothing. He is divided between an identical past and present, and a future without hope. (173)

Freire's observations here are significant inasmuch as they "unveil," if only partially, the underlying causes of the apathy manifested in these borderland learners. His observations echo as well the findings of Adams and Hogan with respect to the cultural disorganization or disintegration experienced in this extremity of bicultural alienation. The extent to which the psychic and emotional world of the Other is destabilized by the experience of marginalization depends on the degree to which identity remains rooted in one culture or the other; its most debilitating effects, however, are evidenced in those students for whom identity is rooted in neither culture.

As evidenced by these writers, these tropes of disenfranchisement—of invisibility, exile, duality, alienation, not-belonging, in-betweeness, and marginality—recur across boundaries of ethnicity, nationality, and gender, signifying a shared experience of marginalization, raising hopes of finding common ground and waging resistance struggle across boundaries. This has important implications for borderland pedagogy as well, for it holds forth the hope that narratives by the Other from diverse cultural contexts might inform one another. I will revisit these pedagogical implications in Chapter 6.

As a place, the reservation is characterized not by a presence, but by an absence; specifically, by the absence of home and self. It is not a real home, but a permanent holding area created by whites in which the Athabascan is not a true self-determining subject, but an object articulated, contained, and controlled by whites and articulated in realist novels like *Call of the Wild* and *Last of the Mohicans*. The Athabascan has been displaced from his or her true home, is in actuality a refugee on her own reservation, homeless in his own home. Native students, some more than others, have a deeply felt sense of loss, of being lost, or of not-belonging. Again, Said's observations are instructive:

> One enormous difficulty in describing this no-man's land is that nationalisms are about groups, whereas exile is about the absence of an organic group situated in a native place.... For exile is fundamentally a discontinuous state of being. Exiles are cut off from their roots, their land, their past. (51)

The grim irony for the Athabascans is that, unlike the Saidean exile displaced from Palestine, their exile and alienation occurs within sight of, if not actually upon, the very land once associated with their roots, their past, their cultural integrity.

A Case of Mistaken Identity

As a consequence of the silence Leo habitually manifested in the classroom, I associated him with his equally silent peers: Velma, Hank, Joey and Pete. I assumed that, like them, he was suffering and manifesting the effects of bicultural alienation. Yet, as I discovered, he didn't drink, didn't take drugs, didn't exhibit any of the nihilistic behavior of his peers, and most importantly, didn't dissociate himself from his native subculture. The silence he maintained in class masked a deep identification with his native culture, which explained his close friendship with Mark, the younger generation's unofficial gatekeeper of Athabascan lore.

I discovered my mistake, not in the classroom, but while out in the woods ptarmigan hunting with Mark, Leo, and Will, who stopped by my house on a Saturday afternoon to invite me along, their .22s cocked over their shoulders. I was struck by the transformation in their personalities outside the classroom, for they exuded the confidence and camaraderie of an adolescent Athabascan militia. These ptarmigan hunting trips became a regular feature of my Saturday afternoons, and underscore the singular nature of teaching in the Alaskan bush. The boundaries that define the locus of the teacher-student relationship get blurred, as that relationship is not only extended into the community, but inverted: the students taught me as much about their culture outside the classroom as I taught them about mine inside it. I not only learned more about the Athabascan culture on these occasions, but about the students themselves. For the older generation of Athabascans, the students act as a sort of barometer, taking the measure of outsiders who are new to the village, and particularly of teachers. They pass their impressions along to their parents, who then communicate them to their relatives, reinscribing in this manner the "moccasin telegraph" tradition of previous centuries.

On these rambles through the woods, I gained a wealth of knowledge about Mark and Leo that respectively confirmed and contradicted assumptions I had made about each of them. In the woods a totally different Leo emerged, as if the oppressive conditions in the classroom had repressed the personality traits he evinced in the outdoors. All the traits associated with the exercise of authority emerged in nature: leadership, ambition, initiative, ingenuity, hard work, fluent communication, and a native wit. He was as talkative in the woods as he was incommunicative in the classroom, though his speech was soft-spoken after the Athabascan fashion. The high esteem with which Mark and Will regarded Leo, as a consequence of his superior woodlore and marksmanship, was evidenced by their willingness to follow his every lead.

It was Leo who solved the riddle of a trail "sign" that had perplexed me on my walks for two years. In those months when the dust lay deep upon the trail to the Dena'ina River, I was always intrigued and puzzled by a series of short parallel lines in the dirt that were obviously the track of some animal, but which one? Crouching over them one day, Leo identified them as the marks left by the wingbeats of a ptarmigan on its "take off." I could see at a glance that this trail sign conformed to his explanation.

"They eat the seeds on the trail."

A little ways further, we came upon one of these game birds pecking its lunch from the path. I froze, afraid that any movement would put the bird to flight. Leo laughed at my precautions.

"You don't have to stop. It won't fly away as long as you keep whistling when you walk toward it."

I gave him a skeptical look.

"Go on. Try."

I did as he suggested, and just as he said the bird let me approach within a few feet.

"Them ptarmigan are the dumbest birds around."

I stopped whistling, and the game bird looked up at me. I stopped. It stared. I took a step forward and it took wing, heading for a nearby spruce with a loud whirring of wings whose short beats were as comical as they were uneconomical. Of the four of us, Leo was the only one able to spot the bird in the dark foliage of the spruce.

"About three-quarters the way up. See it?"

"Where? I can't see it?"

"I'll show you."

With a crack-shot from his .22, Leo brought the ptarmigan to ground. While standing over the bird, he offered me a pinch of snuff. I declined, recalling what others had said about the notorious sting of this ground fungus that passed for "chew." My students cajoled and persisted. I gave in, to my immediate regret, and the face I made gave them a good-natured laugh.

Another page in the very ambivalent process of my own indigenization had been turned. It was evident from such outings as these that my students had as much to teach me about themselves and their culture as I had to teach them about mine. Indeed, the opportunity to continue this process of "going native" in a very real way, as opposed to just studying native ways in books, was one of the more appealing aspects of the experience, and one of the reasons I had accepted this position. I will revisit the process and implications of my own indigenization in Chapter 5.

Leo and Mark made a gift of the ptarmigan to me and they afforded yet another example of the "give away" code that was privileged in the traditional Athabascan culture. They even offered to teach me how to pluck it, an invitation I was quick to accept. Standing over my kitchen sink, they plucked the feathers in a fraction of the time it took me on subsequent occasions, warming it under the faucet to loosen the quills from the flesh. Though I dined alone in the bush that Thanksgiving, I had the rare privilege of devouring this game bird, which when plucked, stuffed, and broiled was as savory as any Turkish game hen I have ever eaten.

These outings were always of an impromptu nature, and while the light was long they often occurred after school. On other occasions, I would hear my name shouted from the gravel street outside my house. Opening the door, I would find them standing three or four abreast, .22s cocked over their shoulders or swinging at their knees. While reading in my rocker, there would sometimes occur a telltale "thump" on the roof. This I knew to be the sound of a ptarmigan tossed there by one of my students, often with a shouted greeting, followed by a burst of laughter as good-natured as it was communal.

The easy and thorough literacy Leo evinced in the ways of the woods stood in sharp contrast to the "illiteracy" he manifested in class. He seemed as empowered in the forest as he was passive in the classroom, as in touch with the world there as he was alienated from it at school, as alive in this natural environment as he was inert in the artificial confines of the classroom. Personality traits that were repressed in the classroom emerged in this familiar, nonthreatening setting. The woods seemed to bring him out of himself, whereas pedagogy had merely driven him deeper into himself, into a shell of self-conscious silence. Why? Was it because in one milieu his innate traits were brought into play whereas in the other it was only his "deficiencies," his shortcomings, his differences that were visible, while his initiative, ingenuity, and leadership languished for lack of exercise, retreated into a sedentary hibernation deep within an introspective space, like a bear slumbering in its December den?

Then I realized I had mis-recognized Leo, as being like Velma, Hank, Pete, and Joey, as suffering from the effects of "cultural disintegration," when in actuality he was more like Mark, his identity deeply rooted in the ancestral traditions of his subculture, inseparable from his native landscape. Though suffering the ill-effects of biculturalism, as they all were, his personality did not evince the same extreme effects of marginalization for the simple reason he still felt an abiding sense of membership in his Athabascan culture. Whereas Hank and Joey devoted their time outside the classroom to nihilistic drinking, drug-taking, and crime sprees, Leo roamed the woods with his peers, retracing the footsteps of his ancestors. His failure to assimilate into the dominant culture was not merely the result of the great disparity between those cultures, but of his desire to remain Athabascan. As I further discovered in talks with him on these walks, Leo was very well versed on the arguments being enunciated on both sides of a series of contentious environmental conflicts, or eco-wars, between the Athabascan and the whites, over logging, oil-drilling, and coal mining activities. These were having an adverse impact on the Athabascan's subsistence hunting and fishing activities, and as an avid moose hunter and salmon fisherman, Leo was deeply invested in the outcomes of these disputes. He held strong and well-informed opinions about the causes of these problems and what should be done to rectify them.

A question then occurred to me: could the functional literacy Leo evinced with respect to his native landscape and the environmental issues associated with it be used as a vehicle for the acquisition of academic and critical literacy inside the classroom? How these local cultural conflicts influenced pedagogy is an issue I will revisit in Chapter 7.

Putting the "Bush" Back Into The Bush Teacher: Implications and Possibilities

These outings influenced my pedagogy in significant ways, providing me with a wealth of observations regarding the personalities of these students, enabling me to fine-tune my understanding of them, to recognize mistakes I had made and adjust my impressions accordingly. These trips afield also planted in my mind the idea of somehow extending the classroom into the woods, of making nature a supplemental "text" to be "read" and written about in conjunction with various classroom texts, as a means of ameliorating the debilitating effects of alienation I observed in the classroom. I began to contemplate the usefulness of a pedagogy foregrounding the Athabascan's holistic and systemic knowledge of nature, using writing themes to "unveil" their natural world, to develop not only critical, but creative writing skills, to foster not only academic but critical literacy. Only then might a new, radical red subject begin to emerge like the native sun from a blanket of white clouds, like the native landscape from its blanket of white snows: visible, eruptive, recolonizing the ground in which it is rooted.

Words, signification, representation when restored to the native are what allow him or her to escape this nightmarish no-man's land of nonexistence, in which they are formed, reformed and deformed as objects to be acted upon, unless and until they can effect their liberation through signification, radically reconstitute themselves as subjects, reclaim their World with the Word, and reestablish the harmony between native signs and the things they signify, between their language and their lived reality. Only then might their alienation give way to reconnection, their disintegration to reintegration, their dismemberment to re-memberment.

In a sense, the borderland classroom resembles a battlefield ward in which the casualties of this violent cross-cultural conflict are gathered, each suffering the "mutilations" of exile, some in silence, others in rage, some with a pleasant smile and a sardonic jest, others with an angry word and a profane gesture. The bush teacher who ventures into this cross-cultural contact zone can expect to be confronted with the myriad effects of marginalization, whether moderate or extreme. Somehow, pedagogy must account for the violence of the effects manifested in those we are charged with teaching; somehow, it must make the healing of those wounds a primary objective; somehow, it must purge from itself those practices that only exacerbate these wounds, which add the insult of pseudo-acculturation to the injury of deracination, which add the insult of neocolonialism to the injury of colonialism.

And so I began to wonder if there might not be some way of combining these two disjointed realms of literacy, the birch forest and the borderland classroom, some way of linking learning to the native landscape, and the conflicts being waged over it between Athabascans and whites, some way of foregrounding what Leo already knew, some way of emphasizing these "texts" whose contents he already knew by heart and could "read" at a glance, some way of not only teaching in the bush, but *to* the bush, some way of putting the "bush" back into bush teaching. By bringing borderland students into "contact" with their native landscape and the conflicts immanent in it, we are in effect bringing them back into contact with lost, uncolonized realms of the indigenous Self, which was historically inseparable from the land. We are in effect fostering the reemergence of an old/new Native American subjectivity from the indigenous ground in which the Tree of Knowledge has been rerooted. The earth at the foot of this Tree of Knowledge is the site for the emergence of this new, radical red subjectivity, a spawning ground as red as the native rivers teeming with salmon. And like the hook-nosed Chinook, not until the Athabascans return to their origins will they too be able to reproduce themselves. Return and reproduction are inseparable processes for the exile, which is why preservation of the originary habitat is essential for the survival of the Athabascan, as it is for all Native Americans. The ground under the native tree of knowledge is as fecund as the soil under the wooden scaffold from which sprang the mythical mandrake, nourished on the blood of sacrificial victims.

To facilitate the rebirth of this radical red subjectivity, the Athabascan must first re-colonize the Tree of Knowledge: those sites where knowledge is made and disseminated. They must take this tree, uproot it from the colonized terrain in which it is now situated, and replant in the good red earth of their own subculture. To regain the paradise he or she has lost, the Athabascan must first regain the signs that name that paradise. To recover the World they must first recover the Word, and those topoi where it is used to oppress them, including the borderland classroom. Only then, will the Athabascan be able to make the word flesh, as red as the meat of the hook-nosed salmon, as red as the snows of a December dawn unfolding from the heart of the Athabascan's darkness.

3

The Bush Teacher
as Cultural Imperialist

To the Indian kid the white boarding school comes as a terrible shock. He is taken from his warm womb, to a strange cold place. It is like being pushed out of a cozy kitchen into a howling blizzard. The schools are better now. . . . They look good from the outside—modern and expensive. The teachers understand the kids a little better, use more psychology and less stick. But in those fine new buildings, Indian children still commit suicide because they are lonely amid all that noise and activity. I know of a ten-year-old who hanged herself. . . . The schools leave a scar. We enter them confused and bewildered and we leave them the same way. When we enter the school we at least know that we are Indians. We come out half-red and half-white, not knowing what we are.

—Lame Deer 24, 25

I n this chapter I want to investigate the complicity of the borderland school in general, and of the bush teacher in particular, in the enterprise of cultural imperialism. Although published over a quarter of a century ago, Lame Deer's description of the violence done to Native Americans in the name of education is significant for a number of reasons. First, it speaks to the lived realities of schooling extant on the reservation today. Though Athabascan students in Nyotek were no longer shipped off to white boarding schools in Oklahoma, many of their parents, older brothers, and sisters had experienced such a forced dislocation, in which they were not only subjected to the violence of "cultural bleaching" in the classroom, but to the brutality of other Native American kids outside it. It was not until the landmark Molly Hooch case in 1971 that this practice was discontinued, the state agreeing to build in every native village a state-of-the-art school.

E. L. Elmendorf School was one of the legacies of this landmark court case, with an estimated worth of $3.3 million and an annual operating budget of $712,000. It was a blue, cinder-block edifice that more closely resembled an industrial plant, and was situated at the geographical center of the village of Nyotek. Its location reinscribed on a physical plane the asymmetrical relations of power that reserved the center for the colonial authorities while relegating the native to the margins, even in his or her own village. The school was an extension of the one-room schoolhouse, for under its single, flat roof, classes were conducted from kindergarten through the twelfth grade. The students were drawn from two distinct and racially segregated communities: the all-white timber camp 4 miles to the south and the Athabascan village of Nyoteck. It was administered by a principal/teacher and ten faculty members (all white) and supported by a staff that included a secretary, a teacher's aide, a nurse, a cook, a cook's helper, and a janitorial staff (all native), once again reinscribing the hierarchical relations of power between whites and Athabascans.

The school featured a state of the art basketball gym, cafeteria, voc-ed shop, biology classroom, business classroom, multipurpose room, administrative office, and teacher's lounge. In fact, but for its location it might have been mistaken for a modern school in Anywhere, U.S.A. And though it too "looked good from the outside—modern and expensive," the Athabascan students were still subjected to the violent effects of cultural bleaching, for its primary purpose was to assimilate the native students into the dominant culture, or lacking this, to tame the insurrectionist impulse of the Athabascan by providing his or her children with a hot lunch and a series of highly regimented activities that kept them off the streets and out of trouble, but which in reality reinscribed the authoritarian regime of the master-slave, colonizer-colonized dialectic. As the educational careers of Hank, Velma, Pete, and Joey evidenced, schooling on the reservation still "leave[s] a scar." The Athabascan schooled in Nyotek in our time is just as confused and alienated as his Lakota counterpart a generation ago. They still emerge from the experience "not knowing what we are." Even though the schools are more modern and the pedagogy less overtly violent than in the boarding schools of old, the goals and the effects remain very much the same: initiation into the dominant culture, suppression of the native subculture.

As I have indicated elsewhere, the school itself was the site of contestation between the dominant culture and indigenous subculture whose representatives fought over the use of its facilities, the nature of its curriculum, and the hiring of its staff, among other things. Not just the classrooms, but the school itself, was a "contact zone" for the collision of these two cultures, a hybridized topos comprised of elements of both cultures, like the native subject and the village itself. It was simultaneously the site of schooling and social activities, of instruction in algebra and Dena'ina, the mother tongue of the Athabascan, of basketball games and potlatches. In short, it was never just a school, a topos of teachers and administrators. The Athabascans claimed as much ownership of the school as the whites. If during the day it was run by whites, then by night it reverted to the hands of the Athabascans, who reoccupied its multipurpose room with their bridge clubs and bingo games, its gym with their basketball leagues and native Olympics, its stage with their native dances and potlaches, and its classroom with courses in Dena'ina, skin-sewing, and native cooking. If by day the subculture was largely suppressed in the school, then by night it reemerged (the dark, repressed, eruptive material of the Athabascan cultural unconscious) in the form of activities associated with their ancestral lifeways. On the other hand, if the school conscripted the children into the dominant culture by day, it recruited their parents by night, as Athabascans converged on it to participate in the extracurricular activities privileged in the dominant culture: its bingo games, bridge clubs, and basketball leagues. E. L. Elmendorf was thus a very ambivalent topos in this bicultural contact zone.

The Bush Teacher as Cultural Imperialist

The pedagogical exigencies of this borderland setting prompted me to ask some difficult questions. What were the social, cultural, political, economical, and educational factors producing these bicultural tensions? More significantly, to what extent was schooling in the borderlands, and my own pedagogy in particular, responsible for reproducing if not producing the alienated consciousness of these students, and the ubiquitous debilitating effects associated with it: confusion, conflict, ambiguity, apathy, hostility, nihilism, alienation, etc.? What is the practical justification for a college-prep pedagogy if not a single Athabascan student had any desire, much less any plans, to attend college? What is the practical warrant for an assimilationist pedagogy for students who are denied full assimilation because of their "inferior" ethnic status? Moreover, what is the ethical warrant for a pedagogy of "initiation" that reproduces the violent effects of marginalization? In short, what is the justification for a pedagogy of the oppressed that is itself oppressive? Could pedagogy in these bicultural borderlands somehow "heal" the mutilations of marginalization? And if so, how? Were there "alter/natives" to these pedagogies of assimilation and initiation, and if so what might they be? Where was I to find the pedagogical arts of this contact zone? In subsequent chapters I will posit an answer to this second category of questions. In this chapter I want to proffer a response to the first category of questions: to what extent was schooling, and my own praxis in particular, complicit in the enterprise of cultural imperialism?

The great disparity between my perception of my mission and the Athabascans' perception of it was just one of the shocks in store for me, though it was a first painful step toward a more liberatory pedagogy, a pedagogy of solidarity with the Athabascan subculture. The borderland classroom, no less than the transnational corporation, is a key player in the enterprise of cultural imperialism. As Ward Churchill argues, the dissemination of knowledge and technology "helps perpetuate the system of global domination from which the genocidal colonization of Native America stemmed and by which it is continued" (226). Knowledge—the production, reproduction, and dissemination of it—is a primary medium for the circulation of power, as Foucault observes. Whoever controls the "sign" and the apparatuses of representation controls a key weapon in the struggle for domination. The classroom, which is nothing if not a site for the production and dissemination of knowledge, is a critical arena in this power struggle. It enhances the preservation of one culture, and by so doing facilitates the annihilation of other cultures, merely by determining what constitutes knowledge, merely by deciding whose language gets spoken; whose history gets written, read, memorized, and propogated; whose codes get mastered and whose get ignored; whose lore gets told and whose gets silenced. Teachers, inasmuch as they are the lightning rods for the transmission of the dominant culture at the ends of Empire, are complicit, whether wittingly or not, in this process.

As the living reincarnation of other outsiders who had come into their village to spread the Word of the dominant culture (missionaries, politicians, bureaucrats, social workers, and representatives of multinational corporations), I was regarded with ambivalence by some Athabascans and with hostility by others. What I viewed as a mission of mercy that would save their children from illiteracy by setting them firmly on the path to the American materialist dream, they regarded as an act of cultural theft. If I saw myself as a teacher of the Euro-American culture, they saw me as a thief of their Athabascan subculture. My teaching posed a double threat to the Athabascan: first, it inevitably implied the suppression of their indigenous culture; second, it threatened to deprive them of the last means by which that culture might propagate itself: their children. Each Athabascan child recruited into the academies of the dominant culture was one less to carry on the ways of their ancestors. Consequently, the natives perceived my motives and my mission in a less favorable light than did I.

Even my long-standing love of things Native American, my keen desire to "go native" myself, was regarded with skeptical disapproval by some Athabascans, who saw it as an attempt to exploit rather than to empathize with them. This disparity between the Athabascans' view of my pedagogical mission and my indigenizing tendencies and my view of these things came as yet another shock. What I saw as a means of celebrating their culture, they saw as yet another brazen attempt to "rip it off," to make it mine, to take possession of it. Consequently, I was regarded by some Athabascans as another incarnation of the "white shaman," the "Indian wannabe," or "the new Age hobbyist" who appropriates traditional Native American holistic beliefs in a quest for his or her own spirituality. Indeed, this quest was one of the motivating factors in my decision to teach on the reservation. The experience, I hoped, would continue if not complete the process of my own indigenization, begun as a child when I joined the "Indian guides" instead of the boy scouts, and fueled by the photos of Edward Curtis, whose book adorned a coffee table in my parents' house, and whose "authentic" images of Native Americans reinforced my stereotypic image of them even as it reinforced my desire to "go native" at a young age. Though unaware of it at the time of my arrival in the bush, I shared a common heritage with these New Age cultural colonists:

> white, mostly urban, affluent or affluently reared, well-schooled, young (or youngish) people of both genders who . . . are thoroughly diseased by the socioeconomic order into which they were born and their seemingly predestined roles within it. Many of them openly seek . . . a viable option with which they may not only alter their own individual fates, but transform the overall systemic realities they correctly perceive as having generated these fates in the first place. (Churchill 230)

This passage is like a mirror constructed of words, one that forces me to gaze upon the colonizing features of my own pedagogical mission into the land of the Athabascan. Was not my disenchantment with the political status quo and the socioeconomic order in the Lower Forty-eight one of the primary reasons I had ventured North in the first place? Was I not fleeing in revulsion from the socio-economic order that I could no longer identify with, whose principles and practices were so at odds with my own? Similarly, I too had turned to Native American spirituality to fill the void created by my own apostasy from Catholicism. Despite this alienation, I was motivated ironically enough by an almost evangelical desire to bestow on these native students the benefits of the college-prep education I had received. As Jenny Sharpe observes in "Figures of Colonial Resistance," "none of us escapes the legacy of a colonial past and its traces in our academic practices" (99). And yet in promoting the advantages of a college-prep education to these borderland learners, was I not encouraging them to seek assimilation into the very socioeconomic order I had renounced?

I was in some respects the living embodiment of the "alienated" outsider, proselytizing an alienating discourse, one which if subscribed to left the native estranged from his or her home culture and ancestral landscape. Alienation is a disease that the colonizer brings into the land of the indigene, one that sweeps through the ranks of the native with the virulence of a smallpox epidemic. In some respects, I was as much in need of a "healing ritual" as my alienated students, as an antidote to the effects of my own political, social, religious, and cultural estrangement.

Initially, I felt alienated from the monolithic Alaskan landscape as well, dwarfed into insignificance by its limitless, cold expanses. This monolithic terrain, however, was an ideal site for the monolithic enterprise of American neocolonialism. Colonialism, as defined by Stephen Slemon, is "an economic and political structure of cross-cultural domination" ("Scramble" 17). Postcolonialism, as Ashcroft, Tiffen, and Griffiths assert,

> does not mean "post-independence," or "after colonialism," for this would be to falsely ascribe an end to the colonial process. Post-colonialism, rather, begins from the very first moment of colonial contact. It is the discourse of opposition which colonialism brings into being. (117)

This definition is significant inasmuch as it establishes postcolonialism as resistance to colonialism, not as an era succeeding it; it is a force that exists in partiality and in opposition to colonialism, not in an autonomous totality. It establishes the temporal contamination of the postcolonial moment by the colonial forces that engender it, and that continue in the post-independent phases through neocolonial apparatuses such as the transnational corporation and the borderland school (Althusser 136). Though the weapons and the field of contestation have changed, the aim remains the same: domination of the indigenous subculture for profit and power. The missionary and the mercenary have merely given way to the mapmaker, the surveyor, the logger, the geologist, the oil-driller, the coal miner, and alas the bush teacher as the instruments for continuing this cultural dominance. In "Women Skin Deep," Sara Suleri posits a similarly agonistic definition of postcolonialism, describing it as a "free-floating metaphor for cultural embattlement" (275).

The Infinite, the Interstate, and the Imperial

I had arrived in Alaska in such a neo/postcolonial moment, almost a decade after the signing of the Alaska Native Lands Claim Settlement (ANLCS) in 1971. This settlement acknowledged the native's claim to a greatly reduced percentage of the land while opening vast tracts of previously held native lands to commercial development. The wealth of natural resources the land contained was as inviting as the land itself was resistant. Ironically, it is in just such limitless spaces that the colonizing impulse finds the conditions suitable for its own reproduction. It should come as no surprise that the imperialist impulse is most rampantly manifested in topoi that seemingly have no bounds, where expanses offer few constraints to the expansive enterprises of the colonizer, just as the limitless acres of the Louisiana Purchase invited rapid Westward expansion in the nineteenth century, even as the limitless realms of outerspace and cyberspace are inviting similar expansion at the close of the millennium.

If there is one thing Alaska has plenty of, it is space. It was therefore an ideal milieu for the expansive enterprises of Euro-American neocolonialism. Frontiers provide an abundance of two things the imperialist impulse requires: space and an absence of rules. What is required to initiate and rationalize the invasion is a void, geographic and legal. This is what both sparks and justifies the impulse to settle, develop, tame, and civilize the "wilderness"— whether it is the unfenced continent of the tundra's open space, the uninhabited reaches of outerspace, or the unbounded dimensions of cyberspace. All possess what the imperialist instinct requires: a seemingly infinite space upon which to impose its infinite appetite for profits and power. As noted in a recent edition of *Science Frontiers*, "when we colonize outer space we are building a timeless world on which the sun literally never sets" (Nov. 28, 1995). Which is why the land of the Alaskan native, and the resources of those lands, became the object of a covetous, colonizing gaze.

Infinity thus becomes a master trope for the colonizing impulse, as Frederic Jameson observes in "Modernism and Imperialism."

Similarly, the Great North Road of E. M. Forster's *Howard's End* is the insidious materialization of that impulse. The road leading to infinity becomes a trope of colonial penetration into the Edenic. As Jameson writes,

> for infinity in this sense, this new grey placelessness, as well as what prepares it, also bears another familiar name. It is in Forster's imperialism, or Empire, to give it its period designation. It is Empire which stretches the roads out to infinity, beyond the bounds and the borders of the national state. (323)

The Great North Road conjoins the infinite and the imperial. Upon just such a road I too had traveled North into the land of the Athabascan: the Alkan Highway. It stretched far beyond the bounds of the contiguous United States, through Canada and the Yukon Territory, ever wending its way toward its Edenic destination like a serpent intent on corrupting the object of its relentless penetration. As with Forster's Great North Road, it too had carried a tide of colonists northward, just as the Inside Passage, the Chilkoot Trail, and the Yukon River had in the gold rush days, though now they flooded north in the guise of oil prospectors, fishermen, loggers, new-age spiritualists, entrepreneurs, tourists, collectors, recreationists, game hunters, and bush teachers. Whether they designated themselves such or not, all bore the tell tale mark of the imperialist pilgrims of Forster's Great North Road:

> In the car was another type whom nature favors—the Imperial. Healthy, ever in motion, it hopes to inherit the earth. . . . Strong is the temptation to acclaim it as a superyeoman, who carries his country's virtues oversees. But the imperialist is not what he thinks or seems. He is a destroyer. He prepares the ways for cosmopolitanism, and though his ambitions may be fulfilled, the earth that he inherits will be grey. (323)

Jameson's observations, like those of Lame Deer and Churchill, comprise a linguistic mirror in which my own complicity in the process of cultural imperialism is reflected. Like the traveler of Forster's Great North Road, my blood was warmed by a spirit of restless industry, a legacy of the Puritan work ethic that is bred into succeeding generations of Euro-Americans, and to which my "education" had been yoked. This adventuresome, pioneering, grass-is-always-greener spirit creates in succeeding generations of Americans a citizenry animated by the settler impulse, lacking only a frontier to invade. I was one such "settler" in search of somewhere to settle where opportunities abounded. Further, like the pilgrims of the Great North Road that led to Howard's End, I too was inspirited by a messianic impulse to carry my country's educational virtues, if not overseas, then at least overland. The Alaska rural school system was the Peace Corps I chose in which to proselytize the virtues of a Euro-American education, even while acknowledging that the socio-economic-political order it served was dehumanizing, if not corrupt, and while failing to see how the educational apparatus was contaminated by the order it helped perpetuate. Thus, the evangelical zeal of my educational mission was a compendium of uncritical contradictions, of colonizing and indigenizing tendencies, of estrangement from the establishment and faith in the value of an establishment education, assuming that what applied to me would apply with equal veracity to these students. All that was lacking was a little inspiration, guidance, and friendly persuasion—all things that I could and would provide in my unofficial role as "gatekeeper" to the American Materialist Dream.

Thus the dominant culture turns even its most alienated subjects into unwitting recruiters, who swell the ranks of its order with fresh conscripts, eager to be assimilated in the name of cultural hegemony, thus extending the empire into the remotest reaches of the realm. No less than the missionary or the field doctor or the technological consultant, I dispensed afar the Euro-American order with a zeal bred into my bones, preaching the value of an assimilationist education, never pausing to question the adverse effects that the deracination associated with such an education might subject the Athabascan student to.

Like Jameson's superyeoman, I too was a contradiction of appearances and realities, was not simply what I thought I was: an estranged individual pursuing his own destiny to the good of others. I failed to see how my mission served the larger mission of the dominant culture, how in my zeal to help the Athabascan, I was only helping the colonizer to further oppress him and her, fostering in them an alienation that superseded my own, for whereas mine was self-imposed, theirs was merely imposed. Whereas my cultural diaspora was an exodus, theirs was an exile I was helping sustain. And given the impossibility of full assimilation and equal participation in the dominant culture, to what good end was this exile directed, to what noble purpose? Where is the nobility in a teenager's suicide? Where is the goodness in an adolescent's drug overdose, or alcoholism, or nihilism, or imprisonment? Where is the humanity amid such violence?

And when the processes of deracination and cultural imperialism had run their course, the earth I inherited would also be gray— a monocultural society for a monochromatic landscape. The red hues of the Native American are subsumed in the cultural sameness of the Euro-American, even as the distinctive features of the Alaskan landscape are effaced each winter under a blanket of snow. Assimilation. Hegemony. Genocide. They amount to the same thing, lead to the same end; gray matter, indeed.

The land of the Athabascan was being overrun by these superyeoman. I saw them all around me: homesteaders, loggers, coal miners, oil riggers, geologists, surveyors, new age hobbyists, part-time prospectors, anthropologists, ethnographers, museum curators, photographers, big game hunters, sports fisherman, recreationists, itinerant nurses, psychologists, social workers, counselors, and yes, bush teachers. All were white, industrious, "ever in motion," and hoping to inherit their portion of the Athabascan's Edenic homeland, their own little piece of the mineral-rich rock. They too carried their culture's values overland; it was part of the equipage that accompanied them north, along with their Kelty backpacks, Nike duffel bags, and Samsonite suitcases. Upon arriving in the land of the Athabascan they did what immigrants and colonizers do the world over: tried to turn it into the home they had left behind, as evidenced by the alien place-names they affixed to this inimitable landscape, mostly honoring the male heroes of colonization: the McKinleys and Berings and Everests and Powells and Pikes and Carsons and Fremonts, whose names adorn the maps made by the colonizer as an initial means of taking possession of the native's land, of making it over in the name of the colonizer's homeland.

Signification plays a key role in the enterprise of cultural imperialism. The Word is the vanguard instrument by which the colonizer seizes possession, asserts ownership of the terrain to be colonized, which is why education is such a critical site for the oppositional enterprises of colonialism and postcolonialism, for the contrary discourses of cultural imperialism and counterhegemonic, resistance struggle. Whomever controls the word, and the right to name the world with it, holds the upper hand in this struggle for dominion on the one hand and liberty on the other. The Word can be used by bush teachers as well for either colonizing or decolonizing purposes, for either oppressive or liberatory ends, a point I will return to at greater length in the second half of this work.

Thus, signification prepares the way for empire, settlement, ownership, possession, and cosmopolitanism. It also prepares the way for the displacement, disenfranchisement, and diaspora of the indigene. Like Forster's imperial, these superyeomen prepared the way for a cosmopolitan lifestyle, which was the chief commodity they sold to the Athabascan who, in subscribing to it, accelerated the eclipse of his or her own subsistence culture. And because the circulation of power is facilitated by an economy of cultures, as well as by an economy of discourses, the society these settlers inherit might very well be "grey" as well. Indeed, the monochromatic appearance of the Alaskan landscape serves as an apt trope for the grey sameness of cultural hegemony that seeks to efface difference from the earth in the service of its own totalizing, "manifest destiny."

The vociferous resistance of some Athabascans to my presence, and the forceful eloquence with which they articulated their resistance, exposed the contradictions of my own position inasmuch as it established my complicity in the erosion of the very subculture I would have preserved. Wasn't my own alienation from the culture in which I had been reared the most powerful argument against assimilation into that order? Moreover, wasn't my attempt to reform that order in my own small way merely another means of reinscribing it along authoritarian lines? As Churchill implies,

> Many of the most alienated—and therefore most committed to achieving fundamental social change—eventually opt for the intellectual/emotional reassurance of prepackaged "radical solutions." Typically, these assume the form of yet another battery of "isms" based on all the same core assumptions as the system being opposed . . . Marxism . . . council communism . . . feminism, environmentalism. . . . (230–31)

To which one might add cognitivism, expressivism, postmodernism, and postcolonialism. Indeed, any "ism" proselytized or packaged in a homogenous form merely amounts to a form of intellectual tyranny, whether students are placed in small, collaborative groups or forced to sit in rows. Further, Churchill implies that the academic, and the alienation that defines his or her critical stance, is perhaps the worst offender in this process:

> A mainstay occupation of this coterie has been academia wherein they typically maintain an increasingly . . . detached "critical" discourse, calculated mainly to negate whatever transformative value or utility might be lodged in the . . . oppositional political engagement they formerly pursued. (231)

As an academic, I contributed to the colonization and alienation of my students as a consequence of my uncritical faith in the alien topics I obliged them to study, and in the act of "study" itself, which presumes an alienating distance from the object being studied. Thus, the adult Athabascans, and many of the students to whom they transmitted their views, were quick to see that to which I was blind: my unwitting complicity in the process of colonization. Churchill writes,

> As long-term participants in the national liberation struggle of American Indians. . . . we have been forced into knowing the nature of colonialism very well. . . . We understand that the colonization we experience finds its origin in the matrix of European culture. . . . Our struggle must be explicitly anti-colonial in its form, content, and aspirations. (233–34)

What Churchill observes of the European applied with equal veracity to myself, as a descendant of Europeans, and as one reared in a Western European ideological climate:

> You have after all been colonized far longer than we, and therefore much more completely. In fact, your colonization has by now been consolidated to such an extent that . . . you no longer even see yourselves as having been colonized. The result is that you've become self-colonizing, conditioned to be so

self-identified with your own oppression that you've lost your ability to see it for what it is, much less to resist it in any coherent way. (234)

The bush teacher is an unwitting accomplice in this process, perpetuating "Europe's synthetic and predatory tradition, the tradition of colonization, genocide, racism, and ecocide" (249). The wary aloofness of most, the utter indifference of many, and the open hostility of a few among my Athabascan hosts engendered in me the shock of recognition, the shock of seeing myself through their eyes, and the shocking disparity between my image of myself and their image of me. In my own eyes I was Mr. Teacher from sunny southern California who had come to enlighten their children, to banish the burden of illiteracy, to work the miracle of transforming them form adolescent Indians living in abject misery to college-bound adults fully invested in the American Materialist Dream, to confer upon them the blessing of a college-prep education with a figurative laying-on-of-hands and a literary version of speaking-in-tongues. I was the knight in shining armor who had come to free them from the shackles of illiteracy, poverty, drugs, alcohol, and low self-esteem, a cultural recruiter disguised as bush teacher, seeking fresh conscripts into the alien, cash-based economy that Lame Deer pejoratively describes as the "green frogskin world" (34).

I would fashion these Athabascan students in my own image. Lacking children of my own, I would seek to eternalize my "self" through them, would seek to reproduce myself, intellectually and ideologically, through them. I would "father" their intellectual "birth," assume a paternalistic role to these surrogate offspring. What did it matter if their skin was brown and mine white, their English "broken" and mine "standard"? This would simply make their ultimate transformation into college-bound intellectuals all the more singular, which would redound to my own credit. It would only raise my value in the eyes of the "suits" who flew into Nyoteck on a regular basis to view the work we were doing with the natives— as if viewing an exotic species of fish being trained to do tricks in a fish bowl. Who could say what benefits might be mine when these administrators beheld the wonders of academic literacy I worked with these natives: awards, letters of recognition, merit pay, a transfer across the water?

I would teach them everything I had learned about academic writing: how to introduce, state, develop, and assess a thesis; how to distinguish a sentence from a fragment; how to write for color as well as for concreteness; how to integrate quotations into their text effectively; how to conduct literary analysis by analyzing passages from *Call of the Wild,* whose realist, action-oriented plot and relevant setting blinded me to its racist stereotypes of the indigenous people, the Yeehats, and its reinscription of the colonial, settler impulse (98). This text constructed both the Alaskan landscape and the indigene in a manner that invited the exploitation of one and the oppression of the Other.

All this I would transmit to my Athabascan wards as if they were indeed no more than so many safe-deposit boxes in which I would store my life savings of knowledge, to paraphrase Freire's banking metaphor for this transactional, colonizing brand of education, which above all seeks to "initiate" the native into the academic discourse community of his or her colonizer through mastery of its discourse conventions. I would teach from the lectern at the front of the class as my teachers had taught me, thereby controlling the discourse, ensuring an "economy" of discourses, while failing to perceive how such a unitary teacherly discourse perpetuates the oppression of the Other by silencing his or her own voice, by divesting discourse of that "heteroglossia" of subaltern signification, thus reinscribing on a microcosmic scale the cultural genocide enacted macrocosmically in the name of monoculturalism. In such a classroom the subaltern may speak, but only insofar as he or she speaks the language of the colonizer, which is not so much a form of speech as a form of minicry, even as the haunting laughter of the loon is not to be confused with the imitative notes of a parrot.

I would further seek to control and manipulate the classroom discourse by reliance on an old pedagogical tool, the Socratic method. I posed questions in order to hear my students recite the answers already in my head, so that they might come to know by heart that which I knew, as a passport for their impending hegira into the dominant culture. Thus, not only were the texts and overall content of instruction accessories to the enterprise of cultural imperialism, but the very manner in which I taught. The lectern stood as a fitting symbol of the centralized, authoritarian, univocal, teacherly discourse I disseminated, a discourse that reinscribed the asymmetrical and oppressive relations of power to which the native was subjected outside the classroom, as well. The podium thus became the classroom equivalent of the judge's gavel: a living symbol of the degree to which discourse was controlled, manipulated, ordered within the very narrow confines of the classroom. This topos for reinscribing the values, mores, and traditions of the dominant culture was every bit as reflective of that culture as the courtroom. Yet, I clung to the lectern like a mariner clinging to the helm of a wooden ship foundering in uncharted seas.

Thus, virtually every aspect of pedagogy reinscribed the asymmetrical power relations of the colonizer-colonized dynamic by placing the teacher in an active position while confining the students to a passive role. Content, methods, goals, texts, lectern, seating arrangements were all critical parts of the apparatus of cultural hegemony, repressing the culture and voices of the native while privileging the culture, codes, and discourse of the colonizer. If there was one voice that was heard above all others, it was mine. And I wanted it this way, not only to teach them what I knew of the dominant culture (its history, discursive codes and linguistic norms), but as a means of retaining control over that discourse. My voice was a means of silencing or minimizing such unsolicited oppositional discourse as enunciated by Erin, or repressing the one thing the colonizer fears above all else, that comprises his or her worst nightmare: the native impulse to insurrection.

The canon, the lectern, the grade book, the Socratic method, the teacher-led "discussion," the quiz bowl, the blackboard, the large desk at the front of the room, the detention slips, the tardy slips, the "progress" reports were all essential props in this theatre of assimilation. The asymmetrical relations of power that prevailed in the community and culture at large were reinscribed along authoritarian lines in the classroom through a pedagogy in which I cast myself in the role of the paternalistic authority figure and the native students in the role of passive objects receiving their daily dose of "discipline." The discipline in this case was the American realist novel as a vehicle for academic literacy, and the discipline of academic writing was a vehicle for assimilation or social control. I was reproducing in the classroom the same hierarchical power relations that oppressed these borderland students in the world at large, where "peasants are under the control of a dominant figure who incarnates the oppressive system" (Freire 176).

The rigid structuring of every aspect of schooling, from the bell-schedule to the alphabetized arrangement of seats in rows, becomes a surrogate for parental authority, as part of that process of socialization that begins with the youth and ends with the adult Other. The adult Other tends to "repeat the rigid patterns in which they were miseducated—the most significant of which is a behavior pattern characterized by passive marginalization and silent despair." For the oppressed borderland learner, these "patterns of domination are so entrenched in them that . . . renunciation would become a threat to their own identities" (Freire 154).

A pedagogy of assimilation is an instrument of social control, for the indigene as for the children of the colonizer. There is one difference: it bleaches out of the native his or her heritage, as well as the impulse toward insurrection, coding onto them instead a passive identity, which is in reality a nonidentity, an indentity founded upon an absence, but one which nonetheless resists sedition because it threatens their identity, pacified as it may be. Freire indicts with insight the hidden and debilitating motives of such a pedagogy of acculturation and the teachers who enact it: "Within the structures of domination, they [schools] function largely as agencies which prepare the invaders of the future" (45):

> Whatever the specialty that brings [teachers] in contact with the people, they are almost unshakably convinced that it is their "mission" to give the latter their knowledge and techniques. They see themselves as "promoters" of the people. Their programs of action include their own "objectives," their own convictions and their own preoccupations. They do not listen to the people, but instead plan to teach them how to "cast off their laziness." (153)

I anointed myself the maker and disseminator of knowledge: in the beginning there was the Word and the Word was mine, and not yours. I own the Word, not you. But I will graciously share the Word with you if you will listen, learn it by rote, and repeat it to me; if you will learn how to write it and say it, like me, and if you will respect me and thank me for giving it to you. Worship it. Memorize it. Recite it. Learn it. And spread it. That is the message I wish to share, and that you must learn. So that some day you can return to this village and spread the Gospel of the Academic Word among your own people, instead of relying on white outsiders, like myself, to do it for you. Freire writes,

> In addition, the dominators try to present themselves as saviors of the men [and women] they dehumanize and divide. This messianism, however, cannot conceal their true intentions: to save themselves. They want to save their riches, their power, their way of life, the things that enable them to subjugate others. (142)

They want to save their history, lore, signifying practices, discursive codes, and linguistic norms, all of which lie within the purview of the assimilationist classroom.

The aim of such authoritarian and assimilationist modes of pedagogy is social control. Argues Freire, this type of "manipulation, like the conquest whose objective it serves, attempts to anesthetize the people so they will not think" (146). In the final analysis, the "dead wood" that accumulates in the borderland classroom is the precise objective of pedagogy, the state of passive alienation evinced by Hank, Joey, Pete, and Velma was the objective of such an assimilationist pedagogy. If they didn't participate, at least they didn't cause any problems either. A pedagogy of acculturation is as tolerant of apathy as it is intolerant of resistance, as evidenced by the manner in which it ignores the silent Other while disciplining the bad Other: who talks back, who disrespects, who cuts school. The Other who comes to school and fails is preferred to the Other who defiantly cuts class for the simple reason that it is impossible to "pacify" a student who is not "present." Those students who could not be assimilated or otherwise collectivized by the dominant culture must be pacified by it. In either case, the genocide of the subculture is accelerated, for those members who are not siphoned off into the dominant culture are put to sleep by it. The borderland classroom has traditionally reinscribed education as the practice of domination, as opposed to the practice of freedom. Freirean borderland praxis seeks to invert or reverse this process, positing freedom, not domination, as the only goal of education in the borderlands (68–69).

It becomes the counterobjective then of resistance pedagogy to reawaken these slumbering souls from the long dormancy of domination and docility, to reactivate this segment of the borderland student population, to reengage the active participation of this disenfranchised, alienated, and all but invisible "subclass" of the borderland classroom. The goal of such a counterhegemonic praxis is not only to reawaken such students but to re-arm them with the decolonizing Word: one that enables them to "answer colonialism back," to "say their own Word," to utter sedition and mount rhetorical insurrection in the classroom as a precondition for carrying such resistance beyond the classroom and into the conflicted world of their people at large, with an aim to making that world more livable tomorrow than it is today.

In the traditional classroom, in the borderlands, as elsewhere, it is the teacher who manifests all the traits privileged for success in the dominant culture: initiative, resourcefulness, ambition, control, assertiveness, authority, agency, the zest for power—all traits we would have out students manifest. Yet, how can they manifest these traits if never given the opportunity to do so? How can saplings grow if they must always stand in the shadow of the tree of knowledge? For the student to grow, the teacher must fall, must step aside, must relinquish the reins of discourse, authority, agency, control, must let the students model these roles for themselves, as active speakers, knowers, writers, and thinkers, as makers and disseminators of knowledge, of their own knowledge, history, lore, signifying practices, not those of the colonizer/teacher.

The greatest obstacle to such a transference of control of the knowledge-making and dissemination process is the teacher. For he or she is reluctant to surrender the reins of authority for a number of reasons: fear of chaos, insurrection, of the disintegration of discipline, of the slippery slope that will end in anarchy, in the reprimands of supervisors, in the recriminations of peers. There is another reason as well: like all who wield authority, they are seduced by its trappings (agency, initiative, attention), and therefore reluctant to relinquish it. The pedagogue, no less than the politician or the priest, is seduced by the aphrodesial effects of power, of being the one in charge, the one in control of the many, the one who is the center of everyone's attention. To stand aside is to step out of the limelight, and into the seeming oblivion of a pedagogical eclipse, is to be marginalized, ghettoized within one's own classroom, relegated to the wings of one's very own theatre. The pedagogical spotlight is as seductive and corruptive as the theatrical spotlight, and the lectern as intoxicating as the down-center mark from which the soliloquy is delivered, and where all the voices are silenced in the presence of one's own. If not careful, we come to love the sound of our own voice more than any other aspect of teaching. But in raising our own, we are perpetuating the silence of others. The raising of their voices can only commence with the gradual silencing of our own, the emergence of their Word can only occur with the eclipse of our own, even as the stars only become visible after the sun has set.

Perhaps the greatest irony of all is that the rhetoric of assimilation I preached to my Athabascan students occurred simultaneously with my own indigenization, as part of a paradoxical process wherein I recruited the natives as I attempted to become more like them. I sought to eject them from their indigenous culture as I sought to inject myself into it. Terrie Goldie writes insightfully of this process of "going native," of "indigenization":

> The importance of the alien within cannot be overstated. In their need to become "native," to belong here, whites in Canada, New Zealand, and Australia have adopted a process which I have termed "indigenization." A peculiar word, it suggests the impossible necessity of becoming indigenous. For many writers, the only chance for indigenization seemed to be through writing about the humans who are truly indigenous, the Indians, Inuit, Maori, and Aborigines. (234)

Goldie's assertions are significant insofar as they call attention to the underlying, even unethical, motives of writing about the Other— of naming, representing, studying the Other as a means of possessing the Other, and as a substitute for the inability to become the Other. Her observations underscore some of the ethical pitfalls of indigenization, of "going native," the most egregious of which is the reinscription of the desire to dominate and possess the indigene even while bonding with him or her, as dramatically evidenced by the climactic phase of Kurtz's career in *Heart of Darkness*. The indigenized colonizer who reduces the Other to an object of academic inquiry merely shifts the arena of tyranny and oppression from the political to the ontological, from the World to the Word, from stigmatization to signification.

Thus, I began to see my long-standing interest in reading books by and about Native Americans as part of a deeper process of indigenization, as part of a desire to "go native." If I couldn't be Indian, I would read about them and live among them, even as I am now writing about them; I would take possession of the Indian through knowledge of the Indian. I would not only seek to possess knowledge about the Indian, but also acquire the artifacts made by the Indian, as a means of possessing the Indians themselves. And these native artifacts I would keep in my own library and living room, as if in a museum, where I could fix them in my possessive gaze. And all of this I did without realizing I was repeating the theft of the native's culture as perpetrated by my forebearers: the soldier, the settler, the missionary, the anthropologist, the photographer, the painter, and the new age spiritualist. My "innocent" search for knowledge about the native Other masked a more predatory desire to "own" the native, to take possession of his or her culture, to devour their lore and make it mine.

Within the classroom, it would remain business as usual until I underwent a pedagogical "conversion" experience similar to the indigenization I was undergoing outside it—"going native" as a teacher, as I had as a resident of the borderlands, utilizing a pedagogy that foregrounded the history, lore, language, signifying practices, and narratives of the Athabascan. It was not enough to bond with the native outside the classroom by learning Athabascan trapping techniques from elders like Nikolai; I also had to evolve a pedagogy that evinced a greater solidarity with the native student. Thus, indigenization on a personal level outside the classroom had to be accompanied by indigenization on a professional level inside it.

Not until I joined the ranks of other Euro-Americans who "are finally coming to terms with who they've been and, much more importantly, who and what it is they can become" could I expect to be accepted and assimilated into the subculture whose values and magical world outlook I shared, yet was in the process of destroying (Churchill 234). If I completed this journey of coming clean with who I was, why I was there, and what I was trying to accomplish, then, and only then, might I expect to be accepted. Churchill writes, "Then, finally, these immigrants can at last be accepted among us upon our shores, fulfilling the speculation of the Dwamish leader Seattle in 1854: 'We may be brothers after all.' As he said then, 'We shall see' " (250). In the meantime, my ideological complicity in the process of deracination as a bush teacher proselytizing a college-prep education could be construed as a form of "genocide with good intentions . . . as a significant component of the final phase of 'genocide' to which American Indian people are currently exposed" (280).

Zest for knowledge, power, leadership, initiative are not things that are easily relinquished, not even when one is using them on behalf of the native, to facilitate liberatory resistance struggle. But even in this seemingly decolonizing context they have harmful effects, reproduce the indigene's oppression insofar as they marginalize him or her, while leaving authority in the hands of the Indian wannabe. The practitioner must thus forever resist the temptation to assume the dominant, down-center position in the theatre of resistance struggle, must be content to let the native assume this sacred ground, which of all topoi in the landscape of oppression marks the generative, eruptive, and liberatory site of the native's reemergence into the theatre of the world. The trope of the emergence motif, recovered, revitalized, and recirculated as a threshold "sign," prefigures the return of the Athabascan to active residency in the borderlands, heralds the return of the native to his or her ancestral landscape, and the earth they inherit shall not be gray, but the good red earth of an Athabascan dawn.

4

Beyond the Contact Zone
Theorizing the Dialogic Classroom

[S]ince the classroom discourse conflicts are local manifestations of social and political ones, teachers of basic writers need to carry this pedagogical work outside their classroom.

—Thomas Fox

W here might the search for the "pedagogical arts of [this] contact zone" lead the bush teacher? The ubiquitous, enduring, and debilitating effects of marginalization that are produced and reproduced in the borderland classroom call into question the aims, assumptions, and activities associated with pedagogies of assimilation and "initiation": the traditional "banking" model and the basic writing paradigm. They underscore as well the practical and theoretical limitations of radical alternative pedagogies: contact zone and conflict-oriented models. What alternative pedagogies then are available to the borderland teacher? Having described some of the conditions that problematize teaching in this conflicted milieu, what can or should the practitioner do to surmount them? In this chapter I will investigate the goals,

103

assumptions, and methodologies associated with pedagogies of "initiation" and pedagogies of "resistance," including basic writing, contact zone, and conflict-oriented pedagogies, as enunciated by their respective pioneers: Kenneth Bruffee, Mary Louise Pratt, and Gerald Graff. I am undertaking this interrogation to enrich, revise, and wed these pedagogies to a more radical, dialogic, emancipatory borderland praxis.

What Happens When Basic Writers Don't Go to College?

The point I wish to emphasize in this section is that the extreme effects of marginalization I observed in these borderland learners, and which have been documented by the research of scholars in diverse disciplines, call into question not only the assumptions of the basic writing pioneers, but the pedagogical aims and methods that are predicated upon those assumptions. The violence and persistence of these effects in native students strongly suggest that we must look elsewhere than to the traditional basic writing model for the "pedagogical arts of this contact zone" (Pratt 40). However, before we can understand how the adverse effects of biculturalism problematize basic writing praxis, we must first define its aims, assumptions, and methodologies. Before commencing this critique, however, I want to acknowledge the profound contribution these pioneering scholars have made to pedagogy by breaking out of the traditional transactional or "banking" approach, establishing a precedent for evolving radical, fresh, interactive, and ethical approaches to composition studies upon which succeeding practitioners might construct a decolonizing, emancipatory borderland pedagogy. Researchers, scholars, and practitioners like Bruffee, Ferrell, Trilling, Rose, Graff, and Pratt have provided the precedent for a pedagogy that breaks with tradition, that is liberatory, dialogic, and relevant to the needs and lived realities of marginalized learners in the borderlands and elsewhere.

What was at first presumed to be the necessary, logical and inevitable end of pedagogy, however, might more usefully be viewed as an intermediary phase in the evolution from univocal pedagogies of acculturation to interactive pedagogies of resistance. In the final analysis, basic writing praxis fails to serve the needs of the marginalized, borderland learner for freedom, membership, integration, and identity by virtue of its similarities to, as opposed to its distinction from, the cognitive, banking model. Its assimilationist aims reproduce in the borderland student the debilitating effects of deracination, acculturation, and marginalization; its methodologies as well, which foreground the small collaborative group as a healing space, fail to achieve the end for which they were designed: the healthful integration of the borderland student into the dominant culture. Finally, its "initiation-based" assumptions are as misguided as they are well-meaning.

The goal of basic writing pedagogy, as enunciated by Bruffee, is the "initiation" of students into an "educated community" (8). The basic writing classroom is thus posited as a vehicle of acculturation, as part of the "process of initiation into membership," into a "new larger, and more complex community" (Trilling, qtd. in Lu 892). The word "initiation" is significant insofar as it connotes the unwitting complicity of basic writing pedagogy in the enterprise of cultural imperialism. Membership in the dominant culture necessarily entails, by virtue of the allegiance that is demanded of the borderland student, renunciation of the subculture. The native student's close identification with that subculture is correctly perceived by the basic writing pioneers to be an impediment to assimilation. One of the goals of basic writing instruction, consequently, is to help minority students "unburden" themselves of their home culture, irrespective of the violence that this "cultural bleaching" subjects them to. Lu continues.

> The word "initiation," Trilling points out, designates the "ritually prescribed stages by which a person is brought into community" (170–71). "Initiation" requires "submission," demanding that one "shape" and "limit" oneself to a "self, a life" and "precludes any other kind of selfhood remaining available" to one. (889)

Such a pedagogy reinscribes the "centralizing" tendency of education in general, which privileges a unitary, uber-discourse over a heteroglossia of subaltern discourses, a single, Euro-American identity over a multiplicity of ethnic identities, and a global monoculture over a diversity of localized, indigenous subcultures. As enunciated in "On Not Listening," Bruffee leaves no doubt as to the assimilationist aims of basic writing pedagogy when he asserts that its purpose is to " 'reacculturate' the student—to help them 'gain membership in another such community' by learning its 'language, mores, and values' " (Bruffee, qtd. in Lu, 894). Richard Courage articulates the rationale underlying these assimilationist aims:

> Champions of academic literacy maintain that class, race, and gender, or other factors have denied many people full access to the cultural capital and credentialling process of which academic literacy is a central component, and that we must challenge this inequity by assimilating these outsiders into the academic discourse community. (485)

When I arrived on the reservation I enthusiastically endorsed this pedagogical goal, believing that initiation into the discourse conventions of academic literacy was in the best interest of these borderland students, that a college education was an essential passport for gaining entrance to the promised land of the American Materialist Dream, and that a college-prep curriculum foregrounding instruction in the Great Books and in the academic Modes of Discourse was the most effective vehicle for achieving this goal. Further, I subscribed to these ideas with a zeal as evangelical as it was uncritical, seeing myself as living proof of their worth. "What I am confronted with here," I told myself, "is a group of basic writers." I grabbed the Great Books and *Warriner's* grammar handbook off the shelves, rolled up my sleeves, and set out with relish on the mission of educating these students for college, as a necessary first step in their assimilation into American mainstream culture, never pausing to question whether they desired such assimilation, or to examine the adverse effects that such acculturation and such a pedagogy of acculturation might subject them to. The classroom conditions I encountered, however, forced me to reexamine not only the goals, but the assumptions they were predicated upon and the activities that were deployed to realize them. In the end, I was obliged to modify or abandon virtually every facet of my pedagogy as hopelessly unrealistic, profoundly irrelevant, or extremely unethical.

The assumptions as well as the goals of basic writing pedagogy were problematic when applied to this particular population of students. As previously noted, basic writing pedagogy is predicated on the assumption that "initiation" into the academic discourse is in the best interest of marginalized students. It is similarly predicated on the assumption that these students desire such assimilation or initiation. It further presumes that such initiation is possible. My experience among the Athabascans prompted me to question these assumptions insofar as not a single native student evinced any desire to pursue postsecondary education. Of what practical purpose then was the acquisition of academic literacy for students who had few plans and no desire to attend the academy? This discovery came as yet another shock, one of many I experienced in the weeks after my arrival on the reservation. In some ways it came as the most violent shock of all, for it rendered irrelevant all of my long-range pedagogical plans. Another question is of more immediate interest to me: what were some of the factors behind this collective refusal to pursue postsecondary education?

For students in Mark's position, who identified strongly with their indigenous culture, a college education threatened his sense of self. As Mina Shaughnessey observes of many basic writers, "college both beckons and threatens them, offering to teach them useful ways of thinking about the world, but threatening them at the same time to take from them their distinctive ways of interpreting the world" (292). Basic writing pedagogy poses a distinct threat to students like Mark and Erin, who identify more closely with their native subculture insofar as it intensifies their fear that "mastery of a new discourse would wipe out, cancel, or take from them the points of view resulting from 'their experience as outsiders'" (Shaughnessey, qtd. in Lu 904).

Another factor in the widespread reluctance of these students to pursue postsecondary education were the communal kinship ties that prevailed on the reservation, and which conflict with the ethos of individual competition that is privileged for success in the academy. Leaving home for college entails a much more violent rupture for the Native American than for the Euro-American, to whom this ethic of rugged individualism is more familiar. As Lame Deer observes,

> The whole reservation was just one big mass of poor relatives, people who called [you] Uncle and Cousin regardless of the

degree of their relationship. . . . We aren't divided up into separate little families—Pa, Ma, kids and to hell with everybody else. The whole damn tribe is one big family; that's our kind of reality. (34)

The strength of these social bonds thus becomes an impediment to assimilation. As Labov affirms in *Language in the Inner City*, "the social bonds between children mean more to them than the opportunities presumably presented by school" (qtd. in Holzman 165). For students in David's position, other factors equivocated against the pursuit of postsecondary education. Although David identified more closely with the dominant culture than with the indigenous subculture, the discrimination he experienced in the metropolis revealed that anything resembling full assimilation was little more than a myth. Though as intellectually equipped as his Euro-American counterparts in the metropolis, such "initiation" was for David an impossibility because his intellectual merits were subsumed by differences of race, despite his own efforts to be the Same, to assimilate the dominant culture's modes of speech, dress, behavior, to meet its academic standards. Cognizant as they were of this asymmetrical code of race relations, many Athabascan students rejected the notion of a college education for the simple reason that the risks were too high and the personal rewards too low to make such a goal desirable. And so the dream of a higher education for them was a dream deferred. As Joanne Devine asserts in *Literacy and Social Power*, if we are to reverse this trend, educators must find ways to "reduce the cultural risks and enhance the personal rewards associated with the acquisition of literacy" (235).

Why risk the loss of identity or the violence of discrimination when one can stay on the reservation and reap many of the same material benefits that a college education purportedly leads to? The monthly checks disbursed by transnational corporations for oil, coal, and timber rights, the twenty years of free electricity donated by the Chuitna Power Co., the free redwood homes built for every native by the Chugiak Timber Co., the annual dividend checks disbursed by the state to every Alaskan resident—all these made it possible for the Athabascan students of Nyotek to circumvent a college education, to leapfrog directly into the American Materialist Dream, Athabascan style. For the Athabascan student, a college education was not a prerequisite for economic survival or social status in the village. As Holzman observes, "Their immediate economic survival does not seem to require the active use of literacy skills and the ideology of the community does not emphasize them" (163). However, it may be the colonizer who laughs last because every Athabascan student recruited into a Euro-American lifestyle is one less who can perpetuate the indigenous culture. Allegiance to a cash-based economy necessarily threatens the Athabascan's traditional, subsistence lifestyle, unless and until the Athabascan can effect a more harmonious conjunction of the two. Thus, instead of privileging assimilation into the dominant culture or repatriation into the indigenous subculture, schooling can emphasize the goal of "doubly educating" the Athabascan, as Luther Standing Bear argues in *Land of the Spotted Eagle* (573), to the values, mores, customs, and discourse codes privileged in either culture, in order to foster a bicultural identity that is an amalgamation or hybrid of both. However, all the literacy in the world will avail the Athabascan little, if he or she is still marginalized as a consequence of differences that nullify merit.

The increasing failure of the dominant culture to make good on the promise of fuller participation in the American Materialist Dream beyond the confines of the reservation resulted in the fact that few if any Athabascan students had any desire to leave those familiar and increasingly materialistic confines. Thus, the basic writing goal of "initiating" these students into the discourse conventions of the dominant culture as a means of assimilating them into it is predicated on the false assumption that such initiation is possible or even desirable among minority students. "Initiation" for these students is a myth and because it is a myth should not be the goal of pedagogy in the borderlands.

If the refusal of Athabascan students to pursue postsecondary education problematized the assimilationist aims of basic writing pedagogy, then the violent effects of marginalization manifested in these students similarly calls into question the assumptions of such praxis, as well as the activities associated with them. Basic writing theorists perceive a student's lingering attachment to an indigenous culture as an impediment to assimilation, as indeed it can be. The more quickly these marginalized learners can "unburden" themselves of the indigenous subculture, the more quickly they can assimilate into the dominant culture, or so it was assumed. In formulating their pedagogical response to this situation the basic writing pioneers assumed two things: that the adverse effects of this cross-cultural journey were transitory, and that they could be reduced if not eliminated by providing the "initiate" with the equivalent of a support group in the classroom, the small collaborative group. Lu writes,

> Bruffee believes that the "trials of changing allegiance from one cultural community to another" demand that teachers use "collaborative learning" in small peer groups. This method will create a "temporary transition or 'support' group that [one] can join on the way." (894)

The primary problem with the education of minority students, according to the basic writing pioneers, was the absence of "support systems to ease him [or her] through the momentary pain, dislocation, and anxiety accompanying his effort to 'unburden' himself" of his home culture (Lu 907). Teachers are urged to use "collaborative learning so that they can use oral discourse to improve written discourse" (Ferrell 252–53) and in order to reduce "the feelings of 'anxiety' or 'psychic strain' accompanying the process of acculturation" (Ferrell qtd. in Lu, 895). The small collaborative group was designed to facilitate this shift from orality to literacy, from indigenous subculture to dominant culture, from functional to academic literacy.

On the surface, the goals of basic writing pedagogy appear similar to those of radical resistance pedagogy: to "heal" or "cure" the violent effects of acculturation. Upon closer examination, however, this pedagogy of assimilation was merely treating the symptoms and not the disease. That it has proven ineffectual in treating those effects should come as no great surprise given the fact that such activities as collaborative learning are predicated on the false assumption that the effects of deracination and marginalization are transitory. As Lu asserts,

> They also suggest that these experiences ... are "temporary" (Bruffee 8). In short they sustain the impression that these experiences ought to and will disappear once the students get

comfortably settled in the new community and sever or diminish ties with the old. (895)

In reality, the effects of deracination and acculturation are far more violent and enduring than these theorists have assumed. Those who have lived through such experiences write of them in a far different light: one that seriously challenges the assumptions of the basic writing pioneers. In *Lives on the Boundary*, Mike Rose provides an account of the effects of marginalization, which would suggest that those effects are anything but ephemeral. As Lu observes, "Rose's account of his own education indicates that similar experiences of 'confusion, anger, and fear' are not at all temporary" (896). Edward Said, similarly, writes of the "mutilations" and "ravages of exile," (50) describing it as a condition of "terminal loss" (49), one that "dehumanizes and quite literally kills" (53), and therefore hardly something to be smoothed away by a classroom support group. He speaks of that "whole complex of pressures and constraints that lie at the center of the exile's predicament, which produces the kind of narcissistic masochism that resists all efforts at amelioration, acculturation, and community" (54), a conclusion that severely problematizes a pedagogy predicated on the assumption that such effects can be "ameliorated" through a makeshift "community" as a vehicle to a fuller "acculturation." Now critics might well argue that the predicament of the Saidian exile is distinct from that of the Native American, and therefore his observations irrelevant to the conditions by which the Native American Other is confronted. I would argue that while differences exist between these two types of exile, the resulting effects are similar: alienation, confusion, nihilism, apathy, loss of identity and membership. Moreover, they are similar because in both instances the Other is subjected to the debilitating effects of deracination and acculturation.

A body of research conducted by scholars in diverse disciplines also attests to the mutilating effects of these dual processes, calling into question the assumptions of basic writing theorists. Irving Howe, for example, writes of the "tensions of biculturalism" and the "crisis in identity" that those tensions produce (110). Lu likewise writes of "the accompanying sense of contradiction and ambiguity" (889), of the "pain and dislocation" such students experience when struggling to "connect with the larger cosmopolitan culture" (898), while Ferrell writes of the "psychic strain entailed in moving from a highly oral frame of mind to a more literate frame of mind." This is a strain "too great to allow for rapid movement" between cultures (252). As Adams concludes, "too few people have reached accommodation that is satisfactory. Consequently, extreme personality traits are manifested to a high degree" (293).

Lu likewise challenges the basic writing assumption that the violent effects of deracination are transitory, that "students are experiencing these trials only because they are still in 'transition,' bearing ties to both the old and the new communities, but not fully 'departed' from one or comfortably 'inside' the other" (894). Such a view of the transcultural journey these students must undertake is reductive inasmuch as it posits that journey as a simple "transition" whose ultimate destination of complete assimilation is a foregone conclusion. The reality is that due to the great disparity between the two cultures and to the unequal code of race relations in the dominant culture, such students will likely never be "comfortably inside" that culture, are likely to never "arrive" at their destination, but be consigned to the margins of both cultures, to the psychic and emotional no-man's land of bicultural alienation as the consequence of a forced dislocation that is not so much an exodus as an exile. Thus, the violence of an induced departure from an old culture is achieved to no useful purpose; the deracination that such pedagogical practices facilitate is accomplished to no practical end. As Howe asserts, for these borderland learners "there must always be some sense of difference, even alienation" (110). Far from providing a solution to the problem of how to teach basic writing students, such practices, well intentioned as they may be, become part of the problem. Drawing on the observations of Gloria Anzaldua, Lu concludes, "the approaches of Bruffee and Ferrell are unlikely to help such students cope with the conflicts 'swamping' their 'psychological borders'" (896).

Thus, the basic writing classroom is complicit in the process of colonization inasmuch as it perpetuates the violence done to the indigene by extending the arena of that violence to the classroom. Not only is basic writing pedagogy ineffectual in ameliorating the effects of bicultural alienation, but it actually compounds them insofar as it perpetuates the very processes of deracination and acculturation that produce so many of the debilitating effects of marginalization. It treats the symptoms instead of the causes of oppression, and this it does ineffectively because it underestimates the violence and ignores the causes of those effects.

If pedagogy is truly interested in ameliorating the effects of oppression, how can it do otherwise than address the causes of that oppression, including itself, first and foremost by seeing that it doesn't perpetuate oppressive relations of power either through its goals, methods, content, or assumptions? Such a classroom must therefore become antiassimilationist, decolonizing, and politicized in its orientation if it is to truly ameliorate the dehumanizing and quite literally fatal effects of deracination and acculturation. That process begins, as Freire asserts, by "unveiling" the "thematic universe" of the borderland student. Since pedagogy comprises a significant part of the borderland student's universe, that unveiling must begin with a cold, hard look in the mirror by the bush teacher. It is not enough that pedagogy in the borderlands hold a mirror up to the world outside the classroom; it must similarly hold a mirror up to itself, to the conditions inside the classroom, to the aims, assumptions, and activities that have produced this lived reality as well.

Beyond the Contact Zone: Toward a Literacy of Resistance

What other pedagogies are available to the practitioner that might more usefully serve the borderland student? Mary Louise Pratt provides a useful, if undertheorized vision of the borderland classroom as a "contact zone." Pratt's trope for such a classroom provides a welcome stimulus for reinventing borderland praxis. In this section I would like to enumerate the uses as well as analyze the limitations of Pratt's "contact zone" model for pedagogy.

Pratt's trope of the "contact zone" is an apt one for the borderland classroom inasmuch as it captures the agonistic bicultural tension of such a pedagogical terrain. In the final analysis, however, Pratt's "contact zone" is more agonistic in theory than in practice. Pratt deploys her metaphor of the "contact zone" to "refer to those social spaces where cultures meet, clash, and grapple with each other, often in contexts of highly asymmetrical relations of power, such as colonialism, slavery, or their aftermaths" ("Arts"

34). At first glance, Pratt's elucidation of her "contact zone" trope would seem to comprise a perfect fit for the colonized, borderland classroom in general, and for the reservation classroom in particular. A writing classroom on an Athabascan reservation is most definitely a site where a dominant culture and an indigenous subculture "meet, clash, and grapple" with one another in a struggle for domination on the one hand and survival on the other. Moreover, this agonistic struggle occurred within the context of "colonialism" and its neocolonial or postcolonial "aftermath." Pratt's elaboration of her "contact zone" trope underscores the agonistic relationship of dominant and indigenous cultures. The "contact zone," as Pratt observes, is also:

> the space of colonial encounters, the space in which peoples geographically and historically separated come into contact with each other and establish ongoing relations, usually involving conditions of coercion, radical inequality, and intractable conflict. (*Imperial Eyes* 6)

It is difficult to conceive of two more "geographically and historically separated" individuals than a white male from California and an adolescent Athabascan from the Alaskan bush. Moreover, the lived realities of the native student were characterized by a series of "intractable conflicts" associated with the environment, with schooling, and with relations between the races.

On the surface at least, Pratt's agonistic trope of the "contact zone" comprises a useful vehicle for signifying the realities of the bicultural, borderland classroom. Indeed, the modifier "contact" is embedded with many agonistic connotations, a few of which I would like to explicate by way of underscoring the relevance of her "contact zone" metaphor for resistance pedagogy. The word "contact" connotes violence in a multiplicity of linguistic contexts. It has been used, for example, to signify the violence of "contact" sports (football and hockey); the violence of military encounters with the Other in the jungles of Southeast Asia, with whom our troops made "contact" in firefights as violent as they were sudden; and the violence of the initial "contact" between new world subcultures and their old world colonizers: Hawaiian history before Captain Cook's "discovery" of the islands, for example, is referred to as "pre-contact."

As deployed here, the phrase also connotes nostalgia for an Edenic moment when the indigene lived in an undifferentiated communion with nature, uncorrupted by "contact" with the European and with the European's alienated and alienating consciousness.

The term "pre-contact" is imbricated not only with chronological and nostalgic connotations, but is a signifier as well of cultural imperialism insofar as it denies the native Other any historical identity apart from the colonizer. Thus, the prefix "pre" performs the work of colonization in the same manner that the "post" in postcolonial does. As Anne McClintock observes, both "pre" and "post" in this context "reduce cultures of people beyond colonialism to prepositional time" (86). Language is thus used to perpetuate the oppression of native peoples who are relegated to the status of prepositions while their colonizers are assigned the dominant syntactical position of nouns and subjects. Discourse, down to the very syntactical structures used to describe the Other, becomes yet another conduit for the circulation of power, and thus for the subjugation of the Other. As McClintock writes,

> The term [post] confers on colonialism the prestige of history proper; colonialism is the determining marker of history. Other cultures share only a chronological, prepositional relation to a Euro-centered epoch that is over (post-), or not yet begun (pre-). In other words, the world's multitudinous cultures are marked, not positively by what distinguishes them, but by a subordinate, retrospective relation to linear, European time. (86)

McClintock here establishes language as the locus of hegemonic domination and of counter-hegemonic struggle, surely an observation with important implications for pedagogy, whether it is used as a tool of oppression or as a vehicle of liberation. Whoever controls the apparatus for the making and dissemination of knowledge—the schools, the textbook and publishing industries, the print and news media—determines whether the Word is to be used as an instrument of "initiation" into the dominant culture or as a vehicle for resistance to and emancipation from that culture. In the colonized terrain of the bicultural "contact zone" there really is no other pedagogical choice. The practitioner is either part of the solution or part of the problem, either teaches in solidarity with the Other or in solidarity with those who oppress the Other.

Pratt's "contact zone" is not without its limitations, however. In the last analysis, it proves more agonistic in theory than in practice, more valuable as a point of departure for reinventing borderland praxis than as the destination of it, more useful as a rhetorical figure for theorizing change than as a master trope for actualizing the aims of resistance pedagogy. Upon closer examination, Pratt's contact zone devolves into a kind of generic, academic, "multicultural bazaar," as Joseph Harris observes, where students "are not so much brought into contact with opposing views as placed in a kind of harmless connection with a series of exotic others" (33). Further, the examples of resistance that Pratt proffers are "either innocuous or esoteric," as Richard Miller asserts. Consequently, "the kind of writing produced in such a contact zone seems oddly benign" (390).

Indeed, Pratt seems to disown her own metaphor insofar as she posits it not as an end in itself but merely as a transitional phase in a process whose ultimate configuration is not a "contact zone" but a "safe house" (40)—a "unified and utopian community" that subsumes difference and represses conflict (Harris 34). As envisioned here, Pratt's contact zone/safe house ironically reinscribes many of the problematic aspects of the basic writing classroom in which collaborative groups are altruistically posited as an antidote to the debilitating and enduring effects of deracination and acculturation, an educational safe house in which "groups can constitute themselves . . . with high degrees of trust, shared misunderstandings, temporary protection from the legacy of oppression . . . Places for healing and mutual recognition" (40).

Upon closer inspection, Pratt's contact zone comprises a sharp departure from Freirean praxis for instead of seeking to "unveil" the realities of oppression, it seeks to "shelter " students from the "legacy of oppression." Instead of bringing students into "contact" with the "existential, present, concrete" conditions that oppress them, not merely as something to be studied, but as problems to be solved, it seeks to smooth over such conflicted lived realities (Freire 85). Instead of bringing students into liberatory contact with the legacies of their oppression, Pratt's safe house loses contact with that reality. As such, it is in actuality a "no-contact" zone: a depoliticized, deconflicted refuge from the lived realities of oppression, one that ironically performs the work of the colonizer by hiding from the Other's eyes the effects of colonization.

And this is its primary flaw.

The Other must reverse the equation of academic inquiry, objectifying the enterprise of colonization that has objectified him or her, making oppression the object of critical inquiry. Instead of being the passive objects of study, borderland students must become the active subjects of the knowledge-making process, and the objectification of their own oppression must become the first text that they "read" and "write," for this truth is as emancipatory when objectified as it is oppressive if left unexamined. It is indeed a truth, which when named and possessed, can set the native free.

Insofar as Pratt's contact zone seeks to shelter students from the legacy of their own oppression, our search for the "pedagogical arts" of the contact zone must ironically exclude Pratt's own pedagogy. We must seek elsewhere for these "alter/native" arts of the contact zone. What promised a dynamic destination for borderland pedagogy amounts in the end to no more than a point of departure from which to initiate the search for the pedagogical arts of the contact zone. We must nevertheless be thankful for that much, for Pratt's contact zone points us in the right direction. If it doesn't comprise the goal of an emancipatory borderland praxis, it is at least a compass for steering a course through the uncharted and conflicted terrain of the borderlands toward such a pedagogy.

Toward a Dialogic Classroom: Teaching the Cultural Conflicts

The search for the pedagogical arts of this contact zone leads me next to conflict-oriented pedagogy. At first glance, Gerald Graff's model for teaching the conflicts provides a pedagogy as agonistic in practice as it is in theory, and therefore would appear to comprise a useful alternative not only to assimilationist pedagogies, but to Pratt's undertheorized contact zone pedagogy. In the last analysis however, it likewise proves too tame for the purposes of this project insofar as it ignores the lived realities of the borderland student as the locus for conflict, foregrounding instead the alien conflicts of the academy and the professorate. In the end, it devolves into a mere academic exercise inasmuch as it shifts the focus of pedagogy from the Great Books to the conflicts of the academy. And while this is one step closer to the lived reality of the college student, it is yet one step removed from the conflicted lived realities of the borderland learner. Nevertheless, Graff's pedagogical paradigm provides a solid theoretical foundation for a pedagogy that is more truly dialogic, and this in my opinion is its most vital contribution to the pedagogical arts of the contact zone. In this section I want to analyze the uses and limitations of Graff's conflict-oriented pedagogy.

In "Teach the Conflicts," Graff argues for a classroom that is "in dialogue with other classrooms," that is truly dialogic, in which learning occurs within the context of a conversation not only between teacher and student, not only between students within a given class, but a conversation carried out between classes as well. Thus, the greatest contribution of Graff's model is that it extends the boundaries of the critical conversation across disciplines. It is a boundary-crossing pedagogy, a pedagogy that dissolves arbitrary barriers between courses, in which pedagogical fiefdoms dissolve into a more holistic praxis: cross-curricular, conflict-oriented, dialogic within and between classes. This is a dynamic alternative to the compartmentalized approach to learning and literacy acquisition. Moreover, whereas a fragmented, specialized, atomized curriculum reinscribes Euro-American values and mores, Graff's dialogic, cross-curricular paradigm reinscribes the more holistic worldview of the Native American in which identity is constructed socially and knowledge is communal. Graff's model thus takes the social construction of knowledge and amplifies it, extends it across the entire curriculum, creating a conversation across disciplines, a dialogue that is mutually reinforced by a series of courses in communication with one another. Thus, while its content is suspect, its methodology is sound. The lived realities of the marginalized learner, not the conflicts of the professorate are the proper destination for such a pedagogy. Graff provides us with the vehicle for reaching that destination. His conflict-oriented model provides the borderland practitioner with both the methodology and the theoretical framework for actualizing a pedagogy that is not only dialogic, but liberatory.

As Graff observes, in a dialogic classroom "questions would not arise in one class only to be abruptly dropped in the next, as tends to be the case now" ("Other Voices" 34). Graff's model is significant not only because it foregrounds cross-curricular instruction, but because it foregrounds conflict as the thematic content of that instruction. In arguing the case for teaching the academic conflicts, Graff provides a strong warrant for extending the focus of that inquiry to include the conflicted lived realities of the students themselves:

> [for] the greater the degree of collective interaction, the more likelihood of generating and sustaining self-criticism of whatever is problematic in that interaction, including its lack of relevance to students' interests and . . . needs. . . . Instead of repressing its own history and politics, such a curriculum would tend to foreground its own history and politics and open it to theoretical debate. (35)

Following Freire's cue, borderland practitioners now need only take Graff's warrant for devising a pedagogy that has "relevance to student's interests and . . . needs," that foregrounds, not the repressed history and politics of the academy, but of the indigenous subculture; not the conflicts of the professorate, but the conflicted "thematic universe" of the indigene (103). Graff's attempt to concretize dialogic theory in the conflicts of the academy provides the impetus for contextualizing dialogic theory in the colonized terrain of an Athabascan Indian reservation, for extending the locus of critical inquiry from the conflicts of the academy to the cultural conflicts of the Athabascan, and studying these conflicts across the borderland curriculum: not only in history and English courses, but in arts and crafts, woodshop, journalism, and bilingual education courses.

Graff's privileging of academic conflict as the locus of critical inquiry and debate, while an important pedagogical move and significant departure in its own right, is nevertheless the principal limitation of his pedagogical model. Like Pratt's model for contact zone pedagogy, Graff's conflict-oriented paradigm is more agonistic in theory than in practice, is more useful as an academic exercise than as a force for meaningful social reform, is more useful for the theoretical framework it provides than for the thematic material it privileges. Instead of orienting inquiry toward the social, political, economic, cultural, and environmental conflicts that problematize the lived realities of the marginalized student, Graff's model for teaching the conflicts foregrounds the "genteel and apolitical" sphere of the professorate: conflicts that he freely admits are irrelevant to the "deep, social divisions of American culture" ("Defense" 220).

Graff underscores the necessity of such a holistic, cross-curricular model if pedagogy is to become truly dialogic, which is to say as dialogic in practice as it is in theory: "I doubt whether the classroom can become effectively dialogic as long as it itself is not in dialogue with other classrooms" (34). Of the two primary ingredients of Graff's model, it is not the thematic material of conflict, but the schematic mechanism of a dialogic curriculum that he deems the most critical: "though my emphasis ostensibly is on conflict, it is ultimately on community and the need for a more integrated curriculum" (220).

Heeding his words, might it not be possible to create a community of courses in communication with one another, to create as well a community that consists of the school and the subculture by which it is encompassed, that extends the locus of academic inquiry into the community, that breaks down the proverbial "fourth wall" dividing classroom from community, bringing students and practitioner alike into direct "contact" with the community and the conflicts imbricated in it? Might it be possible to build on Graff's work, making the conflicts of the bicultural contact zone the locus of critical inquiry and bringing the student into "contact" with those conflicts across the curriculum, by bringing all classes into dialogic "contact" with one another? Moreover, what might such a pedagogy look and sound like? I will revisit these questions in the last three chapters of this work.

This comprises a radical alternative and a sharp departure from assimilationist pedagogies that foreground "initiation" into the "language, values, and mores" of the dominant culture (Bruffee 8). As Cain observes, Graff shows how we can "capitalize upon the conflicts we are warring over, and in the process demonstrates how they can draw us together" (xxxiii). A pedagogy foregrounding the cultural conflicts of the contact zone might heal the wounds sustained by those conflicts with the scar tissue of language, representation, signification, and cross-cultural communication. Ultimately, what is required is that the thematic material of Graff's model be politicized, be resituated in the politicized, colonized, and dehumanized terrain of the borderland student. As Patrick J. Hill argues, "Graff is dealing more with the pale reflection of racial, ecological, and economic conflicts than with their full painful reality" (qtd. in Cain, xxxvi). Papering-over these cultural conflicts, or limiting inquiry to the turf wars of the professorate and the academy, raises the "disturbing . . . possibility that students will remain outside the debates that affect them, missing the opportunities for acquiring skills and knowledge, and for learning to express themselves cogently in speech and writing, that working with conflict can offer them" (Cain xxxix). The classroom will remain a site of oppression that reproduces "alienated consciousness" unless and until it provides the marginalized student the opportunity to say his or her own word, to name his or her own world, as a first critical step toward repossessing both the word and the world (Shor 14). Such a colonized terrain insists that literacy be yoked to the need of alienated learners to "locate themselves in history, to see themselves as social actors able to debate their collective futures" (Aronowitz, qtd. in Graff 240n).

Thus, the role of the critical thinker must be augmented by the role of the social activist. Otherwise, inquiry devolves into mere study for its own sake, divorced from the lived reality it has named, but not endeavored to alter. Analysis must be yoked to action, as Freire asserts: "The more active an attitude men [and women] take in regard to the exploration of their thematics, the more they deepen their critical awareness of reality, and in spelling out those thematics, take possession of that reality" (97). The task of the dialogic teacher is to "re-present that universe to the people . . . and re-present it, not as a lecture, but as a problem," one demanding immediate intervention (101). Understanding the conflicts requires critical inquiry; resolving them requires active intervention. The classroom is the proper site for investigation, but only if it ultimately brings the student into confrontational and liberatory contact with the world beyond the classroom, with those sites where the conflict originates and persists: the logging mill, the oil rig, and the strip mine that degrade local populations of moose and salmon upon which the Athabascan depends for his or her subsistence; the school that accelerates the genocide of the Athabascan's subculture by foregrounding the language, mores, and values of the dominant culture. These are the real conflicts to which we must teach, and we must teach them in dialogic partnership with the student, in dialogic partnership with other courses, and in dialogic partnership with the local community that is oppressed by them.

5

Adventures in Cultural Tourism
Foxfire and the Fetishization of the Authentic

Compositionists are becoming increasingly aware of the need to
tell and listen to stories of life in the borderlands.

—Lu 888

M y search for the pedagogical arts of this contact zone
resulted in the adaptation of some radical alter/natives
to traditional borderland praxis. This search was driven
by a number of persistent questions: was there some other way to
make learning in the borderlands more meaningful to these
marginalized students? Were there not other pedagogical arts that
might somehow "heal" the debilitating effects of deracination and
pseudoassimilation? Was "initiation" into the dominant culture the
only worthwhile objective of borderland pedagogy? Could counterhegemonic resistance become the goal of literacy instead? And if so,
how? If pedagogy had accelerated the genocide of the Athabascan
subculture could it be redeployed to preserve or revitalize that culture by helping students reconnect to its history, lore, customs, mores,
and to the native topoi associated with them? In short, might it not

be possible to reconfigure pedagogy along more ethical, practical, and livable lines? Might it not be possible to foreground the "thematic universe" of the Athabascan as opposed to alien and alienating universe of the Euro-American? Might it not be possible to replace a compartmentalized curriculum that privileges specialization and disconnectedness with an integrated curriculum that reinforces the more holistic worldview of the Native American? Were there not other narratives, other texts, other stories, and other ways of teaching them to The Other? Could local politics, cultural conflicts, and the natural topoi associated with them be "read" as "texts" to facilitate the acquisition of academic and critical literacy?

My search for the alter/native arts of this bicultural contact zone resulted in an apostasy from the dominant Euro-American culture, and a turn toward the Athabascan subculture. I returned the Great Books of the Western Canon to their glassed-in shelves, and turned instead to a series of borderland narratives that I ordered by phone, paid for out of pocket, and had flown into the village on Jimmy St. Claire's bush plane. I returned Warriner's grammar text to the shelves as well, relying instead on the Foxfire project's contextual approach to the acquisition of academic literacy. Back onto the shelves as well went the master narratives of Euro-American history; I relied instead on a series of counter-hegemonic borderland narratives that offered useful rereadings of American history (Dee Brown's *Bury My Heart at Wounded Knee*). These practices could be enriched by other possibilities: for example, the ANLCS could be "reread" as an alter/native "text" that in turn would enable the Athabascan to reread his or her contemporary history. Further, such a reading could be conducted as part of a broader inquiry into the history of colonizer-colonized relations as played out between Euro-American and Native American cultures in a variety of contact zones extending from Plymouth Rock to Trading Bay, from the age of the Columbus to the New Age Hobbyist, from the height of the Renaissance to the twilight of the millennium. I will elaborate on the practices and possibilities associated with these alter/native "texts" in the next chapter.

What emerges is an eclectic, hybridized pedagogy—a compendium of Foxfire, Freirean, and resistance pedagogies adapted to the realities of this bicultural contact zone: a fireweed flower giving in the subarctic wind without giving up the native soil to which it is rooted. It conjoins the dialogic aspects of the Foxfire and Graffian models, in which writing is engaged across the curriculum, is reinforced with reading assignments that foreground alter/native narratives from the borderlands, and finally is linked to a Freirean component foregrounding local cultural conflicts as a vehicle for the acquisition of critical literacy and the recuperation of the indigenous culture. I will devote a chapter to each of these three aspects of borderland pedagogy, though I wish to assert that the distinctions between them are not absolute but indistinct, and bleed into one another as part of a more holistic or integrated learning experience. I would like to add a further qualification: the Foxfire program and the non-canonical reading project were not adopted simultaneously as part of a systematic attempt to integrate instruction across the borderland curriculum. Rather, they were adopted independently, though ostensibly for the same purpose: to make learning more meaningful to these marginalized learners, to facilitate the acquisition of academic literacy, and to help Athabascan students reconnect to their ancestral culture.

Their emergence in the classroom during the same autumn was more the result of coincidence than planning. Though spawned independently, they were nevertheless produced by the same conditions, even as sister twisters are spawned by the same violent forces that prevail over a localized terrain. Therefore, it would be misleading to imply that their concomitant adoption was purely coincidental. The conditions were ripe for a series of pedagogical "events" that would alter the educational landscape of this borderland milieu, at first operating independently of one another then organizing into a more comprehensive system of dialogic instruction as the affinities between them became apparent, and thus the "contacts" between them more deliberate. So that the activities of the Foxfire project and the readings in borderland narratives eventually bled into one another. Thus, what began as a vehicle for the acquisition of academic literacy became a vehicle for the acquisition of critical literacy as well, evolving in directions as unforeseen as they were unintended.

Foxfire Among the Fireweed

When Alicia Taft, the district-wide director of the bilingual education program, approached me about participating in the Foxfire project I was more than willing to lend an ear. In this chapter I will discuss the uses and limitations, the enabling and disabling aspects, of Foxfire pedagogy as adapted to the exigencies of this borderland milieu. The timing of Alicia's approach was serendipitous, for it came at a point when I was desperate for ideas, for solutions, for alter/natives to standard classroom procedures. My morale had reached its nadir; I was not only thinking of requesting a transfer out of the village, but of quitting altogether and returning to California. More than once during that first semester I gazed aloft at Jimmy St. Claire's bush plane as it winged away to Anchorage and I wished I were on it. I was not content with a pedagogy that functioned merely as a form of social control, as an opiate to tame the native's seditious impulses. While this may have calmed my nerves by producing a passive population of native learners, it did little to arouse my pedagogical juices, which required first and foremost that I make strong and continuous "contact" with these students. I could not abide a pedagogy in which I as well as my students were merely "going through the motions" because we had to, because the law required that they be in school and because the terms of my contract required that I do something to earn my paycheck. Aside from that, I could see no useful purpose to what I was teaching them; I could think of no credible answer to the most fundamental of all questions that troubled my mind: Why?

This pedagogical reality was as depressing as the inclement cloud-cover that eclipsed the sun for three hundred days a year. The solution to this problem was equally depressing, for I must either go through the motions of a meaningless pedagogy or abandon it altogether. Yet, without any useful alter/native I could see no choice but to put my head down and blindly blunder ahead with the plans I had been trained to implement, but which alas had no useful currency in this pedagogical situation. This was not why I had chosen teaching as a career, for it reduced pedagogy to pacification. If I couldn't teach with conviction about things that mattered to my students, then I'd rather be digging ditches for the Peace Corps in some "undeveloped" country. Perhaps at the end of my career I could settle for merely going through the motions, but not at its very inception! To be reduced to the aimless drudgery of an ox in harness toiling in the furrows of a fallow field for the next nine months was more than I could bear. However, lacking any practical pedagogical alter/native, I could see no other choice but to grin and bear it, to put my head down and plod blindly ahead with the single-minded resolve of an ox whose world is reduced to the furrows at its feet by the blinders affixed to its eyes. I was driven to adhere to a predetermined ideology by a strong survival instinct that urged me to just serve my time until May 22nd, when I could board Jimmy 's air taxi, bid farewell to the village, and return to "civilization" for whatever fate awaited me.

And then one morning Alicia Taft entered my classroom and showed me there was another way, uttering a word that changed my entire pedagogical landscape, revealing to my eyes an horizon rich with possibilities, and altering the course of my entire career: Foxfire. The more I listened to her explain the unusual features of this pedagogy, in which utterly unconventional assumptions and activities were deployed to realize conventional aims, the more excited I became. It appealed at once to both the adventurer and the traditionalist in me, to the idealist as well as the realist, to that side of me that longed to "go native" and to that side which longed to pass on the rich tradition of my own education. Moreover, here was a possible solution to my most vexing problem, an answer to the myriad questions that had haunted my mind: what to teach these students, and how, and why? Alicia was my Ariadne and Foxfire the thread showing me the way out of this pedagogical labyrinth, similar to the red thread that escapes the pattern of a Navajo blanket, transgressing the borders, regaining the margins and freedom.

For those unacquainted with the Foxfire project, allow me to provide a little background on its origins, aims, assumptions, and methodologies. The project had its roots in the rural mountains of Appalachia, a borderland milieu with enough relevance to my own pedagogical situation to warrant its importation. From its inception in 1972, the Foxfire project attempted to extend the classroom into the local community. As Eliot Wiggington states in the introduction to *Foxfire 2* (1973),

I believe that in most cases the most rewarding and significant things that happen to a kid happen outside the classroom . . . .
The only way I can see to get our kids committed to our

neighborhoods and our communities is to get them so involved in their surroundings that they become determined that the community's destiny will be in their hands, not in the hands of the commercial rapists. They must feel that they are essential to the future of their homes. (14, 16)

The Foxfire project constituted a radical departure from traditional classroom approaches to literacy inasmuch as it foregrounded the local culture of the Appalachian students as opposed to mainstream American culture as the locus of instruction. Thus, the lore, customs, history, dialects, traditions, mores, and values of the indigenous subculture comprised the content of instruction. The vehicle for acquiring this knowledge was a student-centered publication that documented these and other aspects of the subculture.

Foxfire pedagogy comprised a radical shift from traditional classroom praxis in another sense as well, for it was predicated on an active, participatory, and collaborative approach to learning as opposed to the passive, objective, and more individual approach of traditional literacy instruction. Another radical feature of the project was its cross-curricular mode of instruction. Instead of offering courses in isolation from one another, it sought to integrate instruction across the curriculum. It further sought to integrate the community and the classroom in the learning process, to extend the classroom into the community, to establish a direct connection, a living link, between the academic word and the Appalachian world.

The goals, assumptions, and methodologies of Foxfire pedagogy, however, bear some disquieting similarities with those of traditional basic writing praxis. As with basic writing pedagogy, the primary goal of the Foxfire project is the acquisition of academic literacy as a necessary precondition for "initiation" into the dominant culture. The Foxfire pioneers assumed that the acquisition of academic codes in general, and grammatical conventions in particular, would be enhanced if those codes and conventions were taught, not in isolation from the writing process, but as an integral part of it. It was further assumed that the acquisition of such literacy would be accelerated if writing was linked to some real-world application: a student-centered publication foregrounding the recovery of the local subculture. Though the means deployed by these two pedagogies for the acquisition of literacy were radically different, the ends they served were the same. Moreover, Foxfire pedagogy was also predicated on the assumption that such "initiation" or assimilation was not only achievable, but in the student's best interest. As with traditional basic writing pedagogy, such assimilation was further assumed to be "innocent," devoid of any debilitating side effects. The two pedagogies shared a similar methodology as well, foregrounding a more participatory, interactive approach in which small collaborative groups functioned as the principal mechanism for the acquisition of knowledge.

Despite these similarities, Foxfire and basic writing pedagogy differ in significant ways. The Foxfire program is more truly bicultural than the basic writing model. Instead of requiring the native students to "unburden" themselves of their indigenous subculture, they are encouraged to reconnect to it as a means of rescuing it from oblivion. The healing side effects of this reconnection, though not one of the original aims of the project, became yet another benefit of it. Thus, the Foxfire project was more truly hybridized insofar as it simultaneously privileged mastery of the dominant culture's academic codes and the recovery of the indigenous culture's orthodox traditions. As such, it bridged the disjunction between the dominant culture and the indigenous subculture, the schism between schooling and culture that habitually problematizes the acquisition of literacy in the borderlands and elsewhere.

Learning in this context is much more interactive, dialogic, and hands-on than the traditional "banking" approach to education in which students passively absorb the knowledge that the teacher "deposits" in them, or even the traditional basic writing approach that allows students to interact with each other, but not with their home culture. While they are encouraged to get their "hands on" the academic codes of the dominant culture, they are not given the opportunity to get their "hands on" the history, lore, myths, language, and customs of their own native subculture. Perhaps the most distinguishing feature of Foxfire pedagogy is the student-generated publication that functions as the vehicle for the recuperation of the indigenous culture and for the acquisition of academic literacy. Students assume complete ownership of the publication, are responsible for every phase of its production from conducting and transcribing the field interviews to developing and cropping the film, from designing the layout and writing the copy to editing and proofreading the final text.

Having sketched in the origins, aims, assumptions, and activities associated with traditional Foxfire pedagogy, I will now describe how its reincarnation on an Athabascan Indian Reservation both conformed to and departed from that model. What did this Foxfire approach to literacy look and sound like as it was adapted to the exigencies of this particular pedagogical setting? I was invited to participate in this cross-curricular adventure in borderland pedagogy for the simple reason that I had six preps. As the lone generalist on the staff, I was not only charged with administering instruction in English, but in history, arts and crafts, algebra, journalism, and yearbook. I was therefore ideally situated to implement such a cross-curricular model of instruction. Alicia approached me with the idea of devoting my yearbook and journalism classes to the production of the Foxfire publication. She also suggested linking my arts and crafts class to Paul's woodshop, Teresa's home economics, and Max's bilingual education classes. I made the additional decision to establish links wherever possible between my English and history classes and the Foxfire project as well, as much for the preservation of my own morale and sanity as for the benefits of such linkage to the students. Max was an Athabascan elder who was the foremost "gatekeeper" of native lore in the village. He had been working with Alicia for several years to implement instruction in Dena'ina. He was also David's father.

The incorporation of instruction in Dena'ina into the school curriculum resonates with ironic ambiguities. It is just one more example of the peculiar intimacy and the co-option that characterizes colonizer-colonized relations. At first glance, it might appear that the school district was yielding to native demands to "indigenize" the curriculum. A subtler, hidden agenda emerges upon closer examination, however, for assimilating the native has long been the colonizer's preferred mode of co-opting or negating the native's seditious impulses. The autonomy of native resistance is threatened by assimilation; the dominance of the colonizer depends to a significant degree on his or her ability to assimilate the resistance of the colonized. Thus, even the Athabascan's attempt to recover their native language was mediated by the neocolonial apparatus of the reservation school, was conducted within a colonial context, was subsumed in the acculturating experience of schooling.

The Foxfire project solved several of my most vexing pedagogical problems at once: how to engage the interest of native students in the acquisition of academic literacy; how to make learning in general relevant to their borderland existence; how to provide instruction in literacy in ways that did not compound the debilitating effects of acculturation and deracination. Participation in this project not only solved the dilemma of what and how to teach Athabascan students in English and History, disciplines in which I had a certain expertise, but in arts and crafts, journalism, and yearbook, three subjects in which I had no training, little aptitude, and even less interest. The Foxfire project not only supplied the content but the methodologies for these courses. The fact that I had many of the same students in all six classes made such a writing-across-the-curriculum approach that much easier to implement, indeed almost demanded such an approach. I also had the collaborative energy and expertise of Alicia, Max, Paul, and Teresa to assuage my fears of this unknown pedagogical terrain, to ameliorate my unfamiliarity with it. Thus, that which had initially seemed to compound my problems by increasing my preps from six to seven, in the end became the solution to those problems, while generating a series of new problems. Integrating instruction across the curriculum in effect reduced my six preps to one, with some variations from course to course. This dramatically reduced the strain on my nerves, which in turn gave a much-needed boost to my morale. Instead of having to shoulder the burden of pedagogy by myself, that burden was now shared by five of us. The experience of coordinating and sharing instruction was itself a refreshing and invigorating change. The opportunity to get outdoors, to extend the classroom into the woods was another welcome change. The chance to stretch the legs, quicken the blood, exercise the muscles as part of the learning experience made the experience that much more memorable. The acquisition of literacy thus became a more holistic experience inasmuch as it involved not just the use of the brain, but the use of body as well. Learning was shifted from a passive, closed environment to an active, open-air one. The Word and the World, instead of being disjoined, were conjoined as part of a living dialectic.

Praxis Takes to the Bush: The Survival Shelter

What then were the specific activities associated with this Foxfire project? How precisely did this cross-curricular collaboration between the bilingual education, vocational education, home economics, arts and crafts, journalism, yearbook, English, and history classes play itself out on the reservation? Succinctly put, the recovery of the indigenous culture was effected through a series of hands-on projects guided by Max.

On an autumn morning students from Paul's woodshop class and my journalism/yearbook, arts and crafts classes assembled outside the school from which we proceeded by pick-up and van to the site in the forest Max had selected for the "brush camp." Max directed Paul's woodshop students in the construction of the camp while my journalism students documented each phase of the construction with cameras, tape recorders, and notebooks. As a follow-up to this activity, students in my journalism class interviewed Max, who provided a sequential narrative of the camp's construction. The survival shelter, he explained, had to be built with its back to the wind. This would not only provide greater warmth but blow the campfire smoke away from its entrance, once more evincing the Athabascan's innate resourcefulness and initiative: qualities that were also privileged in the dominant culture, but too often repressed in the classroom because there they either had no "survival" value or no opportunity to develop under the regime of a teacherly authority.

Here, the students were active participants in the construction of the brush camp, felling and "limbing" a spruce with their axes, lashing the limbs into a pair of tripods between which another was lashed horizontally like a ceiling-beam, forming the shelter's frame. Between this horizontal beam and the ground other limbs were lashed in place in a vertical position, fleshing out the structure's frame. Over this infrastructure spruce boughs were lashed in place, in overlapping fashion, and in a manner that not only provided shelter from the wind but which allowed smoke to escape. Alder twigs were stripped of their leaves and used as rope to lash everything together. The spruce was sectioned into several stumps, which became makeshift stools, which were then placed in a semicircle around the fire so that their occupants' backs would also be to the wind.

These tasks were executed by Paul's woodshop students working in pairs, as the cameras and tape recorders operated by my journalism students clicked and buzzed. The construction of the camp was a festive occasion, enlivened by the students' native wits and affectionate teasing of one another. Max indulged the pinches of "snuff" that were produced from pockets and slipped into the cheeks of some Athabascan students, female as well as male, establishing a set of rules more in keeping with the indigenous setting and the nature of instruction.

The activity recalled to my mind passages from *Black Elk* and *Lame Deer* describing the festive, communal mood that accompanied the felling, transporting, and raising of the cottonwood tree/sun dance pole ("Looking at the Sun, They Dance" 187), opening up new avenues for linking instruction in reading and writing to this Foxfire project. Students could be asked to investigate the rituals associated with the felling of the sun dance pole, comparing these to religious rites associated with their own ancestral culture. They could be asked to invent similar rituals to attend the construction of the "brush camp," or to interview elders in the village about the nature of ancestral rituals associated with hunting and fishing, and survival in general. Students could likewise be asked to conduct an inquiry into the effects of Christianity on the disappearance of such rituals, or into the revival of such indigenous rites. Thus, the project might give rise to a number of critical and creative writing assignments reinforcing these activities and foregrounding the recuperation of the Athabascan subculture, as well as the acquisition of academic and critical literacy.

To further enhance the live-action, hands-on approach to literacy acquisition, students might be afforded the opportunity to do a little role-playing, performing the rituals they invented or recovered associated with the construction of the survival shelter. Such role-playing activities could even be linked to other activities in the village, such as the regular performance of native dances during the annual potlatch held in the school gym. Finally, such instruction would not only dialogically reinforce learning across the curriculum, but mitigate the effects of bicultural alienation by helping native students reconnect to their ancestral culture. In the next chapter I will discuss how Foxfire pedagogy reinforced instruction in reading and writing.

This initial Foxfire activity also evidenced the efficacy of small collaborative groups as vehicles for the acquisition of knowledge. Knowledge in this sense was more truly socially constructed insofar as it not only involved the literal construction of a survival shelter, but involved collaboration not only within a class, but between classes. Some students, like Mark and Leo, evinced enthusiasm that learning was being yoked to the recovery of their native subculture, and displayed a great deal of initiative and leadership in the building of the brush camp, assuming the role of teachers themselves. The ability to convert the apathy, alienation, or hostility of some students into self-motivated participation is just one example of the transformative power such situated pedagogies of reculturation possess. Students like Diane, Robert, Pete and Velma, who had been paralyzed into apathy by an acute sense of their own inadequacies in an academic setting, suddenly blossomed in the more open, unconventional, interactive, hands-on environment in which learning was now situated. Suddenly, Robert began assuming responsibility for his spelling. Diane and Velma, whose presence had been in reality a silent absence, formed a collaborative interview team, evincing a work ethic they had never manifested when instruction was grounded in *Warriner's* grammar text. Robert suddenly became as vocal as Mark, evidencing the same enthusiasm for the recuperation of the Athabascan culture as previously he had manifested indifference when instruction was oriented toward the great books and discourse conventions of the dominant culture.

The project had the opposite effect on other students however. If it engendered in some students a sense of solidarity with their native subculture, in others it intensified resistance and hostility toward that culture. David, for example, manifested a deep alienation, refusing outright to even participate in the project, even as he had refused to accept instruction in Dena'ina, perhaps because both involved contact with his father, Max, from whom he was estranged. In fact, the close relationship I expected to observe between Max and David, I observed instead between Max and Mark, whom the native elder treated like a surrogate son because of Mark's eagerness to learn the ways of his ancestors, as if Mark was the son Max wanted David to be. Thus, I had to evolve a more individualized plan of instruction for David: one involving more conventional use of the literary canon, as well as the academic codes of the dominant culture, into which David desired assimilation. These differences underscore the group dynamics of the borderland classroom, where students position themselves in a variety of ways relative to the indigenous and dominant culture.

Thus, the Foxfire project not only solidified the subject positions of many native students relative to the dominant culture and the indigenous subculture, but also precipitated shifts between those positions, prompting some to abandon an apathetic or ambivalent stance in favor of one that expressed a more active, participatory solidarity with the native culture. The ambivalence of other students, such as Joey and Hank, remained more deeply entrenched however. They resisted instruction, eschewed participation, whether it occurred in the classroom or the forest, was oriented toward the dominant or indigenous culture.

The brush camp was completed in less than an hour. When finished, it featured a campfire stocked with kindling, a floor lined with spruce boughs for bedding, a cooking pit filled with boulders, and a makeshift clothesline fashioned from an alder twig strung between two spruce trees. That weekend three of my students (Mark, Will, and Leo) returned and used it as an overnight base camp for their ptarmigan hunting forays into the woods, evidencing once again that where industry, initiative, and ingenuity have an opportunity to be exercised, have pragmatic currency and real-life applications, the Native American student will not be found wanting in these characteristics. Where they have no opportunity for utilization, however, they atrophy. I breathed easier knowing these students had a shelter against the unforgiving Alaskan elements, as well as the knowledge to construct such a shelter if circumstances warranted. Thus, this Foxfire project not only increased the likelihood of their survival in the woods, it also enhanced the prospects of the subculture's survival in the immediate future inasmuch as it fostered the transmission of ancestral lifeways from one generation to the next.

How ironic that as the first step toward insuring the survival of the Athabascan culture, Max would have these students construct a "survival" shelter—a literal "safe house" that might indeed, as Pratt suggests, provide them shelter from the "legacy of oppression." Students constructed this survival shelter in the hopes such knowledge would not only insure their own survival in the woods, but the survival of their culture over Time, as part of a pedagogy in which knowledge was acquired quite literally through the construction of it. In this sense, the Foxfire project reinscribed the ambivalent, hybrid nature of life in the bicultural contact zone insofar as the "recovery" of the indigenous subculture was enacted within the educational apparatus of the dominant culture. Yet, it strikes me now that this survival shelter is a fitting trope for the Athabascan's urgent effort to ensure the survival of his or her orthodox spirituality, to fashion a refuge for it deep in the "woods" of the Athabascan's spirituality, a refuge illumined by a pagan flame that blows steady and true in the heart of the native's darkness.

Of Dogsleds and Snowshoes

The second activity associated with the Foxfire program also had as its primary goals the recuperation of indigenous culture and the acquisition of academic literacy. This was a yearlong project involving the construction of model sleds and snowshoes in my arts and crafts classes, and the construction of life-size replicas of these in Paul's woodshop classes. As before, every phase of these activities was documented by my journalism students with cameras, tape recorders, and note-pads. They then turned these materials over to the Foxfire publication/yearbook students who were charged with the responsibility of transposing them into a publishable form. This instruction was reinforced across the curriculum by readings in borderland narratives foregrounding the indigenous cultures of the Inuit, the Lakota, and the Athabascan. In many narratives of the North the dogsled emerges as a primary mode of transportation, and almost every one of Farley Mowat's *Snow Walker* narratives involves lore pertaining to mushing and other native subsistence activities.

Again, the project commenced with the collaborative felling of a tree deep in the forest, this time a birch. The tree was limbed by students and then transported to Paul's woodshop class by pickup where it was placed in a "steamer," a makeshift contraption Max had built comprised of a wide-mouthed, iron pipe to which front legs had been welded so that it stood at a slight angle to the floor. Into it water was poured, and under it a Coleman stove was placed. The classes evinced a collective excitement when they gathered for the steaming of the wood—a process that would initiate the transformation of the birch into a sled. Steam soon began to rise in a steady plume from the iron pipe.

The next morning the work of transfiguring the wood into a sled and snowshoes commenced in earnest when the birch lengths were removed from the steamer. Max showed the students what to do with the steamed birch, now malleable in his hands, before letting them have a try at it. In order to turn the birch into a pair of runners for the dogsled, each length was clamped to a wooden mold, one end of which was curved. Strong wooden clamps secured the birch to the mold, at which point the molds were allowed to set overnight. The process strikes me now as yet another apt metaphor for the manner in which the Athabascan spirit has been formed, reformed, and deformed by the "clamps" of acculturation that shape it in unnatural ways in order to make a better fit with Euro-American culture.

The construction of the model sleds, as with the building of the brush camps, affected students in different ways. Students like Mark and Leo, who were quick to gain mastery of the model-sled-making techniques, assumed more teacherly roles, sharing expertise with peers after the Athabascan's more communal approach to subsistence activities and storytelling practices, in which all commodities, including knowledge, are shared openly, in which ownership is perceived to be collective in contradistinction to the individualized conception of ownership privileged in the dominant culture. I too became a student, learning from Mark and Leo how to bend the railings of the sled to the most aesthetically-pleasing angle, or how to thread the "rigging" of the "basket" through the holes so that the webbing looked symmetrical from one stanchion to the next, or how to bend the "bumper" so that it would not bow forward too much nor too little. It was gratifying as well to observe students like Pete who had struggled with his "inadequacies" in composition suddenly assume a more prominent, active, and self-assured role in the Foxfire program. Instead of being a disinterested spectator of the knowledge-making process, he became a more active participant in it.

The high levels of success enjoyed by some students contrasted sharply with the frustrations experienced by others. In other instances, collaboration turned into competition, as students vied to see who could make the best sled or the most sleds or be the first to finish a sled. As some students worked on their own sleds they kept a wary, and in some cases, an envious, eye on their peers. While some students had advanced to the rigging, others were yet laboring on the bumpers and railing. Thus, the Foxfire project in some respects was contaminated by the mores of the dominant culture that privileged individual achievement and competition over collective goals and cooperation. This was just one more aspect of the hybrid nature of the project, in which the acquisition of academic codes privileged in the dominant culture was contextualized within the recovery of the indigenous subculture.

Such competition bred tensions and dissension among students, some of whom became demoralized at the slow progress they were making with their sleds. Ironically, a certain reversal in success occurred among students. Students like Pete, Velma, Robert, and Leo who had struggled when the focus was on academic literacy met with a greater degree of success when the focus shifted away from the processing of texts to this more hands-on, live-action approach to knowledge acquisition. Similarly, students like Veronica and Jane, who had met with a high degree of success in an academic setting, struggled with this more alien mode of education, became as self-conscious of their "inadequacies" in this realm as Pete and Velma were of their shortcomings in a more academic setting.

Trapping the Native Trapper

Various aspects of the Athabascan subculture were captured and preserved in image and ink and were eternalized on the pages of the Foxfire publication, as a means of rescuing them from oblivion, of resuscitating a subculture that was threatened with extinction. The relationship between the Athabascan culture and the Foxfire project was similar to that between a patient in critical condition and the life support system that sustains the patient's life until his or her last will and testament can be recorded, his or her life-story told. It is similar as well to the relationship between an endangered species and a captive-breeding program that seeks to preserve that which appears doomed to extinction in its indigenous state. An arsenal of technologies was deployed to artificially breed the Athabascan culture in the classroom including: cameras, tape recorders, film, band saws, sandpaper, and hammers. These were all that stood between the Athabascan subculture and the erosive and corrosive forces of deracination and acculturation that threatened it with catastrophic closure.

Thus, a chapter was devoted to documenting traditional Athabascan fur-trapping techniques as practiced by a dwindling number of elders, including Nikolai. Here, I assumed a more active role in the project, as none of my journalism students evinced any great interest in accompanying Nikolai into the snowy woods to observe his trapping techniques. Fur trapping, however, exerted an irresistible lure over me, not only as a means of breaking the monotony of cabin fever, of exercising the muscles and stimulating the senses, but as a means of increasing my own collection of furs in general, and of red fox in particular. Since arriving in the village I had harbored a keen desire to have these furs sewn into a blanket. When I learned through my participation in the Foxfire project that Max's wife, Nellie, was adept at sewing furs into garments, I approached her with my proposal and we quickly agreed on a price. Her skin-sewing comprised yet another chapter in the Foxfire project, along with her expertise in preparing traditional Athabascan dishes: pickled salmon, bear roast, choke-cherry pie, moose-links, salmon jerky, salmon berry wine, squirrel stew, as well as rabbit, ptarmigan, and caribou dishes. The recovery of this aspect of traditional Athabascan culture was undertaken by Teresa's home economics class, Nellie acting as the "gatekeeper" of this lore, as her husband Max did for the indigenous knowledges recuperated by the woodshop, bilingual, and arts/crafts classes.

Over a series of wintry weekends I accompanied Nikolai into the woods as he made the rounds of his traps. Unlike his Euro-American counterparts in general, and several of my white students in particular, he eschewed the iron-jawed traps that crushed the leg bones of their victims, subjecting them to a slow death by freezing. Instead, he trapped martin, mink, lynx, and snowshoe rabbits by erecting a series of ingenious "hutches," placed strategically to take advantage of the seasonal movements of these animals whose "sign" he could recognize at a glance, and whose favorite haunts he knew by heart. Thus, I watched and photographed as he erected a little marten "hutch" at the base of a spruce that stood on the banks of a nondescript, snow-covered creek. It was a place I would scarcely have given a second glance, but it was just the sort of habitat preferred by the marten, and their kin, the weasel. He constructed the hutch in a conical fashion from curls of birch bark and lengths of deadwood that he recovered from the nearby forest floor. He scented the snow with a few drops of a pungent liquid which he had extracted from the glands of a marten. The trap was baited with a ripe chunk of pickled salmon that Nikolai forked from a jar he kept in his knapsack. Though I would sooner have starved than ingested this bait myself, it no doubt comprised an irresistible morsel for any marten that chanced to scent it, and given the strength of the eye-watering whiff I caught, I had no doubt that it would reach the nostrils of any marten between here and Anchorage.

I documented each kind of trap that Nikolai constructed as he made his wintry rounds, setting a spring-pole trap along a trail frequented by snowshoe rabbits, an ingenious device comprised of an alder twig, that when sprung hoisted the rabbit into the air. His beaver trap was just as ingenious, consisting of an underwater snare situated on the banks of the pond at the spot where the beaver habitually hauled itself out of the water. The beaver swam into the snare, which tightened around its throat, quickly drowning it underwater. The beaver pelts were coveted by some for the fine Athabascan mukluks that were fashioned from them. When I informed my friend, Linda, that I was now teaching in the village where she had once lived and taught, she put in a request for several beaver pelts which I then shipped to her in Hawaii. When adorned with beads, they made very fashionable and warm footwear. Nellie excelled in the sewing of these as well. When skinned, the pelts assumed a hooplike shape, and were sold by Athabascans in the village for forty dollars. When Robert informed me his father also trapped beaver, I immediately put in a request for several pelts, which he fulfilled one day, entering class with a paper bag from which he produced the fine, golden-brown furs. I immediately packaged them up and sent them off to Hawaii, where they were converted into Christmas presents by Linda, who had learned the art of sewing mukluks from Nellie.

I recorded notes in my journal of my trapping forays with Nikolai and interviewed him on the subject at his kitchen table. And this too became a separate chapter in the Foxfire publication. Thus, the Foxfire project crystallized and reinforced traditional gender roles, the girls gravitating toward ancestral activities associated with their gender, toward cooking and sewing, while Mark, Leo, Robert and to a lesser extent myself, gravitated toward more physical activities habitually associated with male roles: trapping, sled making, and boat building.

Nothing we did in the Foxfire project was as innocent as we presumed, nor as innocent as it might appear to the reader. My involvement in Nikolai's fur-trapping activities was laden with ironic and ambivalent overtones. Lacking conscripts among the younger generation of Athabascans, elders like Max and Nikolai were eager to impart their native knowledges to anyone who evinced an interest in them, whether white or Athabascan. They no doubt hoped that in passing such knowledge on to me, I would transmit it to the children. Thus, I became an intermediary for the transmission of Athabascan lore from one generation to the next, even as a honeybee unwittingly pollinates flowers that are separated by distances they cannot overcome on their own.

In Paul's woodshop class, in which Vera was the lone female, students were constructing a life-size dory, or whale-hunting boat. Later that spring it was used to kill the first beluga whale taken in decades, a communal and festive occasion in which every family partook. The activity reflected the hybrid nature of contemporary Athabascan life: while the hunters used the dory to stalk and close with the beluga, they used a high-powered rifle to dispatch it. Afterward, the whale was butchered on the beach where its meat was apportioned equally among the Athabascan families, each receiving a large square of its blubber. These activities comprised yet another chapter in the Foxfire book.

The Foxfire project affected the group dynamics in the classroom, altering the positions that some students assumed with respect to the two cultures. Erin, initially one of the most openly hostile students in the class, now manifested a great deal of initiative and leadership, taking charge of the yearbook/journalism class that was responsible for documenting all phases of these Foxfire activities, as well as for producing the publication in which this knowledge was to be embodied. She assumed the roles of principal photographer and interviewer, documenting on film and on tape the construction of the brush camp, snowshoes, and dog sleds. Her agency and involvement contrasted sharply with her earlier alienation and insurrection, and was just one of the metamorphoses I observed in the attitudes manifested by students toward learning. She and Veronica collaborated on a series of interviews with native elders foregrounding the recuperation of ancestral ways, including Max (whose description of the brush camp provided written copy for the pictures they had taken).

Jane and Diane, best friends in life, formed a second interview team. Together, these teams fanned out into the village, interviewing elders on various aspects of their ancestral culture. It was rewarding to observe the responsibility and initiative they manifested when they departed class on these field trips into the village. Noteworthy as well was the attitude of respect they manifested toward these elders, the excitement they evinced about the experience, and the eagerness they exhibited to commence the follow-up activities: transcribing the tapes, developing, cropping, and laying out photos, composing the copy to accompany them, etc.

When writing has real-world significance such as the recovery of a native student's home culture, when it occurs within the context of a real world application such as the production of a book, when it is produced for an audience that is immediate and not abstract, then it can be expected that students will voluntarily undertake the mastery of academic codes: grammatical, rhetorical, and logical, which they resisted when these were imposed in discrete units, in isolation from the writing process, in a text divorced from any meaningful context. The certainty that their text would be read by neighbors, friends, and peers provided the motivation formerly lacking to master these codes. The awareness that they were writing of their own world for a very real audience lent immediacy and purpose to the mastery of academic codes, subsuming that mastery in the broader process of writing, of saying their own Word and writing their own World.

Foxfire and the Fetishization of the "Authentic"

The Foxfire project was problematic in several significant respects, evolving in ways we had neither foreseen nor intended. If it reinforced student inquiries into borderland narratives and local cultural conflicts on the one hand, then it also reinscribed capitalistic practices, accelerating the erosion of the indigenous culture it purported to preserve. The students were required to make at least two sleds and two pairs of model snowshoes—one for themselves and one to sell or give away. This requirement was inaugurated to satisfy the demands of the local residents, Athabascan as well as white, for these "authentic" artifacts of an indigenous culture. Thus, the dogsleds and snowshoes became the objects of a commodity fetishness, one that affected Athabascans as well as whites, students as well as teachers, and which in the final analysis contaminated the Foxfire project itself. Some students became so adept at making these artifacts that they made four or five sleds and an equal number of snowshoes.

As an indication of the extent to which the project was driven by the spirit of commodity fetishness, I offer the following. Not only were students getting requests for dogsleds, snowshoes and birch-burl clocks from teachers and parents, from residents of the reservation and the timber camp, but soon they were getting requests for these "souvenirs" from the administrators across the water, mostly white and male, who saw these artifacts as trophies to add to their collection of native memorabilia. A sort of "souvenir fever" gripped the community as the annual Christmas crafts fair approached. Now I began to see that we, the Foxfire classes, were expected to provide the artifacts for this fair, to sate the materialistic feeding frenzy of Athabascans and whites generated by these artifacts. Each sled, snowshoe, and birch-burl clock became the object of a covetous colonizing gaze, the same gaze that had once fixed itself on the beads and moccasins, the furs and shields, the pipes and tomahawks of the Native American, as if the avaricious spirit of a museum curator or a cultural anthropologist animated the heart ticking in every colonizing chest.

At the time neither Alicia, Paul, Max, Teresa, nor myself paused to consider the ethical, political, or cultural implications of the commodification of these authentic artifacts and our complicity in this process. Indeed, Max himself contributed to this commodification, boarding a plane to Anchorage with a dozen sleds that he sold for $100 each to various buyers: relatives, museums, native crafts stores, etc. Once students caught wind of the windfall Max had reaped, of the prices these artifacts fetched in Anchorage, they ceased regarding the sleds and snowshoes as talismans of their subsistence culture, and saw them instead as commodities to be exchanged in a Euro-American cash-based culture. Profit taking instead of cultural preservation became the driving motive in their construction of these sleds. Thus, instead of conserving the traditions of the indigenous culture, the Foxfire project actually accelerated its extinction by conscripting native students into the dominant culture, by turning them into producers and consumers of commodities.

Upon completion, the sleds and snowshoes were displayed in glass trophy cases. This was a fitting place in which to encase these "trophies" of the authentic native, even as the trophies of big game hunters are hung from walls, even as the pelt of my cross fox and the fox-fur mittens Nellie had woven for me were hanging from the walls of my own home. There, they not only inspired pride in their makers, but something more disquieting: in all who gazed upon them they inspired a lust to possess them. And so these artifacts of an indigenous past were turned into commodities fetishized in a neocolonial present. They became signs for the ongoing capture and containment of the indigene. The category of the "authentic" is problematic inasmuch as it reinscribes structures of domination and subverts liberatory resistance struggle. As Garreth Griffiths writes,

> the mythologizing of the "authentic" . . . is then in many ways itself a construction that overpowers one of the most powerful weapons within the arsenal of the subaltern subject: that of displacement, disruption, ambivalence, or mimicry, discursive features found not in the closed and limited construction of a pure authentic sign but in endless and excessive transformation of the subject positions possible within the hybridized. (241)

The rich possibilities embedded in these artifactual "signs" were closed off in favor of a single meaning that was coded onto them: as commodities. Instead of becoming talismans of anticolonial resistance they became commodities that reinscribed colonialism. Instead of enabling the Athabascan to recover his or her lost origins, they perpetuated the colonizing containment of the native through his or her conscription into a cash-based economy. Mythologizing the native as "authentic" closes off other subject positions, even as it reinscribes reductive representations of the native. Authentic native craftsmanship, like "authentic speech," when it is fetishized as a "cultural commodity, may be employed . . . to enact a discourse of 'liberal violence,' reenacting its own oppression on the subjects it purports to represent and defend" (Griffiths 241). Thus, the reinforcement of this stereotype of the "authentic" indigene, of the native as craftsperson, was the unfortunate by-product of the well-meaning, if misguided attempt by the Foxfire project to recuperate traditional Athabascan culture. As such, it was just another example of what Ward Churchill calls "genocide with good intentions" (280). Moreover, it recalls a similar process of recuperation and representation imposed upon the Australian aborigine. As Griffiths asserts, the construction of the "authentic" Aborigine by the colonist "may be in part the unintentional product of a worthy liberal desire to recuperate Australian Aboriginal culture" (238). In the final analysis, this noble, philanthropic effort to recuperate the indigenous culture devolved into a self-serving attempt to contain it, both literally and figuratively, not only in the libraries, museums, and trophy cases that house indigenous artifacts but in the reductive representations of the "authentic" native as craftsperson that perpetuate his or her linguistic capture. Such practices disable the very liberatory resistance struggle they purportedly support by privileging "authentic" representations of the indigene over "inauthentic" ones. Therefore, while the native craftsperson is celebrated, the political activist is marginalized. The observations of Griffiths are again instructive: this prejudice "frequently results . . . in a media construction of the 'authentic' Australian aborigine in opposition to the 'inauthentic' political activist whose claim is undermined . . . by a dismissal of their right to represent Australian aboriginal culture" (238). The Foxfire project was complicit in this process inasmuch as it privileged the ancestral traditions of the subculture while marginalizing its more contemporary aspects. The traditions of their past were assumed to be the only legitimate representations of the Athabascans while the more reactionary aspects of their contemporary struggle were posited as illegitimate, and therefore unsuited as a focus of academic inquiry.

Foxfire pedagogy thus perpetuated the damaging practice of relegating the "authentic" native to the past, paving the way for his or

her continuing subjugation in the present and future. This privileging of the "authentic" over the "inauthentic" Athabascan, of the
"gatekeeper" over the political activist was reinscribed on a local
level by the relative access Max enjoyed to the school in contradistinction to the marginalization experienced by the president of the
tribal council, David Standmark, whose views reflected a more
contemporary politicized stance. Further, in Max the two prevail-
ing "images of the authentic" were conjoined: "both inscribed under
such legitimating signs as the 'elder,' the local, and the tribal."
(237). Both categories, as Griffiths notes, are "counterposed by the
illegitimate signs of the outsider . . . the fringe dweller," and more
recently, the activist (237). If Max represented the "good" Other,
then to the colonizer David represented the "bad" Other. "Authentic" elders like Max and Nellie occupy very ambivalent terrain in
the borderlands, as do their Athabascan counterparts whose careers are characterized by mimicry of the colonizer. On the one
hand, the sign of the "authentic" native, like the artifacts he or she
produces, has been fetishized and colonized in Euro-American discourse as a means of perpetuating the asymmetrical power relations that characterize the colonizer-colonized relationship. On the
other hand, the "authentic" Other's tendency to work for change
within the matrix of colonialism has also been endorsed as an
effective means of indigenizing the colonizer in general, and the
school curriculum in particular. Native American scholars such as
Susan Gardner rally to the defense of "gatekeepers" in Max's position, and to a pedagogy that privileges a dialogic interaction with
them. For generations natives in Max's situation have been dis-
missed as "Uncle Tomahawks," "apples," or "cigar-store Indians" as
a consequence of their mimicry of and complicity with the colonizer.
Their critics, according to Gardner, designate as a betrayal what is
in fact a radical attempt to "influence institutions through their
politic participation within them" ("Teaching *Mountain Wolf Woman*"
369). Gardner therefore advocates a pedagogy foregrounding collaboration between indigenous "gatekeepers" and quasi-indigenized
insiders: a pedagogy in which "interaction with members of the
culture being 'taught' is built in," in which these "gatekeepers"
have an active role in "course planning and implementation" (368),
a statement that underscores the efficacy of the Foxfire approach
and of the collaboration between Max, Alicia, Paul, Teresa, and

myself. This dialogic interaction between nonnative practitioner and native "gatekeeper" makes it difficult to "divorce the classroom content from contemporary social realities"—a conclusion that subverts the arbitrary binary between "authentic" and "inauthentic" insofar as it makes room in the classroom for the more radical aspects of indigenous culture as well, for those other native voices, for the resistant voices of Erin and David.

Implied in Gardner's assessment is the assertion that such a dialogic pedagogy not only needs to foreground the acquisition of academic literacy but of critical literacy as well. It needs to privilege not only the views of the traditional-minded indigene, but of his or her more political, contemporary counterpart; it needs to privilege a subaltern discourse that is not univocal but polyphonic, and that reflects the complexities and rich heteroglossia of subaltern signifying practices as opposed to a discourse that merely selects the indigenous voices that conform to its own prejudices of the "authentic" native—a discourse which reinscribes the selective breeding programs of conservationists who would preserve for our edification a representation of the native that is simplified, sanitized, and romanticized; that is, a representation fit for consumption by a Euro-American public whose appetite for such a native has for generations been whetted by the images circulated in the realist novels of Jack London, in the "authentic" paintings of Remington and in the photographs of Edward Curtis, in the romanticized images of films like "Dances With Wolves," in the reductive representations of advertising, in the logos of sports franchises such as the Cleveland Indians, and in the stereotypic representations of the strong, silent Indian on television shows like "Northern Exposure." In making her case for such a dialogic, situated, politicized pedagogy, Gardner enlists the forceful discourse of South African scholar Nkomo Mokunburg, who asserts that "committed research and scholarship must eschew neutrality and detachment where the human condition demands drastic amelioration—a scholarship that is catalytic and cathartic is imperative" (303), one that not only functions as a "healing ritual" but that also intervenes in the process of subjugation. It is a pedagogy which, in the last analysis, conjoins the projects of the academic and the activist, in which pedagogy is a precondition of political activism.

Adventures in Cultural Tourism: The Pitfalls of Going Native

In this section I will examine some of the effects of my own tendency toward indigenization, toward "going native," tendencies that
were reinforced by the Foxfire program. The process of indigenization
was for me a very ambivalent one insofar as it was yoked to the
contradictory processes of empowering and exploiting the Athabascan.
As Freire observes, such a "conversion" experience on behalf of the
teacher is a critical step toward a more dialogic pedagogy. In "Relativism, Radical Pedagogy, and the Ideology of Paralysis," Charles
Paine provides a concise articulation of this "conversion experience"
and its pedagogical implications, as enunciated by Freire:

> Freire's well-known works propose "dialogic" education, where
> the teacher undergoes a conversion to the people . . . through
> comradeship with the oppressed," cultivating a knowledge of
> the students' world view. . . . Here no one teaches another. . . .
> Men teach each other, mediated by the world. (562)

Recent scholarship calls into question Freire's assumption that relations between people are mediated by the world, arguing instead
that those relations are mediated by the word (language). This
aside, Freire's observations comment significantly on the peculiar
intimacy of colonizer-colonized relations as embodied in the borderland classroom wherein the colonization of the indigene often occurs simultaneously with the indigenization of the colonizer, as
indeed it must for meaningful transformation of that relationship
to occur. This is the powerful message embedded in the climax of
Conrad's *Heart of Darkness*, a text which if read subversively can
inform the postcolonial borderland classroom. The novel's climax is
a testament to the process of indigenization, of going native, for the
career of the colonialist Kurtz ends in a show of solidarity with the
native. His career commences as a hymn to the alienation of
the modern individual and ends with his attempted conversion to
primitive communism through solidarity with the oppressed native. The trajectory of Kurtz's career is illustrative of the colonizer's
indigenization. It parallels the course of my own career as a bush
teacher, and the careers of many who attempt to carry the values
of the dominant culture overseas and overland, but who end by
becoming at least partially indigenized themselves.

For myself, this process never reached a state of complete identification with the native, as indeed it never could. Complete assimilation into the indigenous culture is as much a myth for the colonizer as absolute assimilation into the dominant culture is for the Athabascan. I could never become one of the natives, only like them. I would always be relegated to a status of "like, but not quite," replicating the marginal social status of some of my native students. If Will strove to mimic the ways of the dominant culture, I strove equally as hard to mimic those of his indigenous subculture. If his mimicry masked the menace of insurrection, mine masked the menace of exploitation. My position was similar to that of Mark and other native students: although I had assimilated the technologies of the dominant culture, I was endeavoring to assimilate the values, mores, and spirituality of the Athabascan subculture, reinscribing colonizing gestures of possession, appropriation, exploitation, and domination. However, unlike my native students, I had not experienced the mutilations of an imposed deracination. The alienation I experienced was self-imposed; theirs was merely imposed; mine was the result of a conscious choice, theirs the result of not having any choices. And therein lay the ineffaceable difference, the invisible barrier that would always stand between us, that would in the end defeat my effort to assimilate into the indigenous culture.

The wellsprings of the impulse to "go native" run deep. By wearing fur mittens, mukluks, and vests made by Athabascan women, by adorning my walls with the artifacts of the authentic Indian, by living and teaching on an Athabascan Indian reservation, by reading and teaching *Black Elk* and *Lame Deer*, by learning the native's fur trapping techniques, by team-teaching with a native elder, by adopting as my own the traditional Athabascan's pagan, pantheistic, holistic, and magical worldview, I was trying to become Indian myself. This goal was as futile as it was long-lived and self-serving. In the last analysis, my desire to go native devolved into a desire to possess the native since I could not become one.

My lust for things Indian, my fetishization of the "authentic" reinscribes what C. B. McPherson calls an ideology of "possessive individualism" (qtd. in Clifford 142). Freire's observations are also relevant here:

> This climate creates in the oppressor a strongly possessive consciousness—possessive of the world and of men. Apart from

direct, concrete material possession of the world and of men, the oppressor consciousness could not understand itself—could not even exist. . . . The oppressor consciousness tends to transform everything surrounding it into an object of domination. The earth, property, production, the creations of men, men themselves, time—everything is reduced to the status of objects at its disposal. *(Pedagogy* 44)

Surrounded by my growing collection of model sleds and snowshoes, ivory carvings, fur caps and mittens, Indian blankets and posters, I was a shining example of James Clifford's "self as owner: the individual surrounded by accumulated property and goods. . . . Thus, the self that must possess but cannot have it all learns to select, order, classify in hierarchies—to make "good" collections" ("On Collecting" 142–143). Perhaps because I couldn't own property of my own on the reservation, I attempted to seize everything else I could get my hands on that was Athabascan, as my own personal property. My acquisition of the texts, artifacts, lore, and spirituality of the Native American in general and of the Athabascan in particular reinscribed the "possessive individualism" of the museum curator, the cultural anthropologist, the ethnographer, the documentary film maker, the native biographer, insofar as it perpetuated the practice of "cutting objects out of specific contexts . . . and making them 'stand for' abstract wholes, a Bambara mask for example, becoming an ethnographic metonym for Bambara culture" (Clifford 144). Thus, fragments of indigenous identity are posited as a whole, enacting the capture of the "authentic" indigene with representations that are at best reductive. This sort of predatory "cultural tourism" is driven by a souvenir-fever consciousness in which the indigene himself is reduced to the status of an artifact to be studied, commodified, owned, possessed, and consumed.

My little house on the reservation (its walls hung with the pelts of indigenous animals, its shelves crammed with texts of indigenous peoples, its closets filled with vests, mittens, mukluks, and hats woven by native women from the furs of native animals) was a monument to my own cultural cannibalism. Clifford elaborates on the disquieting implications of this fetishization of the "authentic," asserting that "collection and display . . . are crucial processes of Western identity formation" (144). The identity of the colonizer to a certain degree is predicated on his or her consumption of the colonized as part of a relation that reinscribes the cannibalistic nature of the predator-prey dynamic. The composition of the colonizing Self requires the decomposition of the colonized Other, ironically reinscribing the relationship between power and cannibalism evinced in many pagan myths and embodied in Native American religious practices in particular. This lust to possess the native drives the colonizer to cannibalize every aspect of indigenous culture, from the native's land to his or her spirituality. The Native American correctly perceives the White Shaman, the New Age Hobbyist, the Indian Wannabe, and all who pose as Cultural Tourists as a threat to the integrity and survival of native spirituality. Having absorbed the native's homeland, artifacts, lore, traditions, and genetic material, these cultural tourists have now affixed their covetous, colonizing gaze on the last bastion of that which is purely Native American: his or her holistic spirituality and magical worldview. Moreover, this impulse to "display" the "trophies" of the cannibalized culture also reinscribes pagan rituals of conquest, the artifacts on display figuratively reinscribing the dismembered body parts of the vanquished culture, as <u>metonyms</u> signifying a culture's dismemberment.

In the last analysis, my fetishization of the "authentic" reinscribed the colonizer's long-standing appropriation of "exotic things, facts, meanings . . . [the] packaging of the past and transference of it to the metropolitan museum," where it is stored in "de-contextualized, collectible forms" (Clifford 161). The Foxfire publication thus was complicit in this process, effecting the metonymic, atomized, dismembered packaging of the Athabascan culture for consumption by teachers, parents, administrators, residents, social workers, academics, historians, anthropologists, ethnographers, museum patrons and anyone else engaged in the predatory practice of cultural tourism. This intellectual cannibalization of indigenous cultures continues today in the form of "conference papers and museum collections and even trendy courses in Native American literature," such as the one I currently teach (Churchill 235). All are complicit in the process which Gerald Vizenor terms "adventures in tribal commodities":

This obsession with the tribal past is not an innocent collection of arrowheads . . . but rather a statement of **academic** power and control over tribal images, an excess of facts, datas, narrative, interviews, template discoveries. Academic evidence is a euphemism for linguistic colonization of oral traditions and popular memories ("Socioacupuncture" 413).

All construct the native, just as intellectuals, travel writers, and politicians in Britain constructed the Asian, as Said asserts in *Orientalism*. All have a hand in metonymically constructing the native as "metasavage"; that is, from the fragments of his or her linguistic dismemberment. The "metasavage" is constructed via a signifying strategy in which the parts are posited as the whole in order to effect the reductive textual capture of the indigene and to meet the tastes of the consuming public for these demonized, idealized, or romanticized images of the Native American Other. Once aroused by these stereotypic representations of the native, the appetites of this readership demand a continual supply of them, so that representations of the indigene become just another commodity in the circulation of goods. Churchill writes,

> The vital, independent cultures of socially subordinate groups are constantly mined for new ideas with which to energize the jaded and restless mainstream of a political and economic system based on the circulation of commodities. The process depends on the delivery of continual novelty to the market. (141)

Academic inquiry, the quest for knowledge about the Other, becomes a means of achieving the textual containment of the Other, of relegating the Other to object status, of reducing the native to a commodity that is fetishized by a consuming public comprised of cultural tourists. As Simon Ortiz observes, this commodification and fetishization of the "authentic" impedes the native's liberatory resistance struggle: "symbols are taken and are popularized, diverting attention from real issues about land and resources . . . The real struggle is really what should be prominent, but no, it's much easier to talk about drums and feathers and ceremonies" (112n). I was not unlike those New Age Hobbyists and White Shamans "who dabble in AIS" (American Indian Spirituality), who "take themselves to be learning or conveying 'truths' about indigenous spirituality, even as they go about buying or selling products generated by the AIS industry" (Whitt 228), and who place their "right to know" above the Other's "right to cultural sanctity or psychological sanctuary" (Churchill and James 210n). The anthropologist's, the ethnographer's, and the academic's right to know is problematic insofar as it perpetuates the "maintenance of their own colonial privilege" (Churchill and James 65).

Thus, the Foxfire program accelerated the erosion of the very culture it was designed to preserve insofar as it perpetuated the commodification of that culture by yoking Athabascan craftsmanship to Euro-American capitalism, by perpetuating the "seizure, repackaging, and profitable sale of highly marketable 'spiritual knowledge'" (Whitt 229). It facilitated the very process of cultural genocide it was designed to arrest by reinscribing reductive representations of the Athabascan as craftsperson, to the exclusion of other representations of the Other, and by excluding others from representing the Other. As Whitt asserts, by "supplanting Indian people even in the area of their own spirituality, it moves beyond physical subordination to effectively secure their absolute ideological/conceptual subordination" (230). In the last analysis, our efforts to preserve the Athabascan culture only hastened its eclipse by the dominant Euro-American culture by reinforcing the cash-based activities of that culture. The native culture is not only threatened by the overtly genocidal practices of the colonizer, but by the invisible genocidal tendencies of the colonizer who undergoes a conversion experience to the native culture. Thus, the erosion of the indigenous subculture is accelerated by the dual forces of colonization and indigenization, one wearing it down from without while the other wears away from within. Is it any wonder then that the Athabascans are wary and mistrustful of outsiders who profess a desire to help them preserve their subculture, for experience has shown that these "friends" pose as great a threat to their survival as gift-bearing Greeks did to the defenders of Troy. Laurie Whitt underscores the severity of the situation:

Spiritual power and objects . . . are being commercialized. Indian spirituality, like Indian lands before it—is radically being reduced to the status of a commodity. It is seized, made over in the image of its appropriators, and sold. Equally startling is the fact that the consuming public seems largely to assume that not only is it getting "the real thing" but that it has been gotten in a morally and politically unproblematic way. The literary and scholarly venues for the commodification of Indian spirituality are extensive. (226)

Whitt concludes that the "crassness of this commodification of indigenous spirituality is stunning... sweat lodges, pipe ceremonies, sun dances and vision quests all have a price tag attached to them and are placed for sale in the marketplace" (227, 235). Lame Deer endorses Whitt's assessment:

The pow wows too have become a green frog-skin business. When I was young there was never an admission charge to a dance... now they dance for the contest money... Imagine charging an Indian to go to his sun dance. The green frog-skin world is closing in, even on our most sacred ceremony. Thus, it is getting more difficult to be an Indian, to preserve the integrity of traditions. (44–45)

Reconfiguring Foxfire Pedagogy

Such a pedagogy is warranted and useful if the acquisition of academic literacy is itself yoked to the acquisition of critical literacy, and if both are yoked to the Other's emancipatory resistance struggle. The ultimate aim of such praxis is not knowledge but reform, is not analysis for its own sake, but actions that alter the conditions by which the Other is oppressed. Unless tied to meaningful action outside the classroom, instruction devolves into a mere academic exercise. A Foxfire pedagogy that perpetuates the fetishization and commodification of the "authentic" is only justifiable if contexualized within a critical inquiry into the ways in which such practices reinscribe relations of domination, and ultimately accelerate the extinction of indigenous culture.

Instead of merely describing the orthodox activities of the indigenous subculture, Athabascan students participating in the Foxfire project could also write about a series of critical themes generated by the project: the corrosive effects of commodification on native culture; the extent to which such practices reinforce the debilitating effects of deracination and assimilation; the manner in which they reinscribe reductive stereotypes of the native as craftsperson; the manner in which they undermine indigenous resistance by marginalizing other native voices and other representations of the native. Thus, a self-reflexive component could be added to the Foxfire project, bringing into play critical discourses that interrogate the complicity of the Foxfire project itself in the enterprise of cultural imperialism, that yoke the acquisition of academic literacy to the acquisition of critical literacy. As before, students could be dispersed through the community in interview teams as part of this inquiry, could be asked to explore the effects of the Foxfire project in writing themes in composition classes, could be invited to assess the advantages and disadvantages of the project.

Further, these writing themes could be conducted in conjunction with readings of borderland narratives foregrounding the theme of cross-cultural contact, examining the influence of a cash-based economy on a subsistence lifestyle. Natives from the village could be invited into the Foxfire class to conduct a forum on the ethics, issues, and implications of such fetishization. David, the tribal council president, could be invited to present his views on the subject, as part of an inquiry that privileged not just the discourses of "authentic" Athabascans like Max and Nellie, but the discourses of their younger, more radical and activist-oriented counterparts, who seek to preserve orthodox traditions while terminating the complicity of those traditions in the colonizing enterprise. Such a polyphonic presentation of Athabascan "signs" and voices would expose native students to the rich variety of indigenous identities and subject positions available to them, would help them avoid containment by reductive representations of the Other, would facilitate their struggle for freedom, which is nothing if not a struggle to escape linguistic and geographic capture. Such a reconfigured pedagogy would acknowledge and celebrate the reality that there is not and has never been one, but many Others. As Foucault's analysis reveals, the circulation of power requires an economy of discourses, an economy of subject positions, and an economy of Others in order to maintain relations of domination.

There is a place in the borderlands for a critical, self-reflexive Foxfire pedagogy. As deployed in Nyotek, the Foxfire project was an ambivalent, hybridized enterprise of enabling and disabling features, of genocidal and liberatory practices. The Foxfire project by virtue of this ambivalence was similar to many aspects of existence in these bicultural borderlands. Like the Athabascans themselves, it was a hybrid of tendencies that reinscribed the practices of the indigenous subculture and the dominant Euro-American culture. It was neither this nor that, but occupied an in-between terrain in which boundaries between good and bad, between liberatory and colonizing effects were blurred.

The Foxfire program was intended to help native students reconnect to their heritage, to make it easier for them "to be an Indian." In our effort to evolve a pedagogy that resists colonization we must be eternally vigilant against the effects of a creeping colonialism that is as ubiquitous as it is unseen, corrupting pedagogies that at first glance seem in the native's best interest, but which in reality reinscribe colonizing gestures of domination. The insidious ubiquity of colonialism stems from its ability to disguise itself as its opposite, to assume the appearance of anticolonialism. Only a vigilant self-reflexivity can insure the integrity of a decolonizing pedagogy of resistance. Pedagogy itself, as well as the manifold enterprises of colonization, must become and remain the object of the bush teacher's critical gaze. Therefore, the most useful tool the bush teacher possesses is not a microscope for studying the effects of colonization on the Other, but a mirror for assessing those self-same effects on his or her pedagogy.

6

Decomposing the Canon
Alter/Native Narratives from the Borderlands

> Representation and resistance are very broad arenas within which
> much of the drama of colonialist relations and postcolonial exami-
> nation and subversion of those relations has taken place. In both
> conquest and colonization, texts and textuality played a major
> part.
> —Ashcroft, Griffiths, and Tiffin 85

body of recent scholarship in postcolonial discourse is radically altering the way we "read" canonical texts, and thus
the way we teach such texts, even as it proffers a body of
"alter/native," noncanonical texts as a more useful vehicle for conducting literary analysis and/or literature-based approaches to writing instruction. Implicit in this postcolonial critique of The Great
Books is the assertion that such texts reinscribe colonizing gestures
of domination through their reductive containment of the Other. It
is erroneous, however, to assume that postcolonial theorists argue
that such canonical texts should not be read; rather, they assert that
these texts need to be reread as the objects of an emancipatory,

decolonizing, critical gaze and in conjunction with a body of counterhegemonic, "resistance" literature that has arisen in reaction to the stereotypical representations of the Other in The Great Books. In short, we not only need to read noncanonical texts by the Other, but to reread canonical texts about the Other.

Such instruction is warranted not only in the multicultural classroom of the metropolitan academy whose readership is comprised of many students who have experienced firsthand the negative effects of racist stereotyping, but in the urban secondary school and in the bicultural, borderland classroom as well where students still experience the direct, enduring, and debilitating effects of racial oppression. These readings and rereadings are thus an essential component of an emerging, liberatory resistance pedagogy in these diverse theaters of learning. In this chapter I want to discuss the radical shift in reading and writing pedagogy that was necessitated by the exigencies peculiar to this pedagogical situation: a shift from appreciative, assimilationist readings of canonical texts to more subversive readings of those texts, and a shift away from those texts to what Min-Zhan Lu terms "narratives from the borderlands" (888). In addition, I want to discuss some of the problems encountered in this shift, my pedagogical adjustments to those problems, and the ways in which this shift affected the group dynamics of this borderland classroom. I want to theorize borderland pedagogy within the context of my own experience; I want to "read" this experience through the prismatic lens of three diverse, yet convergent discourses: radical composition theory, postcolonialism, and Native American resistance struggle. After briefly reviewing the postcolonial critique of the Great Books and modeling a subversive reading of a canonical text, Jack London's *Call of the Wild*, I will articulate a radical alter/native to pedagogy foregrounding borderland narratives.

Composition as a Ceremony of Reconnection

A body of contemporary Native American narratives foregrounds the theme of spiritual redemption through reconnection to an ancestral landscape. As such, these texts comprise useful alter/natives to canonical works for the borderland practitioner inasmuch as they countermand many of the adverse effects of deracination and acculturation. They comprise effective vehicles for conducting an inquiry into the effects of oppression in a colonized terrain. As the careers of Tayo, Abel, and Jim Loney evince in Silko's *Ceremony,* Momaday's *Dawn* and Welch's *Death,* what the subaltern needs is a "good ceremony" to counteract the adverse effects of alienation and to help him or her reconnect to an ancestral topos. As Robert Nelson asserts in *Place and Vision,*

> This view, manifest also in *House Made of Dawn* and *Ceremony,* is that alienation (like Loney's, and like twentieth century humanity's more generally) is a curable disease, and that what Loney needs, like Abel and Tayo both, is a "good ceremony"—involvement in a process of self-rediscovery that for its efficacy depends on reconstellating his individual consciousness to bring it into closer accord with the shape of the land and, thereby, with the life force immanent there. (99)

The fundamental question driving this inquiry is whether reading and writing in the borderland classroom could function in a similar "ceremonial" fashion to ameliorate the debilitating effects of alienation by helping native students reconnect to an indigenous landscape, and to the history, lore, and traditions associated with it? Could writing and reading instruction foregrounding the oppressive realities, past and present, of other native peoples help inaugurate and dialogically reinforce an inquiry into the equally oppressive lived realities of these Athabascan students? Could such a pedagogy also reinscribe the traditional Native American "healing ceremony" and "vision quest" by providing a classroom variant of these ceremonies? Could these and other noncanonical readings raise the consciousness of these students by offering useful rereadings of history and "alter/native" perspectives on their own hybridized existence? Could instruction in such borderland narratives help them articulate their own experience, "say their own Word" (Freire 121)? Could such instruction also be linked to the Foxfire program and to the project of critical literacy, and if so how? Could the writing class in short become another site for the reemergence of a radical, new, red subjectivity? Could pedagogy be deployed not only to facilitate the integration of the borderland curriculum, but the reintegration of the native Self, by effacing once and forever the traumatizing disjunction between Self and Society, schooling and reality, the Word and the World? Finally, might not such readings, and the writing assignments yoked to them, help marginalized learners undertake and complete the difficult transcultural journey from alienated and passive conscripts into the Euro-American culture to a more livable future as "active residents of the borderlands" (Lu 900)?

The Canon and Cultural Imperialism

Implicit in the postcolonial critique of The Great Books is the assertion that the Western canon is complicit in the enterprise of cultural imperialism inasmuch as its texts enact a reductive containment of the Other. In canonical works ranging from Cooper's *Mohicans* to London's *Call*, the native is either romanticized as a noble savage or demonized as a Stone-Age heathen. For example, in the penultimate passages of *Call* the "Yeehats" are stereotypically depicted "dancing about the wreckage of the spruce-bough lodge" after slaughtering John Thorton and his party of prospectors (97). The Yeehats' deflationary treatment by London is signified as well by the bestial and Stone Age imagery the author uses to "capture" them in words. Indeed, killing these natives is figuratively equated with hunting big game: "He had killed man, the noblest game of all. . . . It was harder to kill a husky dog than them. They were no match at all, were it not for their arrows and spears and clubs" (98). Thus, in London's Great Chain of Being the Yeehats are situated somewhere below the Master's pet, in the same category as other big "game." London's mythologizing narratives of the Far North are populated with "superyeoman" types such as John Thorton, who along with their mythic and reductive representations of the wilderness prepare the way for conquest, settlement, and dispossession. As Homi Bhabha argues, such textual stereotypes are a precondition for the subjugation of the Other by colonial and neocolonial institutions: "The objective of colonial discourse is to construct the colonized as a population of degenerate types on the basis of racial origin, in order to justify conquest and to establish systems of administration and instruction" ("The Other" 75).

Further, London's reductive representations of the native reinscribe his equally stereotypic representations of the indigene's land, and in a manner that also rationalizes the conquest, "settlement," or "development" of that land. The romantic works of Fennimore Cooper and Chauteaubriand and the realist novels of London enact the "Orientalization" of the American wilderness, and of Alaska in particular, depicting it in ways that excite the settler impulses of the Empire's readership by conforming to that readership's stereotypic images of both the native and his or her homeland. These realist texts construct the native's homeland in one of several ways, reinscribing the negative stereotypes the colonizer constructs of the native. If the native is romanticized as a noble savage or demonized as a blood-thirsty heathen, the land is similarly constructed as either a barren wasteland in urgent need of development, as a primordial wilderness red in tooth and claw and therefore needing to be tamed, as a boundless treasure of natural resources awaiting exploitation, or as a utopian frontier offering a return to the Edenic and needing only settlers. As Mary Louise Pratt observes, the writer abroad acts as the eyes and ears of the empire, producing "places that could be thought of as barren, empty, undeveloped, inconceivable, needful of European influence and control, ready to serve European industrial, intellectual, and commercial interests" (*Imperial Eyes* 35). The imperial writer abroad not only (mis)represents the Other, but the home of the Other in a manner that invites the colonization of both.

The reductive representations of the imperial writer abroad, these "words" imposed on the "wilderness," are the survey markers by which the writer stakes his or her claim to native soil in the name of Empire. These representations are the red flags the colonizer tags to the trees, the "sign" that marks each for destruction. Thus, words are "part of a more general process by which the emerging industrial nations took possession of new territory" (*Eyes* 35). The reductive images of the native's ancestral topos purveyed by the romantic novelist, the realist storyteller, and the travel writer are as culpable as the buzz saw, the bulldozer, and the bible in preparing the way for the colonization of the Athabascan's homeland.

These and other writers engineer nothing less than a world creation in words, constructing the land of the Athabascan if not the Athabascans themselves in a manner that panders to the prejudices and preconceptions of their settler readership, even as the Orient was constructed for the British readership by the writings of those "subjects" who traveled abroad. Inspired by these images of the native's land, their imaginations embark on the colonizing journey, conveyed into the heart of the native's darkness by the rhetorical roads these discursive superyeomen have built. Thus, the reductive images that effect the textual capture of both the land and its people in realist texts such as London's *Call* and *Fang* are every bit as responsible for the conquest of the indigene's land as the imperial highways built by Jameson's "superyeomen": the Great North Road, the Oregon Trail, the Alkan Highway—all are tropes of conquest. The rhetorical roads of the realist text, which "open" the indigene's homeland to the settlers' imagination long before their colonizing feet set foot on native soil, comprise the "infrastructure" of colonialism as it were: the aesthetic vanguard of conquest which is the counterpart to the military's propaganda machine. They are the "leaflets" scattered throughout the native's homeland that prepare the way for the occupation forces. In the last analysis, aesthetics is as culpable as economics, politics, and religion in the colonization of the Athabascan's homeland. And to the extent that education foregrounds these realist novels, it facilitates the genocidal destruction of indigenous cultures.

The place-names the colonizer imposes on the Athabascan's landscape are yet another example of the manner in which the Word prepares the way for conquest and dispossession. Native place-names are replaced by those of their colonizer, as the indigenous landscape is made over in the image of the invader's distant homeland: Mount Denali, for example, is rechristened Mount McKinley. The place-names along the Alkan Highway signify its colonial origins as well: "Soldier's Summit" and "Contact Creek" commemorate the site where this imperial highway was completed, where the United States Army made contact with its Canadian counterpart in this multinational colonization of an indigenous wilderness. These names are the linguistic monuments they erected to themselves, the discursive counterparts to the statues that populate the native's homeland honoring the white, male heroes of Euro-American colonization. As a prelude to invasion and settlement, to possession and dispossession, the indigene's landscape is given a linguistic face-lift, a signifying makeover that connotes unofficial transfer of "title" from the colonized to the colonizer.

These examples underscore the role signification plays in conquest. Each new name is a rhetorical outpost, a linguistic cache the colonizer constructs in order to inhabit the wilderness, in which to store the ideological trappings of survival and conquest, a linguistic cabin that makes it possible to penetrate, inhabit, and ultimately possess the native landscape. As Paul Carter asserts in "Naming Place," these place-names "do not reflect what is already there: on the contrary, they embody the existential necessity the traveler feels to invent a place he can inhabit. It was the names themselves that brought history into being" (qtd. in Ashcroft, 404–405). To reiterate, the (mis)representations of the realist writer are as complicit in this process of cultural genocide as the more overtly violent means deployed to this end; it is merely violence in an aesthetic guise—the wolf of colonization disguised as the lamb of art. It is significant therefore that Mount McKinley has recently been redesignated Mount Denali, the name by which it was known to Alaskan natives. This is a small, but significant victory for the Alaskan natives in their quest to regain "title" to their ancestral homeland, which is tantamount to recovering "title" to the Self insofar as Native American identity is inseparable from the indigenous landscape.

Insofar as my borderland pedagogy initially privileged appreciative and assimilationist readings of London's *Call* and *Fang,* it too was an accessory to conquest. Postcolonial theorists problematize pedagogies that privilege canonical texts, arguing, as Bhabha does in "Signs Taken for Wonders," that the signifying practices inscribed in these texts and in the pedagogies that celebrate them only serve to perpetuate the "discursive conditions of domination" by proffering a centralized discourse that marginalizes difference (159). The values of the dominant culture, as embodied in the Great Books, are posited as the norm over and against which the mores of the subculture are proffered as abnormal. As Foucault observes, the oppressive circulation of power through discourse requires an economy of discourses if not a univocal language; similarly, the circulation of power through culture requires an economy of cultures if not a monoculture; and finally, the circulation of power through literature requires not only an economy of genres (the realist novel) but an economy of human traits, if not a universal subject that marginalizes and/or subsumes difference ("Power/Knowledge" 85).

In foisting realist novels like *Call* and *Fang* on my Athabascan students, as well as my assimilationist readings of those texts, I was in effect perpetuating representations of those students which were not only stereotypic, but which deepened their alienation from their subculture by "taking us further from ourselves to other selves, from our world to other worlds" (Thiong'o, qtd. in Ashcroft 288). Such depictions not only reinforced racist stereotypes among the white students in my class, thus marginalizing the native students even further, but no doubt deepened the Athabascan students' alienation from schooling on the one hand and from their subculture on the other. As Michael Holzman asserts, "school is seen as the negation of home (and of the street), its values the negation of their values" (165). Instruction in the Great Books in general and the realist novel in particular, as enacted in my own pedagogy, becomes in the words of Ira Shor yet another element in a "mass disabling education" insofar as these texts "reproduce alienated consciousness" ("Educators" 14). I will revisit this relationship between alienation and resistance as manifested in the borderland classroom later in this discussion. In the final analysis, London's reductive representations of the Yeehats constitutes, in the words of Bhabha, an "unproblematized notion of the subject . . . a return of the oppressed—those terrifying stereotypes of savagery, cannibalism, lust, and anarchy which are the signal points of identification and alienation, scenes of fear and desire, in colonial texts" ("Other" 78).

To reiterate, I am not arguing that these canonical texts should not be read or taught, far from it. I am merely asserting that instead of being read appreciatively as vehicles of assimilation into the dominant culture they need to be reread subversively as decolonizing signifiers that facilitate the recuperation of indigenous cultures. The compositionist, in the borderlands and elsewhere, needs to re-deploy these narratives of conquest in order to generate counternarratives of resistance: each colonizing word is a grain of sand with the potential to irritate the oyster of Otherness into producing a pearl of resistance.

Alter/Native Narratives: New Writers of the Purple Sage

To make learning in general, and reading and writing instruction in particular, more meaningful to these marginalized students, I decided to shift the focus from The Great Books to narratives from the borderlands: to read canonical texts like *Call* and *Fang* from an anti- or postcolonial perspective and then only as a supplement to these "alter/native" texts. As Garreth Griffiths affirms in "The Myth of Authenticity," "it is clearly crucial to resistance that the 'story' of the Indian continues to be told. It is only through such counternarratives that alter/native views can be put" (239). Since the Athabascans did not have a body of literature to tell their own story, I decided to import narratives from other Native American peoples so that the "'story' of the Indian [might] be told" in the classroom at least. Stephen Slemon provides a useful name for this growing body of anticolonial, noncanonical literature which he terms "resistance literature . . . which can thus be seen as that category of literary writing which emerges as an integral part of organized struggle or resistance for national liberation" (qtd. in Ashcroft 107).

Like subaltern identity itself, the genres, tropes, and figurative devices of resistance literature are defined over and against those that predominate in the Great Books. Thus, instead of realist novels, the Other deploys magic realist novels as vehicles of resistance: as both a cloak to conceal resistance and as a dagger to enact it. Instead of autobiographies that privilege a monologic construction of the self, Native American as-told-to autobiographies privilege a Self that is constructed dialogically, that is through conversation and dialogue with other voices, as evidenced in the narratives of Black Elk and Lame Deer, two texts that I started using then and that I continue to use in the current course I teach in Native American studies. Magic realism and dialogic modes of identity construction are but two of several signifying practices privileged in resistance literature: others include parody, allegory, and satire, as well as irony, which has been called the master trope of resistance literature. These literary tropes comprise the figurative counterparts to the indigene's linguistic strategy of "sly civility" (Bhabha 78) and "mimicry" that pervade the "counter-discursive" aesthetics of much anglophone literature (Tiffin, qtd. in Ashcroft 97). As reliance on these signifying practices indicates, resistance literature does not exist in a pure, autonomous state apart from colonialism. It is reactionary by definition and thus contaminated by the very literature it purports to resist, defining itself in opposition to the genres and tropes privileged in the Great Books of the Western Canon, comprising yet another example of what Sara Suleri calls the "peculiar intimacy" of colonizer-colonized relations (756).

Readings in these borderland narratives were offered as part of a broader inquiry into the effects of neocolonial oppression on a local level, and as a supplement to writing instruction foregrounding these local cultural conflicts. We therefore read and wrote about native narratives that posited conflict not only as the inevitable result, but as a necessary means of mediating between two cultures. To the as-told-to autobiographies of Black Elk and Lame Deer, I have since added that of Mary Crow Dog (*Lakota Woman*), thus providing the student with a running narrative that spans a century-and-a-half of Lakota history, extending from the precolonial through the colonial to the postcolonial phase, and which represents the perspectives of both genders. In addition, these narratives from the Native American borderlands are the sites of current critical debates over issues of authenticity, representation, marginalization, resistance, and identity. Whose voice for instance is being heard in these as-told-to autobiographies: the Indian's or his or her Euro-American interlocutor's?

I also found Farley Mowat's collection of short stories, *The Snow Walker*, to be a useful vehicle for engaging the interest and raising the critical consciousness of borderland students, native as well as white, in the reading and writing process. Mowat's borderland narratives offer more contemporary, less reductive representations of the indigene than do the realist novels of London. They depict various aspects of existence in the bicultural contact zone, and as such help to "unveil" the thematic universe of the native student. "The Blinding of Andre Maloche," for example, treats the theme of religious imperialism, foregounding the conflict between Christianity and paganism. It recounts the Oedipal-like blinding of a man who renounces paganism in favor of Christianity. "The Iron Men" describes the incursions of the Vikings into the land of the Inuit. It depicts the beneficial and destructive effects of cross-cultural contact with the white man by dramatizing the ruinous impact of modern weapons on native populations. "The Two Who Were One" dramatizes the erosive and corrosive effects that a cash-based economy has on the native's traditional subsistence lifestyle. It narrates the story of an Inuit boy who is forced to kill his pet fox in order to avoid starvation. "Stranger in Taransay" speaks to the mutilations and metamorphoses of exile and displacement, of the Native American diaspora. "Walk Well My Brother" dramatizes the effects of racist stereotyping, as well as the tensions that characterize the colonizer-colonized relationship. It is the story of a native woman who martyrs herself in order to insure the survival of the white bush pilot after they crash in the arctic wilderness.

Insofar as Mowat's borderland narratives foreground the theme of bicultural contact, and the adverse affects associated with that contact, they hold a mirror as it were to the lived realities of the borderland student. They comprise effective vehicles for conducting an inquiry into the lived realities of this bicultural contact zone, for helping the Athabascan student to enunciate his or her own World.

In the course I currently teach in Native American studies I have added other borderland narratives foregrounding the theme of spiritual redemption through reconnection to an ancestral topos: *Ceremony, House Made of Dawn,* and *Death of Jim Loney.* As Timothy Brennan observes in "The National Longing for Form," the careers of many protagonists in this body of resistance literature are extremely relevant to the lived realities of the bicultural borderland resident: their "very rootlessness brilliantly articulates the emotional life of decolonization's various political contestants. It is 'in between'" (qtd. in Ashcroft 175). The exilic, "in-between" careers of these protagonists, as well as the powerful message of their redemption through reconnection to an indigenous homeland, not only speaks to the lived realities of many Native American youths, including the Athabascan student, but offers a positive alternative to their bicultural alienation. Finally, these readings could be offered in conjunction with narratives from other cultures foregrounding the theme of bicultural marginalization, including Chinua Achebe's *Things Fall Apart* and Milton Murayama's *Five Years on a Rock* and *I Just Want My Body Back.*

In this section I want to discuss in greater detail how these borderland narratives were used in the classroom as talismans of reconnection, as vehicles of academic and critical literacy, as antidotes to alienation, as a means of transfiguring reading and writing instruction in the borderlands into a "ceremony" of the native Self, into a "healing ritual" combating the effects of deracination, acculturation, and marginalization, into a quest for "vision" regarding the realities of these students' own hybridity.

Though the shift to these alter/native texts was greeted with enthusiasm by many students, and particularly by those who strongly identified with their indigenous culture, such as Mark, Leo, and Erin, it did engender strong resistance in other students, most notably in David, who identified more strongly with the dominant culture. It met with resistance among some parents and peers as well. Pedagogy in a small, isolated community is influenced to a greater degree by conditions beyond the classroom for the simple reason that a greater percentage of those in the community are aware of what transpires in the classroom, and bring that awareness to bear on administrators, school board members, colleagues, students, friends, and neighbors. Thus, when I made this shift from canonical to noncanonical texts, I quickly heard about it from the principal and from my peers, who spoke on their own behalf and on behalf of those who had spoken to them. For example, some of the white timber-camp parents resented the fact that their sons and daughters were now being forced to read stories by or about Indians. In contradistinction to the views of their parents, some of these same students enthusiastically embraced these borderland narratives, and particularly those of Farley Mowat, because they foregrounded activities with which they had direct experience: trapping, fishing, hunting, raising wild pets, surviving in the wilderness, etc.

The timber-camp parents were joined by some of the Athabascan parents who objected to Mowat's stories because they emphasized the "darker" side of contemporary existence in the bicultural contact zone among the Inuit and Athabascans, or because they reinforced negative stereotypes of the native as a drunk, debilitated, or otherwise dysfunctional Other, because they focused too heavily on the adverse material effects of cultural genocide, displacement, and diaspora in what also amounted to a biting indictment of the Euro-American's contact with the native peoples of the Far North. These parents argued that the preponderance of premature deaths, the ravages of alcoholism, the persistence of pagan religious practices, and the myriad manifestations of cultural dislocation not only constituted a reductive view of the Arctic and Subarctic peoples that reinforced negative stereotypes, but reinforced the self-destructive tendencies of adolescents and preadolescents who were too young to read (and therefore too easily influenced by) these texts. They asserted that these narratives of the borderlands would only intensify the adverse effects of alienation, compound their sense of despair and hopelessness, and accelerate their self-destructive behavior.

As if the resistance of parents and students was not enough, I was also confronted in the teacher's lounge by a colleague who expressed both dismay and disapproval over this apostasy from the Western canon and orthodox pedagogy. Thus, I found myself confronted with censorious voices both within the school and the community, arising from within and beyond the classroom. These experiences served to remind me that in a small, borderland community the walls that delineate the classroom from that community are more permeable than their metropolitan counterparts. If, on the one hand, this leads to greater surveillance of pedagogy, it also creates the possibility for greater articulation between pedagogy and the local population; its greatest curse can also be its most transformative blessing. If it was shocking to discover I was not operating in a vacuum but in a fishbowl, then it was just as refreshing to discover that the pedagogical fish raised in this fishbowl could be released back into the community: into their natural and wild element. In the borderlands the destination of pedagogy should and must be the same as it is for indigenous species that are artificially bred because conditions have led to their precipitous decline in their natural habitat: those wild, local, native conditions that produced the Other must become the destination of a pedagogy that seeks the reintegration of the indigene with an indigenous place. Students released back into their local, lived realities like hook-nosed salmon running swift and red upstream to spawn.

While these resistant voices did not make me abandon my plans, they did make me alter them, did make me stand back, look at these alter/native narratives from these resistant viewpoints, and pose some self-critical questions: were these criticisms warranted; was there some way of incorporating them into pedagogy; was there room in the classroom for these Other voices in counterpoint to my own; could these alter/native narratives also be read "against the grain," as it were, by students inclined toward such a reading; could alter/native narratives as well as canonical texts be read subversively, as well as appreciatively, as part of a reconfigured reading/writing program that was sensitive to the cultural affiliations of *all* students—that reinforced the loyalties of David as well as Mark, that invited subversive as well as appreciative views of any given text? Were my own views merely a new form of orthodoxy, and could that orthodoxy tolerate views that comprised the negation of it: as enunciated by parents, peers, and students?

Or was the force of public opinion in this instance merely another form of censorship, another threat to the principle of academic freedom that should itself be resisted? Given the great level of awareness (or surveillance) of pedagogy in this extremely colonized and politicized terrain, was it wise to turn a deaf ear to such dissonant voices? Would it not be wiser, indeed fairer, to assimilate such voices into my pedagogy? If one of the ways to reconfigure borderland pedagogy is to foreground local cultural conflicts, why not foreground this conflict? Yet, by so doing would I not be reinscribing the oppressive practices of the very colonizers I purported to resist, who for centuries have co-opted native resistance by permitting its lawful expression in the courtrooms, the boardrooms, and the classrooms, in poetry, painting and political pamphlets, so long as it conformed to the literary tropes, the legal codes, and the linguistic norms of the Empire? Would it not be wiser to leave the wild fireweed of native resistance rooted in its natural terrain, instead of transforming it into the political equivalent of a potted houseplant?

In the final analysis, I resisted the efforts to abandon these alter/native texts while inviting resistant, alter/native readings of them. There is no solution to these paradoxical questions that is absolutely beneficial to indigenous resistance: all come with a price. In my assessment, the partial co-option of resistant voices was a smaller price to pay than the absolute silencing that accompanies a genocidal indoctrination in the canonical works of Empire. Better that the Other finds his or her voice in counterpoint to the colonizer, even if it is within the colonizer's classroom, than the silence and mimicry that historically attends the colonizer's totalizing discourse in the classroom and elsewhere.

As I have stated, resistance arose not merely from some segments of the community, but within the classroom as well. This shift to noncanonical narratives by or about the native was vociferously resisted by David whose classroom discourse evinced an "almost phobic denial of the distinctive elements of indigenous culture" (Hogan 88), as evidenced by his earlier refusals to accept instruction in Dena'ina or participate in the Foxfire project, and now by the rhetorical insurrection he mounted against me: "Why do we have to read this junk?"

Why indeed? David's question raises an even more critical one: how to respond to such resistance in the classroom? The first response such resistance demands of the teacher is to find a way of incorporating it into pedagogy, of making room in the classroom for such unsolicited oppositional discourse. Thus, it is the first obligation of the borderland practitioner to disclose the reason for such a shift, as well as one's complicity in reproducing the "discursive conditions of domination" through a pedagogy foregrounding The Great Books. Second, it is incumbent upon the borderland practitioner to make room in the classroom for such resistance voices, to make the oppositional questions students raise part of the critical inquiry as well, as part of a pedagogy in which difference is validated instead of violated, that legitimates instead of marginalizes such oppositional voices. The question thus arises: how do we teach to resistance? And why should we?

I would like to address the second question first. It seems paradoxical at best, hypocritical at worst for a pedagogy arguing the efficacy of foregrounding conflict, of teaching to hybridity, of privileging polyphony over homogeneous discourse to then silence or otherwise marginalize voices of dissent. Far from silencing such resistance, pedagogy should seek for ways to foreground it. Instead of ignoring the questions raised in resistance to such borderland narratives, those very questions should be seized as "generative themes" and posed to students as subjects for critical inquiry, as directed freewriting activities in journals, as themes to be further researched and developed in lengthier, more formal writing assignments, as topics to be debated in class, in small collaborative groups, or in more global discussions, as questions to be carried into the community by students operating in small teams and in conjunction with the Foxfire project, or as part of a broader pedagogical focus on local cultural conflicts.

Thus, David's discourse, and the resistant questions driving it, instead of being silenced or marginalized, should be foregrounded as yet another subject of critical inquiry. A number of critical questions or "generative themes" could drive such an inquiry, and be posed to students like David, remembering of course that the things to be "generated" are critical consciousness and political intervention. Otherwise, the entire project degenerates into a mere academic exercise: which should be read, canonical or noncanonical texts, London's *Wild* or Mowat's *Snow Walker*; do Mowat's borderland narratives indeed misrepresent the native; do they reinscribe the stereotypic signifying practices of the dominant culture; do they present an accurate or inaccurate image of the indigene; do such readings provide negative reinforcement to native students; do they heal or intensify the effects of deracination and acculturation; are Junior High school students too young to read such stories? High school students? Are such resistant discourses merely another form of censorship? What are the implications of teaching the Western canon, and of departing from it?

Pedagogy should seek for ways to stimulate rather than silence these untamed tongues, should foster an environment where students like David can develop their resistant, critical voices through subversive readings of borderland texts in contradistinction to the appreciative readings I proffered of them, and as a counterpart to the subversive readings I modeled of canonical texts. Indeed, though Mowat's narratives foreground an indigenous culture (The Inuit) they signify many aspects of that culture that students in David's position resist: its pantheistic, nature-worshipping religion, its subsistence lifestyle, its defeated and dispirited souls who have abandoned all hope to the bottle or the syringe, its feathers, beads, and drums. Tradition-resistant students in David's position could thus be given the opportunity for discovering, defining, and developing their voices not just as back-talkers on the margins of the classroom but as writers and communicators actively involved in the classroom conversation. Their resistant discourse could be incorporated into the classroom conversation as part of a pedagogy that privileges the heteroglossia of subaltern signifying practices in subversive opposition to the centralized, unitary, teacherly discourse of the dominant culture. David's resistant discourse would thus help other students, native as well as white, to position themselves with respect to canonical and noncanonical texts and the generative themes they raise, discovering their own voices, defining and redefining their own identities in the process.

How specifically did these texts relate to the lived realities of borderland students, Athabascan as well as white? If these alter/native texts intensified the alienation that some Athabascan students felt toward their ancestral culture, they had the opposite effect on other native students, ameliorating the effects of alienation by helping them reconnect to their indigenous culture. If they aroused David's resistance toward his Athabascan heritage they similarly reinforced Mark's strong identification with his indigenous culture, as evidenced by a series of unsolicited anecdotes he offered in response to these readings. For example, Black Elk's description of his career as a medicine man elicited from Mark the following observation: "We have the same thing only we call him a sha-mon," he said, accenting the second syllable. The comment is instructive for it not only evinces Mark's ability to make connections between the abstract and the concrete, between Black Elk's narrative and his own experience, but the "we" underscores his solidarity with the traditional aspects of his own subculture in contradistinction to David's renunciation of those traditions.

The narratives of Black Elk and Lame Deer also helped Athabascsan students reconnect to their own history. While reading Black Elk's description of the long-standing blood feud between the Lakota and the Crow, Mark offered a bit of anecdotal discourse that not only solved a riddle in my mind, but also shed light on his people's own history. He told me of his people's blood feud with the Aleuts, adding that a battle had once been fought on the shores of nearby Dena'ina Lake in which the waters ran red from the blood of the victims, adding that his people never frequented this lake, believing that the island in the center of it was still frequented by the spirits of the dead. These readings not only helped students in Mark's position reconnect to the customs and history of their subculture, but to its lore as well. For instance, Mowat's description of Paija, a blizzard-wandering giantess of Inuit lore, reminded me of the Sasquatch legend of the Pacific Northwest. When I related this to the class, Mark was quick to respond with the Athabascan counterpart to this legend.

"We have the same thing only we call him the Bushman."

I was taken aback, for I thought the lore of the Sasquatch was confined to the Pacific Northwest. Yet Mark's matter-of-fact, if unsolicited comment suggested a far greater dispersion of this myth, implying a common heritage between his people and those of the Pacific Northwest. This in turn led to a discussion of the Hawaiian myth of the "little ones" or "menehune," which as I soon learned from Mark also had an Athabascan counterpart in the lore of "The Shorties." Pointing to a nondescript, weather-beaten tree outside the classroom, he informed me that this tree was home to The Shorties who emerged from it one night every February to wander the streets of the village, which consequently remained deserted on this occasion.

The affinities Mark uncovered between the myths of his people and those of the Lakota, Inuit, the Hawaiians, the Kwakiutl and the Iroquois could serve as a springboard for a writing assignment foregrounding a comparative study of myths across cultures, enabling students to reconnect to the history and lore of their own culture while simultaneously making connections between it and other indigenous cultures. Joseph Campbell's *The Hero With a Thousand Faces* could not only be read to illumine Native American versions of the hero's journey in general and of Black Elk's career in particular, but to facilitate the recovery of Athabascan versions of the hero's quest. Students, for instance, could be invited to compare the phases of the hero's journey as enunciated by Campbell (separation, initiation, and return) with the trajectory of the careers of several protagonists in contemporary Native American novels: Tayo, Abel, and Jim Loney.

Writing activities of a more creative variety were also assigned in conjunction with these narratives from the borderlands, in which students were invited to create their own myths of the Far North, reinforcing traditional Native American storytelling and signifying practices as they explained the origin of the aurora or the moose's dewlap, of the salmon's hooked nose or the rabbit's snowshoe feet, of the ptarmigan's changing plumage or the eagle's bald head or the grizzly's humanlike hind foot. Thus, writing functioned like a "healing ritual" by reducing the alienating effects of traditional reading and writing activities, by helping Athabascan students reconnect to their ancestral landscape and indigenous cultures, by facilitating the retrieval of Athabascan history, lore, and customs, and by enabling these students to author their own narratives from the borderlands which reinscribed traditional Athabascan storytelling practices. As students enunciated in speech and writing their diverse positions with respect to canonical and noncanonical texts, and the issues raised by them, a number of discourses emerged. Students positioned and repositioned themselves relative to the two cultures. In the final analysis, instruction in these alter/native texts helped solidify a multiplicity of subject positions insofar as they reinforced the identities of some students while revealing alternative positions to others, helping borderland students to discover who they were, who they were not, or who they might become. Thus, these con/texts had a significant impact on the group dynamics of the classroom, not only exposing those dynamics but altering them as well, not only generating discourse but facilitating movement between diverse subject positions.

Among students who initially identified closely with neither culture, such as Robert and Will, some aligned themselves more definitively with the dominant or indigenous culture respectively as a consequence of these year-long readings and the debates they generated. For other students, such as David and Mark, these readings solidified initial positions assumed relative to the dominant culture and the indigenous subculture. These readings likewise reinforced the attitudes of students like Erin, who denounced the orthodox traditions of her subculture because they were complicit in the process of colonization while embracing the more reactionary, contemporary aspects of it. Still other students, like Velma, moved from a position of acultural alienation to one of closer identification with the more political aspects of contemporary Athabascan culture. These borderland narratives had little effect on other students, such as Joey and Hank, who resisted such instruction, perhaps seeing it as a threat to their group identity, which emanated from a sense of nonmembership in either culture.

These alter/native readings not only reduced the effects of bicultural marginalization by reducing the disjunction between academic text and cultural context, but they generated as well a series of comparative writing themes privileging the recuperation of the indigenous subculture in general, and its history, lore, and traditions in particular. Lame Deer's autobiography was particularly useful in this regard. Whereas Black Elk's narrative speaks to the more traditional aspects of Lakota culture, Lame Deer offers a more contemporary vision of reservation life. Lame Deer's many passages depicting the debilitating effects of alcoholism, the

oppression of schooling (24), of police brutality and racial discrimination (60–79), and of cultural genocide (80–95) all triggered reso-
nances in the lived realities of mixed-race students like Erin who
had been "schooled" in Anchorage, of full-blood students like Joey
who had embarked on nihilistic crime sprees of their own, or like
Hank and Pete who had witnessed firsthand the ravages of alcoholism among their parents and who were in danger of becoming
teenage alcoholics themselves, and of native students in general
who experienced firsthand the racial slurs of white timber-camp
students, or whose parents had encountered the racist hiring practices of the Chugiak Timber Co.

Lame Deer's career, like Tayo's, is relevant to the lived realities of
these students for other reasons as well. He puts into words many
of the experiences and emotions that characterize the exilic, in-between existence of such students. He writes of many of the same
bicultural tensions: of the tension between past and present, between the need to preserve the past and to resist the oppressive
"capture" of the Native American in contemporary society. He writes
of the fragmented, unstable, shifting, and multiple identities of hybridity that are at one and the same time its worst curse and its
greatest blessing. For if such fragmentation deconstructs the Self, it
also preserves a measure of autonomy for the indigenous Self by
preventing its capture in the reductive signifying practices of the
dominant culture. As Lame Deer writes, "I was always hopping back
and forth across the boundary line of the mind. . . . Being a kind of
two-face, I then wanted to find out how it looked from the other side"
(54). In his quest to escape containment in racial stereotypes, to
discover his own identity, Lame Deer embarked on a boundary-
crossing odyssey through the dominant culture and the indigenous
subculture, assuming many roles, playing many parts. This journey,
which he calls in his own inimitable language the "find out," lasted
his entire life, reinscribes the traditional Native American's life-long
search for knowledge, and underscores the fragmented, multiple,
unstable nature of hybrid identity. Lame Deer writes,

> I was getting older and had tried almost everything. I was
> like a big jig-saw puzzle. Year by year new pieces were added
> to form the complete picture. A few pieces are still missing. . . .
> It was almost as if I were several different people—a preacher,

a spud-picker, a cowhand, a clown, a sign-painter, a healer, a bootlegger, a president of the Indian YMCA. I managed to be both a Christian and a heathen, a fugitive and a pursuer, a lawman and an outlaw. (54–55, 68)

Lame Deer's self-reflexive observations underscore many of the tensions of biculturalism: tensions that problematize the contemporary search for identity. In this rogue's gallery of hybrid identities are roles that are quintessentially assimilationist: preacher, spud-picker, clown, and president of the Indian YMCA. Not to be overlooked is the bittersweet irony of Lame Deer's career as a "sign-painter": for an Indian who has been made captive by "signs" to find employment constructing those signs is as grimly ironic as a prisoner finding work in a factory that produces his ball and chain. Yet, this litany of selves also contains identities that are more traditionally indigenous: the healer and the hunter. At the time, he couldn't say what he was hunting for "or how long the hunt would last"; he only knew that the search was a necessary part of "finding out who I was" (30). More importantly, passages like these provide generative writing themes foregrounding the native student's search for identity. Students could be invited to respond to such passages in reading response journals or in lengthier inquiries, relating it to their own experience, or to that of their parents.

Lame Deer's narrative also articulates the tension between divided loyalties insofar as he assimilates on a technological level to the dominant culture while assimilating on the deeper level of spirituality and mores with his ancestral culture, an accommodation that reflects the reality of many native students. In short, his career has much to offer borderland learners lost in the contact zone between two cultures, searching for a way to negotiate the problematic terrain between them. If it helps some students reconnect to various aspects of indigenous culture, it helps others effect a useful amalgamation of both cultures.

His insightful passages regarding the causes of his own nihilistic crime sprees can help students like Joey and Hank understand the origins of their own nihilistic impulses. These passages provide insight as well for the practitioner inasmuch as they afford a glimpse into the lived reality of the marginalized student. As Lame Deer observes,

We didn't want to be nothing. We wanted to be something. I felt that I was only half a man, that all the old, honored, accepted ways for a young man to do something worthy were barred to me. Just as there was a fence around the reservation, so they had put a fence around our pride. Well, I had to invent a new way of making a name for myself, of breaking through that fence. . . . Going on that joy ride was for me like going on the war path. It was my way of saying, "Look, I'm a man. I exist. Take notice of my existence!" This was worth going to jail for. (78-79)

Lame Deer's narrative has important implications for borderland pedagogy insofar as it not only raises the consciousness of students, native as well as white, by re-presenting to them the material conditions of oppression on the reservation, but models as well an action-plan for intervening against those effects, as evidenced by his peaceful occupation of Mount Rushmore to protest the unsolicited intrusions of cultural imperialism. Such alter/native texts comprise useful vehicles for yoking critical literacy to political resistance, for linking instruction within the classroom to action beyond it.

These alter/native texts can help ameliorate the debilitating effects of alienation by helping students reconnect to their indigenous culture. As Rodanzo Adams asserts, the ability of marginalized students to "imaginatively enter into the past" of their people through its lore, history, and traditions is a critical part in the process by which membership is conferred, identity constructed, and subject status regained. Adams continues,

the demand of children for the "once upon a time" . . . is a demand for full membership in their social group and the story is not satisfactory unless it helps the hearer to conceive of himself as a worthy member of a worthy society. Myths and legends are especially valuable in that they help define ideals, to set up standards, and to create bonds of unity. (94)

Inasmuch as these borderland narratives foreground the local lore, myths, history, customs and knowledges of the native, they comprise useful vehicles for the recuperation of indigenous identity, and as such are effective alternatives to canonical texts. Further, these alter/native readings dialogically reinforced the Foxfire project insofar as they also foregrounded the Athabascan subculture and facilitated the acquisition of academic and critical literacy. While documenting Nikolai's traditional Athabascan fur-trapping techniques in the Foxfire publication, the same students were reading stories like "The Two Who Were One," about an Inuit boy and his pet fox, and the tensions between his people's subsistence lifeways and the cash-based economic system of an incursive Euro-American culture. Other borderland narratives foregrounded other contemporary tensions between the dominant and the indigenous cultures: between Christianity and paganism, between the preservation and the exploitation of the environment, tensions that generated conflicts in their own homeland. If canonical texts weaken the bonds of unity between native students and their indigenous culture, noncanonical narratives from the borderlands conversely strengthen those ties, facilitating the reintegration of the indigene with his or her indigenous culture, and insofar as they do these texts become talismans of healing instead of pharmakons of exile and alienation.

7

Teaching the Cultural Conflicts
Toward a Literacy of Resistance

It is to the reality which mediates men, and to the perception of
that reality held by educators and people, that we must go to find
the program content of education. The investigation of what I
have called the people's "thematic universe"—the complex of their
"generative themes"—inaugurates the dialogue of education as
the practice of freedom.

—Paulo Friere 86

The violent conflict between the Athabascan subculture and
the dominant Euro-American culture was played out in a
number of critical arenas. The environment was one of the
most volatile sites of this cultural clash. It became its own "contact
zone" of bicultural conflict—a topos that reinscribed the hierarchical, asymmetrical power relations between dominant culture and
indigenous subculture. The violence of these environmental conflicts
evinced the high stakes that were in play: huge profits for the
Transnational Corporations vs. the viability of the Athabascan's
subsistence lifestyle. Both sides were thus dependent on the resources of the land for their economic survival, though the resources

181

on which they depended were different. In the case of the transnational corporations, the vast reserves of timber, coal, and oil were the bedrock of their economic survival in the borderlands; for the Athabascans, on the other hand, subsistence was intimately linked to the strength of the moose herds and the salmon runs. Thus, these environmental conflicts were contested across a broad field of topoi, ranging from the offshore oil rigs to the remote moose habitat and the logging roads that penetrated them, to the equally remote Beluga coalfields. Further, these conflicts revealed the peculiar intimacy that characterizes colonizer-colonized relations inasmuch as the Athabascans were complicit in the commercial exploitation of the oil, timber, and coal reserves, having "sold" the rights to them to the transnational corporations as part of the ANLCS.

What were the pedagogical implications of the local cultural conflicts associated with the environment and with schooling in this borderland setting? Could these conflicts similarly serve as vehicles for the acquisition of academic and critical literacy, and if so how? Could they be linked to the Foxfire project and to the noncanonical reading program to dialogically reinforce literacy across the borderland curriculum? More importantly, could an inquiry into local cultural conflicts be yoked to the Athabascan's resistance struggle? Could analysis of these conflicts within the classroom be yoked to actions aimed at resolving them beyond the classroom?

In this chapter I want to posit some responses to these questions, while articulating a model for a conflict-oriented pedagogy, for a pedagogy privileging the constructive uses of local cultural conflicts in general, and particularly the conflicts associated with the environment and with schooling on the reservation. The conflict-oriented pedagogy I am describing here is as equally dialogic, though more politicized than the model enunciated by Gerald Graff inasmuch as it foregrounds not the alien conflicts of the professorate, but the immediate environmental and educational conflicts of the Athabascan. These conflicts lie at the heart of the Athabascans' contemporary resistance struggle, which is nothing if not a struggle for agency, identity, and authority, for the right to govern their own affairs and say their own Word. The resolution of these conflicts will determine the fate of their ancestral culture in both the immediate and foreseeable future. In the effort to fashion a borderland pedagogy foregrounding local conflicts and political resistance, I will not only draw on my own experience, but on the theories of Paulo Freire's radical Marxist pedagogy, of Mary Louise Pratt's contact-zone pedagogy, and of Gerald Graff's dialogic model for conflict-oriented pedagogy.

The ANLCS: The Violence of Signification and Transnational Corporatism

In an effort to establish the role that signification plays in the enterprise of cultural imperialism, the Alaska Native Land Claims Settlement (1971) could be revisited, could be "read" as a "text" in the classroom. This notorious, neocolonial "settlement" reinscribed the duplicitous signifying practices historically deployed in "treaties" with the Native American. As with the treaties "signed" by their counterparts in the lower forty-eight states, the language of this "settlement" contained ominous implications for the subsistence lifeways of the Athabascan—implications which became realities in the years following the agreement. For signing the settlement the Athabascans were awarded a lump sum of $350,000 and "title" to 120,000 acres of land that was already theirs. What they surrendered, however, had even graver implications: their status as a "separate nation," as recognized by the Indian Reorganization Act of the Nineteenth Century, and title to all the surrounding lands. This was the real, hidden agenda of the government agencies negotiating on behalf of transnational corporations: to wrest title of the land away from the Alaskan native in order to gain possession of the vast quantities of natural resources embedded in those lands. Thus, the "settlement" was not an enlightened act of "recognition" that signaled a new dawn in colonizer-colonized relations, but rather a document that legalized the theft of native lands, thus reinscribing the historical treachery of the treaty-making process while perpetuating the asymmetrical power-relations that have for centuries characterized colonizer-colonized relations.

The settlement reinscribed traditional colonizing strategies of domination inasmuch as it offered the Alaskan natives immediate material rewards (cash taking the place of alcohol, blankets, beads, and rifles), and insofar as it used a divide and conquer strategy, inducing a few Athabascans (whom the colonizer designated to be the "official" representatives) to sign away the rights of the entire people, and to the extent that it masked a theft as a trade.

Colonialism had merely assumed a more innocent, but no less geno-cidal, neocolonial guise.

One of the most debilitating legacies of the ANLCS was the loss of nation status it signified. This was accomplished with nothing more than the devious stroke of a pen, and underscores yet again the culpability of signifying practices in colonization. Until the indigene is able to wage resistance in the arena of signification, he and she fight a losing battle, or at least fight at an extreme dis-advantage. Thus, with nothing greater than a blot of ink, the Athabascan nation was transformed into a corporation: the Nyotek Native Corporation, complete with a governing board whose mem-bers were selected by the colonizer, whose "business" was situated not in the native village but in the metropolis of Anchorage, whose bylaws naturally were drawn up by the colonizer, and whose votes were cast in the absence of the people they represented. This is the mechanism by which the conquest of native lands and the genocide of native lifeways are achieved today. It is conquest by signification, by linguistic sleight-of-hand; it is conquest by "trade," oppression by "partnership," and theft by "recognition." Though the arena of contestation has shifted from the battlefield to the boardroom, the end is just the same. The native's lands wind up in the possession of his or her colonizer; the indigene's subsistence lifeways are sup-planted by the cash-based lifestyle of his or her oppressor.

However, the extension of this conflict into the realm of signification has profound implications for the borderland class-room, and for the composition classroom in particular. The very name, "Nyotek Native Corporation," signifies the Athabascan's lin-guistic conscription into the cash-based economy of the colonizer. It is the corporate badge that identifies the Athabascan as a player in Transnational Corporatism. It is a signifier that also effaces their difference as a people: instead of a nation, they are now a corpora-tion. Like their ancestral homeland, the Athabascans themselves have been given a linguistic face-lift by their colonizers: one that signifies their reduction from separate nation status to the status of a minor business partner to transnational corporations.

The colonizer succeeded in shifting the contest to an arena in which the colonizer enjoys a distinct advantage. Thus, possession of the Athabascan's land was gained not through military occupa-tion or even through the influx of settlers, but with the stroke of a pen in a distant glass skyscraper, with the deployment of three little words: Nyotek Native Corporation. The name itself reflects the asymmetrical power relations of the colonizer and the colonized. The words "Nyotek" and "Native" are subsumed by the word "Corporation" inasmuch as they are reduced to the status of modifiers while the word "Corporation" is accorded a more dominant syntactic position as a noun and subject, a linguistic relationship that reenacts on a microcosmic plane the macroscopic marginalization of the Athabascan in the culture at large. This name "Nyotek Native Corporation" signifies not only the loss of separate nation status, but the loss of indigenous identity and the genocide of traditional Athabascan culture insofar as it connotes recruitment into a cash-based economy: one that directly threatens the Athabascan's subsistence lifestyle.

This shift in signification embodied in the ANLCS was meant to signify the dawning of a new era between native and whites in Alaska. What it signified, however, was that the more colonization changes, the more it remains the same. That which was represented as a new dawn in those relations was in reality a twilight that signified the impending eclipse of the Athabascan culture.

Surrendering their status as a separate nation was not the only negative legacy of the ANLCS for the Athabascans. Surrendering title to the surrounding lands to a consortium of transnational corporations had an even greater impact on their subsistence lifestyle. These lands were discovered to contain vast reserves of resources long coveted by transnational corporations: coal, bauxite, oil, natural gas, and timber. It is a legacy the Athabascans share with their Native American counterparts in the lower forty-eight. As Ward Churchill observes, "Alaska native peoples are being converted to landless village corporations in order that the oil under their territories can be tapped" (41). The transference of title to these lands from the Athabascan to these corporations, as well as the harvesting of the resources on those lands, reinscribes the unethical collusion between big business and government agencies, such as the Bureau of Indian Affairs, that has historically exploited the native. Again, Churchill's observations are instructive:

The BIA has utilized its plenary and trust capacities to negotiate contracts with major mining corporations "on behalf of" its "Indian wards" which pay pennies on the dollar of conventional mineral royalty rates. Further, the BIA has typically exempted such corporations from any obligation to reclaim whatever reservation lands have been mined, or even to perform basic environmental cleanup of nuclear and other forms of waste. (41)

The transnational corporations that gained title to the lands surrounding the Nyotek reservation similarly paid a price far below the market value of that land: $3.00 per acre for the 321 million acres in Alaska which the natives surrendered title of. The corporations were similarly exempted from reclaiming the areas they had logged, mined, or drilled. As Gerry Mander asserts,

> just like the Allotment Act, the Indian Reorganization Act, and the Indian Claims Commission Act, The ANLCS was a fraud in concept and execution. It was created by a Congress that was essentially acting as a surrogate for U.S. oil, mineral, and fishing companies. In terms of effective, efficient robbery and scale of deception, ANLCS makes the Allotment Act look like a dimestore burglary. (287)

The primary aim of the "settlement" was not to inaugurate a "new dawn in United States-Indian relations," but to "destroy native title" to the land (290). This it achieved by awarding "title" to 10 percent of the Alaskan landscape, "whereas they had formerly owned 100 percent" (291). The State of Alaska was given three times that amount (30 percent) which was "earmarked for development"(291). Even the cash and the title the natives were given, however, proved to be intangible rewards. Mander continues,

> not one dollar nor one acre of land was actually placed in the control of any native person. Instead, native lands were divided among twelve regions, each under the control of a native-owned corporation. . . . The people would get some money if and when the corporation made a profit by developing the wilderness (as the non-natives wanted them to do). They would never again, as a people, own or control the land. (291)

Thus, even the terms of the cash settlement were yoked to the development of their homeland. It was bad enough to have sold much of their land to the government acting as a purchase agent for various transnational corporations. Now, the natives discovered that in order to receive any money for this sale they had to "develop the wilderness." Before one dollar could be distributed to the residents of Nyotek, the new native corporation into which these monies were funneled had to turn a profit by selling rights to the resources on their lands to these larger corporations. The ANLCS was as ingenious in its predatory design as the iron-jawed traps the white settler sets for the native fur-bearing animals he hopes to turn a profit from. The Alaskan natives were thus victimized by a catch-22 that forced the Athabascan to profit from the destruction of his or her own homeland, and from the destruction of the subsistence lifestyle that was dependent on that land.

This was their "reward" for "signing" the ANLCS. It was a bitter legacy indeed, and when the Athabascans began awakening to the realities of the "settlement" their growing resentment was akin to the violent forces building within the volcanoes that dot the Athabascan's homeland. This was the political climate into which I flew on Jimmy St. Claire's bush plane the day I arrived in Nyotek. The ANLCS did nothing to quell the eruptive force of indigenous discontent. The more that discontent was repressed, the more inevitable its violent return became, for as Arnold Krupat argues, "there is always a return of the repressed in one form or another" (3). In Nyotek, the explosive return of the repressed, the violent eruption of the cultural unconscious, would assume the form of a protracted racial conflict in which long-simmering conflicts over the environment fueled hostilities over education.

The ANLCS was a subject of contentious debate among Athabascans: some congratulated themselves for having profited off the white man's greed; some argued for its repeal; some expressed keen regret that it had been signed in the first place; some directed their rage at the relatives and board members living in Anchorage who had betrayed their best interests to the whites, who had been duped by the terms of the agreement; others directed their hostility toward their white colonizers, in whatever form they assumed: loggers, bush teachers, state troopers, geologists, anthropologists, and social workers. The air was rife with racial tensions, which the ANLCS and its aftermath intensified.

The Transnational Corporation versus The People of Nyotek

A look at the contents of the environmental impact study commissioned by the Nyotek tribal council and conducted by Darbyshire and Associates reveals the reasons for the Athabascans' deep concerns for their homeland. Placer Amex Inc. had placed before the tribal council a proposal to buy the rights to the huge deposits of coal discovered in the nearby Beluga Coal Field. The discovery of vast deposits of coal on Athabascan lands came as no surprise to anyone. I could hardly go for a walk along the Cook Inlet or the Chuitna River without stumbling across large chips of coal. They littered the surface as cow-chips once littered the prairie, and were an even greater source of fuel. Yet, these black chips became markers in a high-stakes struggle between Placer Amex and the tribal council. As Darbyshire and Associates' study indicates, the fate of the Athabascan's homeland was yoked to the fluctuations in the global marketplace:

> As a result of the oil price increases of the mid-to-late 70s, major decisions were made by government and industry to shift emphasis from oil to coal fuels. . . . This explosive demand for coal is the single most important factor affecting Beluga development. Because the field does not have the benefit of existing infrastructure, the area needs a rapidly growing and concentrated market to warrant development. . . . Quantities of at least 750 million tons of coal have been identified as economically extractable for initial field development. This quite stable and predictable supply . . . is a very favorable element. (3)

Additionally, the study shows that 71,000 acres in coal leases were held by four corporations: Mobil Oil, Placer Amex, Diamond-Chuitna, and Amax Inc. The lands held by Placer Amex Inc. were located "25, 15, and 8 miles, respectively, from the village of [Nyotek]" (5).

The study then offers a "review of potential development scenarios" (4). For instance, Placer Amex' plans included the development of a Coal-to-Methanol Plant, the coal to be "transported via rail or conveyor belt . . . to a methanol plant at Granite Point on the east end of Trading Bay." In addition, "a self-sufficient townsite would be constructed to house . . . 1,500 workers plus their families and support personnel" (5). This portion of the review concludes with the assessment that the project "could be in operation as early as 1987" (6). The potential environmental impacts from this development were as foreboding as they were numerous. According to Darbyshire and Associates, they included the following:

- Small amounts of air pollution from coal dust particulates resulting from handling;
- Interruption of wetlands and groundwater drainage;

- Potential degradation of stream water quality if regulations of Surface Mining Control and Reclamation Act are violated;

- Biological disruption of the Chuitna River;

- Potential loss of approximately 50 percent of salmon stock in the area if precautionary measures are not taken, according to Alaska Department of Fish and Game;

- Rerouting of creek beds and surface water;

- Displacement of brown bear population;

- Moose will coexist with most mining activity but increased moose kills are expected on the railroad tracks; overall moose population may increase due to increase in pioneering vegetation. (13–14)

Thus, of the eight potential "impacts" listed, only one is advantageous to the Athabascan: the alleged increase in the moose population.

Oil drilling and natural gas operations included similar development scenarios, as interviews with personnel at Diamond-Chuitna, Mobil Oil, and Amex revealed. These included plans for an "industrial enclave such as Prudhoe Bay . . . within the Chuitna lease area," as well as the construction of a "permanent townsite" (7). It included as well the construction of a "transportation corridor" to the proposed "stockpile area and port site." These plans were similar in their configuration to the infrastructure of the lumber mill, which had been up and running since shortly after the signing of the ANLCS in 1971. These corporations even had plans for the development of the mouth of the Chuitna, which was perhaps the favorite destination of my walks. On many occasions I had observed families of ocean otters playing in its bore tides. A bald eagle pair nested in the crown of an old cottonwood that commanded a view of the wetlands that were home to many species of migratory bird. To imagine an environment that was home to otter, eagle, muskrat, and goose converted into a deepwater port with rails and stockpiles and conveyor belts and who knows what other heavy machinery had a leaden effect on my spirits. The images of wildness contrasted so sharply with the images of this heavy equipment I could scarcely associate both with the same landscape.

If it came to pass, the Athabascan village would be bracketed by the lumber mill to the south and the coal plant to the north, each operating a deepwater port, with its constant output of noise and traffic of cargo ships. What disruptive effect would these operations have on the migratory habits of the salmon, whose species returned to the Chuitna River each summer in a series of three runs beginning in May and lasting until late August? Was the day fast approaching when those returning to the reservation in late August might look down from Jimmy St. Claire's bush plane and see not a single column of woodsmoke rising from the huts in which the Athabascans smoked their salmon? And what would be the effect on the local moose population, already dwindling, of all this commercial development? Somber speculations indeed. The facts go on: "2,000 people employed during construction of the D-C operation; mining facilities: 500 employees; port facility: 70 employees; maintenance of transportation corridor: 25 employees; camp maintenance: 35 employees" (8).

Development scenarios for oil drilling were just as ominous. These included, "30- to 35-foot exploratory holes to be drilled in the next three years" at the Beluga Lake site, "some 55 miles northwest of the village of [Nyotek]" (9). As the study concludes, the result of "both large-scale coal and large-scale oil and gas development . . . would mean a regional population increase to more than 40 times the current population level. This fact alone will make for many changes in village lifestyle" (11). It is difficult to imagine how any of these changes would benefit the Athabascan's subsistence hunting and fishing activities. The study cautions that these figures are the result of a "worst case scenario" in which the "potential negative social, economic, and environmental effects depicted herein would be the result of unrestrained development" (11).

The study then couches most of the anticipated effects in positive terms that are problematic at best. For example, it notes that there would be "more long- and short-term local job opportunities for the [Nyoteks]," while failing to account for the racist hiring practices that habitually deny Native Americans equal opportunity in the job market, whether local or otherwise. The study likewise posits economic changes in a positive light, deploying such signifiers as "growth" and "diversification," as if these are assumed to be good for the Athabascans in and of themselves. The study notes the "potential" for lower prices that increased competition would bring. However, while this might benefit some natives, it would hurt others. The Standmarks, who ran the only local store on the reservation, would suffer a loss in profits, while the natives to whom they sold their goods would benefit from the lower prices.

The study admits outright that there would be "less emphasis on subsistence economy; more emphasis on cash economy," and quickly passes on to the next point as if this dramatic change was to be easily achieved, while ignoring the adverse effects of it: loss of identity, confusion, ambivalence, alienation, nihilism, apathy, alcoholism, drug abuse, and all the other concomitant effects long associated with deracination and acculturation. Thus, the genocidal effects of such development are not only taken for granted but freely admitted. Perhaps Darbyshire and Associates should have added another "bullet" to the list of environmental impacts: cultural genocide.

Again the study reinforces the language and terms of the ANLCS, unwittingly underscoring the collusion between big business and the native corporations. It notes for example the "potential financial benefits to residents accrued from lease of subsurface estate and surface rights-of-way through regional and village Native corporations" (12). It further notes the genocidal impact of this development: "If the majority of new residents are white, [Nyoteks] could be reduced to minority status. Local values, beliefs, customs, traditional authority lines, and group norms could be challenged," which is indeed the unstated objective of such development.

The study also notes the potential for increased racial strife, of "intergroup conflicts at work and school" (13), thus resulting in "lower productivity at work and school, due to preoccupation with conflicts." The study quite freely admits that such development can be expected to have a negative effect on the acquisition of literacy.

In assessing the potential impact of oil and natural gas development, the study makes the following ominous observation:

> should a major oil discovery be made at existing exploratory wells ... or should there be a considerable increase in world market demand for natural gas thereby warranting production, it is highly likely that the increased levels of activity will create a considerable impact on [Nyotek] and its residents. (21)

The study goes on to forecast the potential impact of oil and natural gas development on the environment, noting that "degradation of the regional and local environment can be expected to accompany oil and gas development in the area." A number of "accidental occurrences" could have ruinous effects, including the following: "loss of well control, pipeline breaks, tanker accidents, and failure of storage tanks" (22). In light of the natural disaster inflicted on the entire region by the Exxon Valdez "accident" several years later, these assessments were indeed prescient, underscoring the tendency of potential impacts to become real ones. The study concludes that "in addition to these accidental occurrences, a considerable degree of degradation can be expected as a result of the routine day-to-day operation of the production facilities. These impacts include:

- short-term disturbance from the discharge of drilling mud, cuttings, and solid waste;

- long-term shoreline alteration;

- soils displacement from dredging and filling;

- flow of water across wetlands blocked by access roads;

- waterfowl nesting areas disrupted by high noise levels;

- potential for contamination of drinking water; and

- potential for disruption of essential fish and wildlife reproductive habitat. (22)

Thus, in a grimly ironic twist of conquest, the Athabascans were induced to "sign" their own death warrant. If the ANLCS acted as a birth certificate for the exploitive enterprises of transnational corporations in these borderlands, it similarly signified the eclipse of the indigenous culture. These legalistic words had a more violent impact on the wilderness of the native than any natural disaster, influx of settlers, or military invasion ever had, insofar as they prepared the way for the invasion of the Athabascan's homeland by a consortium of corporations: Diamond-Chuitna, Placer Amex Inc., Mobil Oil Inc., Chevron USA, Chugiak Timber Inc., and Simasko Production Co, with their skidders, bulldozers, buzz saws, drilling rigs, and strip-mining equipment—the mechanized arsenal with which the colonialist conquers native lands. Instead of helmets, these New Age neocolonialists wear hardhats, but the genocidal effects of their activities are as violent if not more so. If not "genocide with good intentions," it is at least genocide with a smile and a "settlement" check.

Although the conflicts over the oil drilling and coal mining operations were significant, it was the conflict over the logging operations that became a flashpoint for racial tensions on the reservation and its immediate environs. Even the deployment of the word "environment," however, reflects an ideological bias that privileges the signifying practices of the dominant culture as opposed to those of the indigene. While the term "environment" connotes the holistic, systematic relations of the Athabascan's natural world, it is empty of the spiritual content that governs the Athabascan's relationship to nature. The Athabascan would use the term "environment" only reluctantly, for it signifies nothing of his or her spiritual relationship to "the land" or the "earth," terms that more effectively signify the bond the Athabascan traditionally experienced relative to his or her homeland. This identification is so strong it is virtually synonymous with nature. Signification, thus, underscores the fundamental difference between the Euro-American and Native American in their respective attitudes toward nature: while the colonizer names nature after himself, the native names himself after nature. For the Athabascan, not only "subsistence," but identity itself is inseparable from the land. Therefore, the conflicts that threaten this relationship, that weaken the native's bond with nature, strike to the very soul of the Athabascan inasmuch as they diminish his or her sense of self, of identity, by cutting off the Athabascan's identity at its very source. The Athabascan severed from the earth is a disconnected signifier, an empty and vulnerable signifier, a dandelion loosed on the wind and severed from the stem that is rooted to its native soil.

Little wonder then that the Athabascans should resist with such violence the violent impact that drilling rigs and chain saws are having on their native lands. Before describing the pedagogical implications of these cultural conflicts, I want to describe the most volatile and contentious of these eco-wars.

The Chugiak Timber Company versus The People of Nyotek

The roads penetrating the seemingly infinite spaces of the Alaskan natives did not end with the Alkan Highway or the North Slope Haul Road. They merely gave way to a network of narrower, unpaved roads that granted the colonizer in general, and loggers in particular, access to the heart of the native's darkness, even as they deepened that darkness. Like the "superyeoman" who ventured to the ends of the British isles on the great North road of E. M. Forster's *Howard's End*, the loggers of the Chugiak Timber Mill were as industrious and as eager to profit from the native's homeland as their counterparts employed by Placer Amex Inc., Shell Oil Company, ARCO Alaska, DYCO Petroleum Corporation, Chevron USA, Inc., Alaska Gas Exploration Associates (AGEA), and a host of other transnational corporations whose covetous, colonizing gaze had become fixed upon the lands of the Athabascan as a consequence of the proven reservoirs of natural resources those lands contained. The entire region was on the verge of an economic explosion, of yet another boom, the latest in a series of "booms" that have characterized the history of Alaska and impacted the subsistence lifeways of its native peoples, who if not the least, were often the last to benefit from these "booms." The tribal council consequently commissioned Darbyshire and Associates to conduct an environmental impact study (1981), to analyze the effects of these proposed commercial enterprises on the native's natural habitat. The findings of Darbyshire and Associates relative to the operations of the Chugiak Timber Mill are significant:

[Chugiak Timber Mills, Inc.] has run a logging operation and a chip mill in [Nyotek] for 7 years. In addition to the areas covered by the plant, the dock, and the camp, the company's timber sales cover 275,000 acres. According to [Jim Douglas], Senior Vice President, Chugiak Timber Mills has no plans for any type of expansion of operations in or near [Nyotek]. The company anticipates continued operation at the same level indefinitely. At present the mill employs between 50 and 75 persons on a year round basis. [Douglas] stated that, as always, the company is interested in hiring local people. (27)

Darbyshire and Associate's assessment is significant for a number of reasons. First of all, it contains several claims that are problematic at best. For example, the assertion that Chugiak Timber Mills has no plans "for any type of expansion" is called into question by a statement in the preceding paragraph that informs the reader that "The Alaska Department of Natural Resources will conduct a bid-sale for 5-year timber rights on 48,000 acres located just east of the Chuitna coal fields and north of the Nyotek Native Corporation Lands" (27). This is precisely the sort of expansion that sparked the concerns of the Nyotek natives, and prompted them to commission the environmental impact study in the first place. The announcement of this sale of lands for timber harvesting would seem to directly contradict the reassurances of the Senior Vice President that the lumber mill had no plans "for any type of expansion of operations in or near Nyotek." This is just the sort of intentional double speak Native Americans have had to contend with for centuries in their dealings with their American colonizers, and underscores yet again the role that signification plays in the enterprise of cultural imperialism.

Signification underscores the disparity between assertions and reality in other areas of Darbyshire and Associates "study." They permit the Senior Vice President of the logging mill to offer the native another assurance, which if not false, was at least questionable: the assurance that, "as always, the company is interested in hiring local people" (27). As the Athabascans would assert, however, that while Chugiak Timber Co. may be "interested" in hiring them, it rarely did. Given the large population of available Athabascan males, enough to more than meet the demands for a labor pool of fifty to seventy-five workers, why were never more than a handful ever employed by the mill? Those in charge of hiring at the mill countered that they did not hire Athabascans because those they had hired tended to show up for work drunk or skip work altogether, thus reinscribing the negative stereotype of the Native American as a drunk, and further reinforcing the Athabascans' claim that the mill's hiring practices were racist.

The Nyotek Athabascans had long complained of the lumber mill's racist hiring practices. Yet, their grievances were compromised by yet another example of the "peculiar intimacy" that typifies colonizer-colonized relations: the mill had constructed for free a series of redwood homes in the village to offset the needs of its growing population for affordable housing. Thus, a part of the village took on the aspect of a quiet, affluent cul-de-sac in suburban American. Yet even in this, the superyeomen of the lumber mills took on the visage of gift-bearing Greeks, for the new homes the natives inhabited accelerated the erosion of the very subsistence lifestyle they were fighting to preserve by enmeshing them even deeper in the lifestyle of their colonizers, to say nothing of deepening their debt of gratitude to the lumber mill. With this single act, the Chugiak Lumber Mill defused the insurrectionist attitudes of many Athabascans, driving those feelings underground. The repression of these animosities, however, only enervated them, assuring that their inevitable eruption would only be the more violent.

Darbyshire and Associate's study is significant for the things it omits as well. It says nothing for example of the lumber mill's adverse impact on the Athabascan's subsistence moose-hunting practices. I was witnessing a reenactment of the same history that had been played out on the Great Plains a century earlier, wherein the buffalo herds, upon which the Lakota and other tribes depended for their food, shelter, clothing, and spirituality, were slaughtered by whites for their tongues and their hides. This arena of conflict between the Athabascan and the logger was also characterized by a grim irony: once "logged-out," the forest comprised an ideal browsing habitat for the moose, which were unwittingly attracted into these "kill zones" in such large numbers every family in the timber camp could count on a freezer full of moose meat to see them through the winter, while the freezers of many of their Athabascan counterparts in the village remained empty. This topos of conflict thus also reinscribed the asymmetrical power relations that privileged the colonizer over the colonized. While the Athabascans had to patrol the logging roads for hours on end in hopes of a chance encounter with a moose, the loggers had merely to run to their "skidders," grab a high-powered rifle from the cabin, take aim and fire. While Athabascans had to spend hours quartering and transporting the meat back to the village, the loggers merely had to winch the half-ton carcass onto the bed of a logging truck and transport it back to the "shop" where it was quartered and converted into steaks, hamburger, jerky, and sausage in a fraction of the time it took the Athabascan to achieve the same end.

These differences produced animosities between the races. For many Athabascans it was more than they could bear in silence. Not only was the lumber mill denying them jobs, it was taking the meat off their tables. Yet, the Athabascans found themselves in an ambivalent and divided position, for it was hard to criticize the enterprise that had built their new homes. In this fashion, the lumber mill purchased the freedom to continue its oppressive and genocidal practices. Their logging practices thus contributed directly to the sharp decline in local moose population, despite the shortening of the moose-hunting season to a three-week period in September. Bulls with trophy-sized racks were taken from the Athabascan's homeland. Once word reached Anchorage that these Boone and Crockett giants were being taken from the lands encompassing the Nyotek reservation, a different breed of hunter began appearing on the scene: the recreational, big-game hunter. Thus, there were not only fewer bulls to mate with the cows, but instead of being mated by the biggest and strongest bulls, the cows were mated instead by the younger and weaker ones.

The heard inevitably went into sharp decline, a fact observed to me by Jimmy St. Claire, the bush pilot who serviced Nyotek from Anchorage. Whereas he used to count sixty or seventy moose on a typical "run" from Anchorage, now he was lucky if he saw one or two. As a result, the Athabascans were obliged to shoot moose on sight, whether it was in season or not, in the woods or in the village. If they wanted to supplement their diet with this traditional staple they had no other choice. A single mature bull when dressed out could yield four hundred pounds of meat: enough to feed an extended Athabascan family for a year.

Emotions over the situation were raw, simmering at or near the surface. For many Athabascans the loss of this source of meat was not worth the homes they had gained. These feelings were exacerbated by the allegedly racist hiring practices of the mill that denied them the opportunity to offset this loss through gainful employment. To this segment of the Athabascan population, the advantages of the lumber mill were far outweighed by the disadvantages. Their sentiment was further exacerbated by the fact that the mill was under no obligation to "reclaim" the forests it had logged. However, the Athabascans were willing to overlook this, since these areas comprised ideal moose habitat, which they could then hunt once the loggers had moved on. The impending sale of adjacent lands for logging further alarmed them, for instead of eradicating or even containing at current levels these logging operations, they were now faced with the potential expansion of logging activities, despite the Senior Vice President's assurances to the contrary. Like their counterparts in the lower forty-eight, they had been lied to one too many times to have any confidence in those assurances and indeed took them as proof that their own worst fears were warranted.

Another aspect of the lumber mill's operations rubbed more salt in the Athabascans wounds: the mill was situated on the same hallowed ground as the Athabascans' ancestral village. The tsunamis generated by the epic quake of 1964 had forced the relocation of that village to safer and higher ground: the bluffs four miles to the north that marked its present location. In this pre-ANLCS period, the Athabascans could not have foreseen that this historical site in a few short years would be occupied by their colonizers. More than a few Athabascans found this to be a galling and intolerable affront to their heritage.

For these reasons then the Athabascans felt increasingly resentful of the lumber mill and its employees, many of whom bussed their children to the reservation school. It was a volatile situation, lacking only a spark to ignite it. Ironically, that spark was provided not by the lumber mill, but by the school itself, whose principal hired a logger's wife instead of a native woman as his secretary. This touched off a racial conflict that consumed the entire village-timber camp community in a two year legal battle whose repercussions spread throughout the district, the region, and the state, involving in due course the Board of the School District, the Alaska State Trooper's Office, the Alaska Human Rights Commission, the Alaska State Supreme Court, and the Federal Bureau of Investigation. Whatever animosities had been repressed to that point, erupted into the open in an escalating conflict that divided teacher from teacher, student from student, Athabascan from Athabascan, white from white, Athabascan from white, student from teacher, parent from student, principal from faculty, tribal council president from principal, and teachers from parents, fracturing this bicultural contact zone along virtually every conceivable fault-line and adversely affecting not only friendships, but careers.

The sad irony is that the desire to protect their ancestral ways, which depended upon subsistence hunting and fishing, is what induced the Athabascans to sign the ANLCS in the first place. However, once profit taking and not subsistence became the prime motive for the native corporation, the pressure to abandon the traditional, nonprofitable subsistence lifestyle and to "develop the wilderness" instead was intensified. In the last analysis, the dominant culture got the Athabascans themselves to do what they had been unable to do: sign a "settlement" that required them to eradicate their own subsistence lifestyle in order to receive payment for the lands they sold. The ANLCS is a monument to the insidious ingenuity of the colonizer's signifying practices, as embodied in the treaty-making documents that have for centuries been deployed to wrest "title" of native lands away from the native. As Mander writes,

> profit, growth, expansion, and conversion of natural resources to dollar-producing income were now the managers' driving motives. It was quickly obvious to the new class of native business people that traditional subsistence activity would not turn a profit—unlike cutting down forests, mining for minerals, drilling for oil . . . and promoting high impact tourism. (293)

The legacies of the ANLCS are as notorious as they are numerous. It not only ended native title to the land, but seriously threatened indigenous subsistence lifestyles, increased the welfare dependency of the native population, intensified the frictions between native peoples, subverted indigenous structures of government, undermined the autonomy of native peoples, and opened the door to rampant commercial exploitation of the resources on native lands by transnational corporations, which are among "the most economically voracious organizations in the world" (294). Argues Mander, "the ANLCS has affected everything: family relations, traditional patterns of leadership and decision making, customs of sharing . . . the entire native way of life. The village has lost its political and social autonomy" (295).

The neocolonial institutions of the transnational corporation and the borderland school have had a far more debilitating impact on the Athabascan subculture than the more overtly colonizing activities of the militarist and the missionary. Observes Paul Ongtooguk, "now, when they are coming in after the land they come not with soldiers, but with people carrying briefcases" (qtd. in Mander, 294) as part of an attempt to "re-create Main Street on the tundra" (296). Consequently, what is being effaced in the borderlands of Alaska is not only the ability to be different, but the right to be different. Speaking on behalf of the Yupik Eskimo leaders, Art Davison underscores the Other's desire to remain as such: "Please try to fathom our great desire to survive in a way somewhat different from yours" (qtd. in Mander 297). Mander reinforces the assertion that one of the arenas of bicultural conflict stems from the native's desire to remain native: "It is their profound desire to be themselves, to be true to their own values, that has led to the present confrontation" (302).

Yet the Indian's attempt to be Indian threatens the hegemony of the colonizer, intensifying efforts to eradicate Indianness. The very act of self-assertion is itself an insurrection against the assimilationist aims of the colonizer. For the Other, identity and insurrection are inseparable: I am, therefore I am subversive. Further, without "title" to their land, the Athabascans cannot be themselves insofar as indigenous identity is inseparable from the land. Thus, any attempt to reassert themselves as natives is inevitably yoked to reestablishing their autonomy over the land—a struggle that brings them into direct conflict with the interests of the transnational corporations. Thus, the landscape itself is the site of a violent contest between the mutually opposed interests of these two parties—it remains the prize to be possessed in this violent, bicultural tug-of-war. On the one hand, Glacier Amex, Chevron USA, and Chugiak Timber working through the Nyotek Native Corporation, are seeking to establish their "title" to land; on the other, the Nyotek tribal council is seeking to "reestablish tribal control over the land," as well as the autonomy of tribal forms of government and the preservation of ancestral lifeways (300). For the Alaska native, wealth and profit are defined in terms of a holistic relationship to the earth that foregrounds a subsistence, as opposed to a cash-based, lifestyle. Argues Antoinette Helmer of Craig, Alaska, "profit to natives means a good life derived from the land and sea . . . This land we hold in trust is our wealth. It is the only wealth we could possibly pass on to our children. . . . Without our homelands we become true paupers" (qtd. in Mander 301).

Composing the Eco-Wars

To be not only relevant but ethical in such a milieu, pedagogy must somehow seek for ways to foreground the native's landscape and the conflicts immanent in it, not only as a vehicle for a more active residency in the borderlands, but as a means for overcoming the debilitating effects of bicultural alienation through reconnection to an ancestral topos. Further, composition instruction foregrounding the local cultural conflicts could not only reinforce instruction in borderland narratives, but in the Foxfire project as well, privileging the acquisition of critical, as well as academic literacy. In the search for the "pedagogical arts of [this] contact zone," I had to look no further than the local cultural conflicts associated with the environment and with schooling (Pratt 40). These too became the "alter/native" texts to be read and written, the "generative themes" which not only help native students to "unveil" their colonized world, but to alter it as well.

What then are the pedagogical implications of these local cultural conflicts? What are the constructive uses of cultural conflict in the composition classroom? How might the conflicts immanent in the environment and in schooling be used in the composition classroom as vehicles of academic and critical literacy? How might the acquisition of these literacies be yoked to native resistance struggle, as part of an effort to make learning in the borderlands more meaningful to these marginalized students, to make the borderland residency of such students more participatory and their futures more livable? If one of the goals of resistance pedagogy is to orient instruction, not to the lived reality of the colonizer, but to the experiential base of the colonized, than do not these local cultural conflicts comprise a facet of that experience that warrants inquiry? Can not these conflicts, in short, be posed as a series of problems to native students to be studied, analyzed, read, debated, and written about, as a preliminary means of solving them? Could not the inquiry we had launched into the conflicted contact zone of the Inuit and the Lakota, as embodied in the borderland narratives of Black Elk, Lame Deer, and Farley Mowat serve as a springboard for an inquiry into the Athabascans' own environmental contact zone, and the conflicts associated with it?

Before elaborating this model for conflict-oriented pedagogy, however, I want to offer a qualification: in this chapter I am not merely writing of my borderland experiences of yesteryear, but of the possibilities I see for enriching borderland pedagogy in the future. The focus of this chapter, therefore, is not merely descriptive but illustrative. My purpose here is not merely to describe the constructive uses to which these local conflicts were put in the classroom, but to illustrate as well the pedagogical possibilities for foregrounding cultural conflict as a vehicle for the acquisition of literacy, critical as well as academic, and for a more participatory residency in the borderlands. With regard to the pedagogical possibilities enunciated here, I share James Berlin's hope "that teachers will find in them suggestions for developing course materials and activities appropriate to their own situations" (115).

One implication of these eco-wars was the effect they had on the group dynamics of my classes. An inquiry foregrounding cross-cultural conflicts has the potential to become contentious in the extreme, especially in a classroom comprised not only of Athabascan students who lived on the reservation, but of white students who lived in the timber camp, and whose fathers worked as loggers, roustabouts, and foremen at the mill, the oil rig, and the hydroelectric plant. Further, virtually every student, Athabascan as well as white, female as well as male, had participated in family moose hunts as part of a lifestyle that was a hybrid between subsistence and cash-based practices. Many of the boys and a few of the girls were good shots with a rifle and had "taken" their own moose. All were knowledgeable in the intricacies of the moose hunt; and most held strong opinions on the politics of moose hunting that divided almost exclusively along racial lines. Many shared the attitudes of their parents regarding the viewpoints enunciated by the other side. Thus, these eco-wars served to reinforce the racial divisions of the timber-camp/reservation community, transforming the classroom into a microcosm of that community.

These environmental conflicts, however, affected much more than the group dynamics in the classroom. They provided the "alter/native" texts for a Freirean approach to borderland pedagogy: one that afforded students of both races the opportunity to "read" these conflicts and then write about them, to read and write their own world as a means not only of naming, but of transforming it.

Words in the Wilderness: Praxis Takes to the Woods

This inquiry into cultural conflicts foregrounds a number of goals. By mastering the signifying practices of their colonizers, as embodied in "texts" such as the ANLCS, Athabascans might avoid being victimized by them. By learning to read between the lines of those texts they might avoid the further reduction or loss of their autonomy; by "reading" the white spaces in between the colonizer's words, they might maintain their own "space," might more effectively resist the colonizer's intrusions into that space—intrusions that are habitually initiated with the Word, that is through signification, through a rhetoric of negotiation that disguises disadvantages as advantages, theft as trade, conquest as autonomy, and a "rip-off" of the land as "title" to it—negotiations that accelerate the Other's slide down the slippery slope of signification, a descent which ends with the catastrophic closure of cultural genocide. Such a resituated pedagogy encourages native students to assume a more active role in the preservation of their homeland and their traditional lifeways, and in the resistance struggle their people were waging to achieve those ends, not only when they graduated to adulthood themselves, but now. Analysis of cultural conflicts in the academic arena should not be confined to a mere academic exercise, but will hopefully generate actions in the broader and more immediate political and cultural spheres: actions aimed at resolving those conflicts.

If white students could be made aware of the adverse effects upon the environment of logging, coal-mining, and oil-drilling activities, then their future complicity in these activities might be modified, or at least made contingent upon a commitment to re-claim the lands by these corporations. Such a repositioned peda-gogy raises the possibility that the future participation of students in logging, coal-mining, or oil-drilling activities would not be di-vorced from ethical concerns or from the negative impact these activities traditionally were having on the moose populations, on salmon migrations, and hence on the indigenous peoples who de-pended upon these for their subsistence. Environmental corporatism is not necessarily incompatible with the subsistence needs of the Athabascan; it is only incompatible with those needs if its practices take no account of them.

In this section I would like to articulate some of the possibilities for the constructive use of cultural conflicts in the composition classroom. Following Freire's cue, these environmental conflicts could be posed to students as a series of problems not just to be studied, investigated, debated, and written about within the classroom, but to be acted upon and resolved beyond it. What possibilities does such a focus present for the practitioner, in the borderlands and elsewhere?

As part of an ongoing focus on the signifying practices of the colonizer that have historically oppressed the Native American in general, and the Athabascan in particular, the ANLCS could be revisited. The signifying practices embodied in this "settlement" could be interrogated within the context of an historical inquiry into the signifying practices extant in other treaties between the United States government and Native Americans. A series of criti-cal questions could be posed to students linking this text to recent Athabascan history, and positioning both within the broader his-torical context of colonization through treaty-making: Should the ANLCS have been signed by Athabascans? Should it have been signed by all Athabascans? What were the advantages and disad-vantages of signing it? Do the disadvantages outweigh the advan-tages? What are the negative legacies of it? Does it pose a threat to the subsistence lifeways of the Athabascan, and if so how? Should Athabascans actively seek its repeal, and if so how might this goal be achieved? Should Athabascans have surrendered "separate na-tion" status conferred by the designation of "Reservation"? Should they have accepted corporate status? What are the legal, political, cultural, and ethical implications of this shift in signification from reservation to corporation? What are its implications for the construction of Athabascan identity? How does the ANLCS reinscribe other treaties "signed" by other Native American peoples in other places and in other times? Does it reinscribe a history of colonization dating back five hundred years, and if so how? Were Congress and big business guilty of collusion in the ANLCS for the purposes of colonization?

These questions could drive a semester-long inquiry into the origins and legacies of the ANLCS that could not only be linked to instruction in American history, but that could dialogically reinforce instruction in the Foxfire program and the borderland reading project. Students in the Foxfire publication class, for example, could be dispatched into the local community to document the attitudes of Athabascans concerning the ANLCS, adding a contemporary chapter to a Foxfire publication that heretofore privileged the recuperation of the "authentic," "orthodox" Athabascan to the exclusion of all others. A pedagogy foregrounding local cultural conflicts could not only be linked to Foxfire pedagogy, but could reconfigure it in significant and useful ways: appropriating it as a vehicle for critical, as well as academic literacy, for the recovery of contemporary as well as traditional Athabascans culture, and for participatory as well as literate residency in the borderlands.

Such a conflict-oriented pedagogy could also dialogically reinforce instruction in the reading and writing class. The ANLCS could be reread as a text that reinscribes the colonizing effects of the realist novel, reinforcing subversive readings of London's *Call*, Forster's *Howard's End,* and Conrad's *Darkness*, as part of a broader indictment of the signifying practices the colonizer deploys to justify the theft of native lands. This is an inquiry into the role of representation that would extend from the aesthetic to the political realm, dialogically reinforcing instruction in reading and writing. Indeed, Berlin argues that an inquiry into the signifying practices of the dominant culture comprises a central focus of social epistemic pedagogy: "Social-epistemic rhetoric is the study and critique of signifying practices in their relation to subject formation within the framework of economic, social, and political conditions" (77), to which I would add the category of the aesthetic. A pedagogy foregrounding cross-cultural conflict would be remiss if it did not include an inquiry into the signifying practices that characterize the colonizer-colonized relationship, as Berlin asserts: "signifying practices are always at the center of conflict and contention" (82).

Further, this inquiry into the signifying practices and negative legacies of the ANLCS could be linked to a broader inquiry into the conflicts associated with the environment. Again, a series of problem-posing questions related to coal mining, oil drilling, natural gas exploration, and logging would drive such an inquiry: should the corporations that engage in these activities be required by law to "reclaim" the land? Does logging have an adverse impact on local moose populations? Does it pose a threat to native subsistence hunting? What should be done to curb or eliminate this threat? Should loggers be prohibited from hunting moose on lands the Athabascan sold to the logging company? Should they be prevented from killing moose in the areas they log? What legal rights do nonnatives have on native lands? Does the Constitution of the United States apply on an Indian Reservation? Do the normal guarantees of freedom apply to nonnatives? Should whites in other words be free to hunt, fish, and trap on native lands? Is the Athabascans' attempt to prohibit these activities a form of reverse discrimination? Are the hiring practices of the Chugiak Timber Co. discriminatory, as has been alleged? Should the Chugiak Timber Co. be obligated to hire more natives, all natives, or a certain percentage of natives? What is wrong with logging practices as they are currently conducted on lands adjacent to the reservation? And what should be done to eliminate those "wrongs?" How have the Athabascans benefited from logging activities? Do these benefits offset the adverse environmental, social, and economic impacts of logging? Should the timber camp be relocated to less politicized terrain? Do the Athabascans have a legal or ethical right to insist on such relocation?

A series of similar questions could drive inquiries into the proposed development of the Beluga coalfields, offshore oil deposits, and natural gas reservoirs. Moreover, these inquiries could be linked to a number of critical writing activities. In the prewriting phases, students could be given the opportunity to discover their own voices on these issues through a series of directed freewrites in journals. They could be asked to conduct semester-long inquiries into one or more of these issues. As part of this inquiry, they could be required to interview adults in both the reservation and timber camp communities, and these interviews could comprise yet another chapter in the Foxfire publication foregrounding contemporary aspects of Athabascan existence. They could likewise be required to devise an action plan for resolving the problem or conflict, and to initiate steps to implement that action plan. Students could be grouped in small collaborative teams or pairs to conduct phases of the inquiry, to write up the results. Questions generated by this inquiry could become the subject of small group discussions or broader classroom debates, in a further effort to help students come into voice on a particular "theme." In order to develop their own critical voices, students could be asked to keep a running response journal in which they recorded their own evolving attitudes on a given issue. Thus, the recovery of local cultural conflicts could be associated with every phase of the writing process, from prewriting to brainstorming and research, from independent to collaborative writing activities, from solitary reflection to group discussions. Members from the community, Athabascan as well as white, representing the views of opposing sides could similarly be invited into the classroom as part of the inquiry: loggers as well as native moose hunters, the foreman of the lumber mill as well as the president of the tribal council.

When students had reached a level of mastery relative to an issue they could be given the opportunity for disseminating that knowledge to their peers in the form of oral presentations, could be allowed to model the role of an arguer, of a public intellectual, of a civic-minded citizen, of a knower and a knowledge-maker, as a means of preparing for presentations in more public forums: town hall meetings, tribal council meetings, school board meetings, environmental impact hearings, land lease sales hearings, commencement addresses, etc. These public forums, not the composition classroom, are the necessary destination of critical inquiry and the agonistic discourses that evolve from it. Students could be allowed to model the role of public intellectual in the classroom as a prelude to assuming that role in reality, in the community at large, thereby entering and shaping the public conversation being waged over these conflicts.

A more live-action approach to the acquisition of critical literacy could be adopted as well, one that allowed students to model the roles of those engaged in these debates: a School Board member or

Tribal Council President, concerned parent or Athabascan resident, logger or native moose hunter, sports recreationist or Fish and Game board member, Senior Vice President of Chugiak Timber or Nyotek Native Corporation board member, game warden or Athabascan poacher, modeling the discourses associated with these diverse viewpoints at a mock press conference, a public hearing, a courtroom trial, or a school board meeting. These role-playing activities could be expected to empower students' public presentations insofar as they would allow the students to challenge, defend, rebut, refine, and develop their viewpoints in classroom debate. The classroom could thus be transformed into a "contact zone" of persuasive discourses, where the diverse opinions of potential rhetoricians are brought into "contact" with one another. As Cain states,

> stage the debate itself, involve the students in it, and represent the polarized positions along with any that fall between. Expose students to what their elders are squabbling about, and empower them to grasp and articulate why these issues matter so they can gauge where they stand themselves. ("Teaching" xix–xx)

Cain's views are similar to those articulated by Min-Zhan Lu in "Writing as Repositioning," in which she advocates a pedagogy that enables students to "reposition" themselves relative to a heteroglossia of discourses, as opposed to being the passive objects to which knowledge is transmitted as part of a unitary, teacherly discourse. Graff theorizes a similar position foregrounding the constructive uses of conflict:

> So let's instead seize upon the conflicts that separate us and define them as issues that we can explore with one another and with students. Let's make the institution a place for serious learning and for political self-consciousness without insisting that it become single-mindedly politicized, captive to a single ideology. (124–27)

Instead of screening students from these local cultural conflicts, instead of sheltering them from the legacy of oppression, we should evolve pedagogical arts of the contact zone that enable them to directly confront that which oppresses. As Cain argues, teachers need to "imagine how we can profitably make education coherent through foregrounding conflict and empowering it as a principle" (xxxii). These activities could also be expected to foster a stronger sense of voice, purpose, and audience in their writing. Letters addressed to editors of metropolitan papers, speeches addressed to members of the tribal council or school board, petitions addressed to the principal, all might function as a more action-oriented complement to the consciousness-raising, "reflective" component of Freirean pedagogy.

This is why it is paramount that the "unveiling" of the indigene's world through analysis be followed by the alteration of that world through action. In the final analysis, literacy must become resistance, or it withers on its intellectual vine for want of any useful role to play in the Other's conflicted existence, for want of any relevance to his or her lived reality, for want of the stimulus of activity. Like any appendage that has no use, it atrophies for want of exercise in an apolitical climate.

Toward a Literacy of Resistance

The white man takes such things as words and literatures for granted. . . . He has dulled and multiplied the word, and words have begun to close in on him. He is sated and insensitive; his regard for language—for the Word itself—as an instrument of creation has nearly diminished to the point of no return. It may be that he will perish by the Word.

—Momaday 89

Instead of being used only as an exit, the door that leads from the composition classroom must be used instead as an entrance into the conflicted topoi of the contact zone where resistance is already being waged. Instead of being viewed as a door that closes off academic conversations, it should be viewed as a threshold for extending that conversation into those other, nonacademic sites where cultural conflicts are being contested. Ultimately, analysis must acquire legs, must get off its sedentary intellectual behind and onto its recolonizing feet, must introduce the world at large to its wild native tongue, if it is to stand any chance of recolonizing the world with the word. Otherwise, it must be content to have no more relation to the world than a bowl of cold, alphabet soup sitting on a table in the colonizer's kitchen. In the bicultural contact zone, literacy that does not lead to resistance is merely another form of nonexistence.

What actions then are available to the borderland student seeking to devise an action plan for resolving these cultural conflicts? When converted to resistance, what forms might such critical literacy assume? The first phase involves organization on the local level, beginning at the school and expanding outward to include the community. To this end, students could form a society of their peers whose stated mission is the preservation of ancestral lifeways and the environmental habitats upon which they depend—a society whose goals are the reassertion of indigenous autonomy over the land, the responsible development of that land, and/or the productive coexistence of the Athabascan and the transnational corporation. They could recruit members throughout the school and the community. They could sponsor consciousness raising activities, elect officers, dispense flyers, circulate petitions, call for public meetings, address the tribal council and the policymakers of the Chugiak Lumber Mill, write letters to the editors of metropolitan papers, stage protests as media events against environmental degradations, expand membership to include adults from the community. They could call for town meetings in which Athabascans could confront the corporate hierarchy of the lumber mill with their concerns over the impact of logging on subsistence moose-hunting activities. They could form a bridge of activism and consciousness raising with the tribal council, joining its effort to resist the incursions of the colonizer. They could seek to engage the corporate echelons of Glacier Amex, Chevron USA, and Simasko Corp., in similar public dialogue, seeking guarantees of environmental reclamation, for employment, and for safeguards against environmental degradations that negatively impact their subsistence fishing and hunting activities. Ultimately, they could run for political office, on the local, regional, or state level. They could invite speakers already invested in the struggle to preserve the environment, to act as consultants sharing their knowledge of tactics and grass roots organization, with a proven history for waging similar resistance in other places: in the redwood forests of Northern California, in the wetlands of

Florida, on the coastal communities of California where offshore drilling is degrading the environment, on the open seas where fisheries are being depleted through gill-netting.

The conflicted topoi of the lumber mill, the logging road and the clear-cut forest, of the coal field and the oil rig could be picketed with placards expressing their concerns. Metropolitan media could be contacted to give coverage to such activities. Corporate offices in Anchorage could become the sites of similar activities. Symbolic activities depicting the degradation of the Athabascans' homeland could be "staged" for the media as part of these activities: events involving role-playing and costumes, satire, parody, and song. Public hearings could be held in Anchorage as well, in an effort to recruit others to their cause, natives as well as white. In short, the indigene must wage his and her struggle on two fronts, in two directions: the native must struggle to repossess all that is ancestral; concomitantly, the native must master the signifying practices, must mimic the discursive strategies of the colonizer in order to avoid being victimized by them in the future as they have in the past. Thus, with one arm the indigene must hold onto the past; with the other they must fend off the blows in the present. Their resistance on one front makes possible recovery on the Other.

Once solidarity had been generated on the local level, it could be pursued on the regional and state level. A systematic campaign to form an alliance of Alaskan natives against the encroachments of transnational corporations could be initiated by phone, by mail, and by e-mail, in an effort to extend the debate from the localized community of the Nyotek Athabascan to a much broader political and cultural arena, in an effort to broaden their base of support, to widen their stance so that it not only encompassed the ground under their feet, but the lands of all Alaskan natives.

Such solidarity is a critical step to the long-term health and prospects of such a movement. One of the critical strategies the colonizer deploys to perpetuate the subjugation of the Other is to fragment the native population and then deal with their resistance piecemeal, thus minimizing resistance by localizing it. The native must recognize and resist this tendency of the colonizer to confine resistance to the local level. The ANLCS affords abundant evidence of this strategy of subjugation inasmuch as it divided Alaska's native population into fourteen regions, each with its own "corporation," each of which was then recognized by the colonizer as the representative or spokesperson for the peoples of that region. This strategy reinscribes the colonizing practices of the last four centuries wherein the United States government negotiated separate treaties with the subsects of various tribes (Iroquois, Shoshone, Lakota) instead of treating them as a nation. As Freire observes,

> It is in the interest of the oppressor to weaken the oppressed still further, to isolate them, to create and deepen rifts among them. This is done by varied means, from the repressive methods of the government bureaucracy to the forms of cultural action with which they manipulate the people by giving them the impression that they are being helped. The more a region or area is broken down into "local communities" . . . the more alienation is intensified. And the more alienated people are, the easier it is to divide them and keep them divided. These focalized forms of action . . . (especially in rural areas), hamper the oppressed from perceiving reality critically and keep them isolated from the problems of oppressed men in other areas. (137-38)

The strategy of designating a corporate board to represent the native population of a region underscores Freire's observation that "the oppressors do not favor promoting the community as a whole, but rather selected leaders":

> the latter state, by preserving a state of alienation, hinders the emergence of consciousness and critical intervention in a total reality. In addition, the dominators try to present themselves as saviors of the men they dehumanize and divide. This messianism, however, cannot conceal their true intentions: to save themselves. They want to save their riches, their power, their way of life: the things that enable them to subjugate others. (142)

This is why the organization of the people is a first critical step away from subjugation, a step that the colonizer fears almost as much as the native's open insurrection, for it weakens the colonizer's position, destabilizes it insofar as the colonizer's control of the Other no longer tends toward totalization. Argues Freire, "In the dialogical theory of action, the organization of the people presents the antagonistic opposite of this manipulation" (176).

Therefore, to be truly dialogic pedagogy must not only integrate instruction across the borderland curriculum, it must integrate analysis and action, literacy and resistance, consciousness and conflict, pedagogy and politics, instruction and insurrection. One form this activism can therefore take is organization, on the local, regional, state, national, and even international level. For example, the Athabascan's quest for agency could be accompanied with an analysis of the Hawaiian's quest for sovereignty. Thus, the effort to organize on the local level of the school, by forming "clubs" or "societies" that actively seek the preservation of the Athabascan's subculture and local environment, by building bridges to other organizations in the Athabascan community, such as the tribal council, could serve to stimulate organization on a broader scale, between Nyotek and other Athabascan villages, between the Athabascans and the Aleuts and the Eskimo, between the native peoples of Alaska and the Inuit of Canada, and between these native peoples and their cousins in the lower forty-eight and Hawaii. The borderland school, or at the very least, some of the classrooms within it, can provide some of the infrastructure for the native's liberatory struggle. Historically, these schools have functioned "within the structures of domination . . . as agencies which prepare the invaders of the future" (Freire 45). Let them help prepare instead the liberators of the indigenous landscape. In freeing their native earth, they are freeing themselves to emerge from it, and what emerges will be a new, radical red subjectivity, rooted to its native soil, saying its own Word in a native tongue, mingling its voice with that of a loon laughing on an unnamed lake, of the wind soughing through the shifting leaves of an Athabascan autumn, each a shield of light raised to the sun: unfettered, unfallen, and unquiet.

Foregrounding these local cultural conflicts can comprise an effective "alter/native" for education in the borderlands and elsewhere. Friere's words are again inspirational on this point: "I can affirm that the concept of culture, discussed imaginatively in all or most of its dimensions, can provide various aspects of an educational program" (119). Conflict is one of the dimensions of culture that pedagogy can appropriate as a vehicle of critical literacy and participatory residency. As Graff asserts in "Other Voices, Other Rooms: Organizing and Teaching the Humanities Conflicts," "if the aim is to help students become interested participants in the present cultural conversation instead of puzzled and alienated spectators— the aim should be to organize such conflicts of principle in the curriculum itself" (23). Though speaking of the conflicts associated with the academy, Graff's goal of using conflict to make education more participatory can be seized as a warrant for shifting the focus of this inquiry from the turf wars of the professorate to the cultural conflicts of the community. As with Graff's model, the aim of such a situated pedagogy would be to make students "articulately aware of the controversies surrounding them" so that they can "take an aggressive part in them" (30).

Providing a forum in the classroom for students to speak and write on such issues today increases the chances they will become spokespersons for their communities tomorrow. By mastering the literate practices of the colonizer, his academic codes and signifying practices, these students will be better able to resist the oppressive ends to which these codes and practices are often put. Only by answering colonialism back in its own tongue will the indigene be able to effectively wage such resistance, be able to secure autonomy over his or her affairs.

This presumes that borderland students today acquire such literacy in order to be spokespersons and advocates of their people's resistance struggles tomorrow. It presumes as well that resistance is the only justification for the acquisition of literacy in the borderlands. The worst thing the Athabascans can do is to remain alienated, aloof, or apathetic, uneducated, uninvolved, or unaware, disenchanted, passive, and silent: a spectator to the eclipse of their ancestral culture and the degradation of their natural environment. Activism, intervention, involvement, advocacy, and literacy are the only viable options for the marginalized faced with the threat of cultural extinction, the loss of self-determining autonomy, and the "capture" of their native lands by transnational corporations.

This is really the only practical justification for literacy in the borderlands, but it is enough to warrant such instruction. The aim of literacy, therefore, should not be conscription into the academies of the dominant culture as a precondition for assimilating into that culture; rather, the purpose of literacy in the borderlands should be a more active, participatory, and liberatory citizenship in those borderlands. Such students must be taught not only to read and write, but to reread and rewrite: to reread the texts that have led to their subjugation, to rewrite the history of that subjugation. The acquisition of academic and critical literacy must not be privileged as ends in themselves, but only as the means to a more livable future and participatory citizenship in the borderlands.

Who will become the David Standmarks of tomorrow if not the Erins and Marks of today? Who will become the tribal council leaders of tomorrow, if not the students of today? Who will write the letters and deliver the speeches protesting the erosion of Athabascan autonomy if none are prepared to assume the mantle of advocacy for their people, if none are prepared to "answer colonialism back" in its own tongue? If they are not prepared to speak and write and act themselves, then others will speak and write and act on their behalf, and to their further disadvantage. If they do not seize control of the Word, they will be victimized by it. If they do not gain control of the discourse, the discourse will control them.

It is in this sense and in this sense only that the acquisition of academic and critical literacy are of any use to these students. How can they hope to enter the conversations that determine their future "if the powerful vocabularies in which the controversies are fought out remain in control of the faculty" (Graff 30), or the school board, or the transnational corporation, or its legal experts and its "settlement" writers? In this context, a college education is critical as well insofar as it does not become a vehicle of assimilation into the dominant culture, but is yoked to the Athabascan's resistance struggle, insofar as it doesn't sever the ties between the student and his or her home culture, insofar as it preserves the hyphen of hybridity that perpetuates two-way traffic between the dominant culture and the indigenous subculture, insofar as education does not compromise the integrity of the signifying bridge by which the indigenous culture can be regained by the cross-cultural traveler. If the hyphen is allowed to collapse, all is lost: the native academic to his people; the people to the indigene-as-intellectual. But as long as the cross-cultural sojourner can dance on the hyphen of hybridity, he or she can still reconnect to an ancestral topos, can still experience the spiritual redemption that comes with such "contact," can still wage the resistance that is required to regain a paradise that has been lost.

Thus, literacy must not be purchased at the cost of hybridity. Only by preserving his or her hybridity, will the educated native be able to dance along the hyphen that alone preserves "contact" with the ancestral culture. An education that severs this link, that destroys the hyphen of hybridity exacts too high a price on the Athabascan student insofar as it accelerates the process of cultural genocide. Literacy for the indigene is only justified if the integrity of hybridity is preserved, for this alone allows the educated native to retain contact with the subculture, to contribute to its liberatory struggles. In the final analysis, pedagogy among the oppressed is not about the transmission of knowledge; it is about the transference of power. It is not about the patronizing transmission of knowledge that is already made; it is about the making of knowledge-makers. It is not about the recruitment of pacified citizens into the heartland of Euro-American culture; it is about the construction of active [rez]idents in the heart of the native's darkness. Such a pedagogy seeks to foster not merely the subsistence, but the resistance of the indigene. The first critical step toward changing the native's world is to return to him or her the freedom to name it. By returning to the Athabascan the "signs" that were taken from him or her, we are in effect giving the native back his or her world, for when the subaltern then speaks what will emerge is a world creation in words—a new world, a linguistic utopia authored by the indigene's signifying practices, in which wonders are reborn from signs retaken.

❖ References ❖

Achebe, Chinua. *Things Fall Apart.* New York: Fawcett Crest, 1959.

Adams, Rodanzo. *Interracial Marriage in Hawaii: A Study of the Mutually Conditioned Processes of Acculturation and Amalgamation.* New York: MacMillan, 1937.

Allen, Paula Gunn. *Studies in American Indian Literatures.* New York: MLA, 1983.

Althusser, Louis. "Ideology and the State." In *Lenin and Philosophy.* Translated by Ben Brewster. London: NCB, 1971. 123–173.

Angelou, Maya. *I Know Why the Caged Bird Sings.* New York: Bantam, 1969.

Anzaldua, Gloria. *Borderlands/La Frontera.* San Francisco: Aunt Lute, 1987.

Ashcroft, Bill, Gareth Griffiths and Helen Tiffin. *The Post-Colonial Studies Reader.* New York: Routledge, 1995.

Bakhtin, Mikhail M. "Discourse in the Novel." *The Dialogic Imagination: Four Essays by M. M. Bakhtin.* Translated by Caryl Emerson and Michael Holquist. Edited by Michael Holquist. Austin: University of Texas Press, 1981.

Bartholomae, David. "Inventing the University." *When a Writer Can't Write.* Edited by Mike Rose. New York: Guilford, 1985, 134–65.

Berlin, James A. *Rhetorics, Poetics, and Cultures: Refiguring College English Studies.* Urbana, IL: NCTE, 1996.

218   ❖   REFERENCES

Bhabha, Homi K. "The Other Question: Difference, Discrimination and the Discourse of Colonialism." *Out There: Marginalization and Contemporary Cultures.* Edited by Russell Ferguson, Martha Gever, Trinh T. Minh-ha, and Cornel West. Cambridge, MA: Massachusetts Institute of Technology Press, 1990, 71–87.

———. "Signs Taken for Wonders: Questions of Ambivalence and Authority Under a Tree Outside Delhi, May 1817." *Critical Inquiry* 12.1 (1985): 144–65.

———. "Sly Civility." *October* 34 (1985): 71–80.

———. "Of Mimicry and Men: The Ambivalence of Colonial Discourse." *October* 28 (1984): 125–133.

Bizzell, Patricia. "Marxist Ideas in Composition Studies." In *Contending with Words: Composition in a Postmodern Era.* Edited by Patricia Harkin and John Schilb. New York: MLA, 1991. 52–68.

Brennan, Timothy. "The National Longing for Form." *Nation and Narration.* Edited by Homi Bhabha. London: Routledge, 1990.

Bruffee, Kenneth A. "On Not Listening in Order to Hear: Collaborative Learning and the Rewards of Classroom Research." *Journal of Basic Writing* 7.1 (1988): 3–12.

Cain, William E. *Teaching the Conflicts: Gerald Graff, Curricular Reform, and the Culture Wars.* Edited by Cain. New York: Garland, 1994, x–xxxix.

Carter, Paul. "Naming Place." *The Road to Botany Bay: An Essay in Spatial History.* London: Faber, 1987.

Churchill, Ward. *Indians Are Us: Culture and Genocide in Native North America.* Monroe, Maine: Common Courage Press, 1994.

———. and M. Annette James. *Fantasies of the Master Race.* Monroe, Maine: Common Courage Press, 1992.

Clifford, James. "On Collecting Art and Culture." In *Out There*, 141–169.

Conrad, Joseph. *Heart of Darkness.* Harmondsworth: Penguin, 1983.

Courage, Richard. "The Interaction of Public and Private Literacies." *College Composition and Communication* 40 (1989): 484–96.

Crow Dog, Mary and Richard Erdoes. *Lakota Woman.* New York: HarperCollins, 1990.

Darbyshire and Associates. "Socioeconomic Impact Study of Resource Development in the [Nyotek]/Beluga Coal Area." Anchorage, AK: Darbyshire and Associates, 1981.

Deane, Seamus. *Nationalism, Colonialism, and Literature: Terry Eagleton, Frederic Jameson, and Edward Said.* Introduction by Deane. Minneapolis: University of Minnesota Press, 1990.

Devine, Joanne. "Literacy as Social Power." *Literacy Across Languages and Cultures,* 221–237.

Dowling, William C. *Jameson, Althusser, Marx: An Introduction to the Political Unconscious.* Ithaca: Cornell University Press, 1984.

Fanon, Frantz. *The Wretched of the Earth.* Trans. Constance Farrington. New York: Grove Press, 1963.

Ferrell, Thomas J. "Open Admissions, Orality and Literacy." *Journal of Youth and Adolescence* 3 (1974): 247–60.

Foucault, Michael. "Two Lectures." *Power/Knowledge: Selected Interviews and Other Writings, 1972–1977.* New York: Pantheon, 1980: 78–108.

Fox, Thomas. "Basic Writing as Cultural Conflict." *Journal of Education* 172 (1990): 65–83.

———. *The Archaeology of Knowledge and the Discourse on Language.* Translated by A. M. Sheridan Smith. New York: Pantheon, 1972.

Freire, Paulo. *Pedagogy of the Oppressed.* Translated by Myra Bergman Ramos. New York: Continuum, 1989.

Gardner, Susan. "And Here I Am Telling in Winnebago How I Lived My Life: Teaching Mountain Wolf Woman." *Order and Partialities: Theory, Pedagogy and the "Postcolonial."* Edited by Kostas Myrsiades and Jerry McGuire. New York: State University of New York Press, 1985.

Giroux, Henry A. "Paulo Friere and the Politics of Postcolonialism." *Contemporary Theory for the Postmodern Classroom.* Edited by Gary A. Olson and Sidney J. Dobrin. New York: State University of New York Press, 1989. xi–xxxv.

Goldie, Terry. "The Representation of the Indigene." *Fear and Temptation: The Image* of the *Indigene in Canadian, Australian and New Zealand Literature.* Kingston: McGill-Queens University Press, 1989.

Graff, Gerald. "Teach the Conflicts." *South Atlantic Quarterly* 89 (1990): 51–67.

————. "Other Voices, Other Rooms: Organizing and Teaching the Humanities Conflicts." In Cain, 17–44.

————. "In Defense of Teaching the Conflicts" In Cain, 219–228.

Green, Michael K. "Cultural Identities: Challenges for the Twenty-First Century." *Issues in Native American Identity.* Edited by Michael Green. New York: Peter Lang, 1995.

Griffiths, Gareth. "The Myth of Authenticity." *De-Scribing Empire: Postcolonialism and Textuality* Edited by Chris Tiffin and Alan Lawson. London: Routledge, 1994.

Harris, Joseph. "Negotiating the Contact Zone." *Journal of Basic Writing* 14 (spring 1995): 27–42.

————. "The Idea of Community in the Study of Writing." *College Composition and the Communication* 40 (1989): 11–22.

Heath, Shirley Bryce. *Ways With Words.* New York: McGraw-Hill, 1983.

Hobson, Geary. "The Rise of the 'White Shaman' as a New Version of Cultural Imperialism" in *The Remembered Earth.* Albuquerque: University of New Mexico Press, 1990.

Hogan, Linda. "Who Puts Together." *Studies in American Indian Literature: Critical Essays and Course Designs.* Edited by Paula Gunn Allen. New York: MLA, 1983, 169–177.

Hogan, Patrick Colm. "The Gender of Tradition: Ideologies of Character in Post-Colonization Anglophone Literature." In Myrsiades and McGuire.

Holzman, Michael. "Nominal and Active Literacy." *Writing as Social Action.* Edited by Marilyn M. Cooper and Michael Holzman. Portsmouth, NH: Boynton/Cook, 1989: 157–173.

hooks, bell. "Postmodern Blackness." *Yearning: Race and Gender in the Cultural Marketplace.* Boston: South End Press, 1990, 22–31.

————. "Marginality as Site of Resistance." In *Out There.* Edited by Russell Ferguson et al. Cambridge: Massachussetts Institute of Technology Press, 1990: 341–343.

————. "Talking Back." in Ferguson et al., 337–340.

Howe, Irving. "Living with Kampf and Schlaff: Literary Tradition and Mass Education." *The American Scholar* 43 (1973–74): 107–112.

Hutcheon, Linda. "Circling the Downspout of Empire: Post-colonialism and Postmodernism." *Ariel* 20.4 (1989): 149–75.

Jameson, Frederic. "Modernism and Imperialism." *Nationalism, Colonialism, and Literature.* Edited by Seamus Deane. Minneapolis: University of Minnesota Press, 1990, 43–66.

———. *The Political Unconscious: Narrative as a Socially Symbolic Act.* Ithaca: Cornell University Press, 1981.

Knoblauch, C. H. "Critical Teaching and Dominant Culture." *Composition and Resistance.* Edited by Mark C. Hurlburt and Michael Blitz. Portsmouth, NH: Boynton/Cook, 1991, 13–20.

Krupat, Arnold. *The Voice in the Margin: Native American Literature and the Canon.* Berkeley: University of California Press, 1989.

Lame Deer, John (Fire) and Richard Erdoes. *Lame Deer: Seeker of Visions.* New York: Washington Square Press, 1972.

Lewis, Tom J. and Robert E. Jungman. *On Being Foreign: Culture Shock in Short Fiction.* Edited by Lewis and Jungman. Yarmouth, ME: Intercultural Press, 1986.

London, Jack. *The Call of the Wild.* New York, Bantam, 1963.

Lu, Min-Zhan. "Conflict and Struggle: The Enemies or Preconditions of Basic Writing?" *College English* 54 (1992): 887–913.

———. "Writing as Repositioning." *Journal of Education* 172 (1990): 18–21.

———. "The Teaching of 'Usage' in the Contact Zone." Conference on College Composition and Communication. San Diego, CA, 1993.

Lunsford, Andrea and Suellyn Duffee. "Graff's Project and the Teaching of Writing." In Cain.

Mander, Jerry. "The Imminent Theft of Alaska." *In the Absence of the Sacred.* San Francisco: Sierra Club Books, 1991, 387–402

McClintock, Anne. "The Angel of Progress: Pitfalls of the Term 'Post-Colonialism.'" *Social Text* 31/32 (1992): 84–98.

Miller, Richard E. "Faultlines in the Contact Zone." *College English* 56 (1994): 389–408.

Milton, John. *Paradise Lost.* New York: Rinehart, 1966.

Minh-ha, Trinh T. "No Master Territories." *Where the Moon Waxes Red: Representation, Gender, and Cultural Politics.* New York: Routledge, 1991.

Mokunburg, Nkomo. "Post-Apartheid Education: Preliminary Reflections." *Pedagogy of Domination: Toward a Democratic Education in South Africa.* Trenton, NJ: Africa World Press, 1990, 291–323.

Momaday, N. Scott. *House Made of Dawn.* New York: Harper, 1968.

Mowat, Farley. *The Snow Walker.* New York: Bantam, 1975.

Muir, John. *Travels in Alaska.* Boston: Houghton Mifflin, 1915.

Myrsiades, Kostas and Jerry McGuire. *Order and Partialities: Theory, Pedagogy, and the Postcolonial.* New York: State University of New York Press, 1995.

Neihardt, John G. *Black Elk Speaks: Holy Man of the Oglala Sioux.* Lincoln: University of Nebraska Press, 1979.

Nelson, Robert M. *Place and Vision: The Function of Landscape in Native American Fiction.* New York: Peter Lang, 1993.

Ortiz, Simon. "Interview." in Laura Cotelli. *Winged Words: American Indian Writers Speak.* Nebraska: University of Nebraska Press, 1990.

Paine, Charles. "Relativism, Radical Pedagogy, and the Ideology of Paralysis." *College English* 51 (1989): 557–570.

Parry, Benita. "Problems in Current Theories of Colonial Discourse." *The Oxford Literary Review* 9.1–2 (1987): 27–58.

Pratt, Mary Louise. "Arts of the Contact Zone." *Profession* 91 (1991), 33–40.

———. *Imperial Eyes: Travel Writing and Transculturation.* New York: Routledge, 1992.

Proust, Marcel. *A La Recherche du Temps Perdu.* Translated C. K. Scott Moncrieff. New York: Random, 1922.

Rose, Mike. *Lives on the Boundary.* New York: Penguin, 1989.

Said, Edward W. *Orientalism.* New York: Vantage, 1979.

———. "The Mind of Winter: Reflections on Life in Exile." *Harper's* (September 1984): 49–55.

Scientific Frontiers. Nov. 28, 1995.

Sharpe, Jenny. "Figures of Colonial Resistance." *Modern Fiction Studies* 35.1 (1989): 137–155.

Shaughnessey, Mina. *Errors and Expectations: A Guide for the Teaching of Basic Writing.* New York: Oxford University Press, 1977.

Shor, Ira. *Critical Teaching and Everyday Life.* Boston: South End Press, 1980.

———. "Educating the Educators: A Freirean Approach to the Crisis in Teacher Education."

———. *Freire for the Classroom: A Sourcebook for Liberatory Learning.* Edited by Shor. Portsmouth, NH: Boynton/Cook, 1987, 7–32.

Silko, Leslie Marmon. *Ceremony.* New York: Viking, 1977.

Slemon, Stephen. "The Scramble for Post-colonialism." *De-Scribing Empire: Post-colonialism and Textuality.* Edited by Chris Tiffin and Alan Lawson. London: Routledge, 1994.

———. "Unsettling the Empire: Resistance Theory for the Second World." *World Literature Written in English* 30.2 (1990): 30–41.

———. "Magic Realism as Postcolonial Discourse." *Canadian Literature* 116 (1988): 9–23.

Spivak, Gayatri Chakravorty. "Can a Subaltern Speak? Speculations on Widow-Sacrifice." *Marxism and the Interpretation of Culture.* Edited by Cary Nelson and Lawrence Grossberg. Urbana: University of Illinois Press, 1988, 271–313.

———. "Three Women's Texts and a Critique of Imperialism." *Critical Inquiry* 12.1 (1985): 43–61

Standing Bear, Luther. *Land of the Spotted Eagle.* New York: University of Nebraska Press, 1933.

Suleri, Sara. "Woman Skin Deep: Feminism and the Postcolonial Condition." *Critical Inquiry* 18.4 (summer 1992): 756–69.

Thiong'o, Ngugi wa. "The Language of African Literature." *Decolonizing the Mind: The Politics of Language in African Literature.* London: James Currey, 1986.

Tiffin, Helen. "Post-colonial Literatures and Counter-discourse." *Kunapipi* 9.3 (1987): 17–34.

Trilling, Lionel. *The Last Decade: Essays and Reviews, 1965–75.* Edited by Diana Trilling. New York: Harcourt, 1979.

Trimbur, John. "Consensus and Difference in Collaborative Learning." *College English* 51 (1989): 602–616.

Vizenor, Gerald. "Socio a Cognitive: Mythic Reversals and the Striptease in Four Scenes." In *Out There.* Edited by Ferguson et al. Cambridge, MA: Massachusetts Institue of Technology Press, 1990, 411–419.

Walcott, Derek. "The Muse of History." *Is Massa Day Dead? Black Moods in the Caribbean.* Edited by Orde Coombs. New York: Doubleday, 1974.

Welch, James. *The Death of Jim Loney.* New York: Penguin, 1979.

Whitt, Laurie Anne. "Indigenous Peoples and the Cultural Politics of Knowledge." In Green, 223–271.

Wigginton, Eliot. *Foxfire 2.* Garden City, NY: Anchor Press, 1973.

Wilson, Lucy. "European or Caribbean: Jean Rhys and the Language of Exile." *Frontiers* 10 (1989): 68–72.

Young, Robert. *White Mythologies: Writing, History, and the West.* London: Routledge, 1990.

Index